THE BEST OF

CORWIN

RESPONSE TO INTERVENTION

The Best of Corwin Series

Classroom Management
Jane Bluestein, Editor

Differentiated Instruction
Gayle H. Gregory, Editor

Differentiated Instruction in Literacy, Math, and Science
Leslie Laud, Editor

Educational Neuroscience
David A. Sousa, Editor

Educational Technology for School Leaders
Lynne M. Schrum, Editor

Equity
Randall B. Lindsey, Editor

Inclusive Practices
Toby J. Karten, Editor

Response to Intervention
Cara F. Shores, Editor

THE BEST OF CORWIN

RESPONSE TO INTERVENTION

CARA F. SHORES
Editor

With contributions by
William N. Bender ▪ Cara F. Shores ▪ Kim Chester
Catherine Collier ▪ Susan L. Hall ▪ Evelyn S. Johnson ▪ Lori Smith
Monica L. Harris ▪ Martha J. Larkin ▪ Paul J. Riccomini
Bradley S. Witzel ▪ Bob Algozzine ▪ Ann P. Daunic
Stephen W. Smith ▪ Daryl F. Mellard

CORWIN
A SAGE Company

CORWIN
A SAGE Company

FOR INFORMATION:

Corwin
A SAGE Company
2455 Teller Road
Thousand Oaks, California 91320
(800) 233-9936
Fax: (800) 417-2466
www.corwin.com

SAGE Ltd.
1 Oliver's Yard
55 City Road
London EC1Y 1SP
United Kingdom

SAGE India Pvt. Ltd.
B 1/I 1 Mohan Cooperative
Industrial Area
Mathura Road, New Delhi 110 044
India

SAGE Asia-Pacific Pte. Ltd.
33 Pekin Street #02-01
Far East Square
Singapore 048763

Acquisitions Editor: Jessica Allan
Associate Editor: Allison Scott
Editorial Assistant: Lisa Whitney
Production Editor: Melanie Birdsall
Typesetter: C&M Digitals (P) Ltd.
Cover Designer: Rose Storey
Graphic Designer: Nicole Franck
Permissions Editor: Karen Ehrmann

Printed in the United States of America

Library of Congress Cataloging-in-Publication Data

A catalog record of this book is available from the Library of Congress.

978-1-4522-1741-3

Contents

Preface

Cara F. Shores

In the years since its national debut in IDEA 2004, response to intervention (RTI) has undergone significant growth and change. In its infancy, RTI was a somewhat controversial means for identifying young students with reading disabilities, and significant debate occurred for several years regarding whether RTI on its own could be a valid and reliable tool for identification of students with specific learning disabilities. As individual states adopted the process, RTI took on numerous forms, including three-, four-, and five-tiered models that would or would not include special education. The process received new monikers, including pyramid of interventions (POI), multi-tiered system of support (MTSS), and response to instruction and intervention (RTII), to name just a few. These name changes were indicative of more significant alterations in process and implementation; RTI is now used for a variety of purposes throughout the United States and is gaining strength in areas of Canada.

In essence, RTI has reached adolescence. The process is no longer limited to its original narrow scope for identifying students with reading difficulties. Instead, it is widely used to provide targeted interventions for students in the areas of math and behavior, and it has proven effective for students in preschool through high school. It has been meshed with professional learning communities, differentiated instruction, and enrichment for high achievers. Implementation models are as varied as the schools in which they are implemented and the students served through those processes, and we now have a wider assortment of intervention and assessment tools from which to choose. We know more about using appropriate tools, monitoring instruction, and making adjustments based on student outcomes. In most cases, RTI is now implemented as a school improvement model designed to address the needs of all learners. In many schools, RTI is proving a highly effective umbrella under which all school improvement initiatives are aligned, and schools with good RTI models in place are making significant gains in student achievement.

However, three basic factors have remained constant in effective RTI models. First, instruction and intervention must be supported by valid and reliable research. Second, instruction and intervention must be data driven and responsive to individual student needs. Finally, instruction and intervention must be implemented with fidelity. If any of these factors is weak or missing, the process becomes ineffective for improving student outcomes.

Corwin has created this *Best of Corwin: Response to Intervention* resource to guide practitioners through this challenging and rewarding process. As editor, it is my goal to provide you with the best and most relevant information available relating to quality RTI implementation. The chapters included in this book were carefully chosen to address the essential factors listed above. They offer a variety of perspectives for all educational practitioners and leaders and focus on elementary through high school grade levels, reading, math, behavior, and English learners. In addition, they provide information on assessment, data-based decision making, and fidelity of implementation. Each chapter was carefully selected to provide a comprehensive view of an effective RTI process. It is my hope that this resource will enable you to develop and implement RTI to have a powerful impact on your students.

Introduction

Cara F. Shores

This volume is an overview of the concept of differentiated instruction, featuring excerpts from nine works by recognized experts. The following is a synopsis of what you will find in each chapter.

Chapter 1. Response to Intervention

William N. Bender and Cara F. Shores

It is a common belief that response to intervention (RTI) began in 2004, when it was included in the Individuals with Disabilities Education Act. However, research had begun on components of the process about forty years earlier. Chapter 1 provides a comprehensive history and definition of RTI, placing specific emphasis on its use to identify students with specific learning disabilities. It is important for educators to see the full picture of where and how RTI began in order to understand where it is going in its evolution.

Chapter 2. Determining Appropriate Research-Based Interventions

Cara F. Shores and Kim Chester

Too many times, schools fail to address the quality of core instruction when developing their RTI process. Instead, educators focus on identifying interventions to be used with students after they fail to achieve. In reality, there must be equal focus on both core and additional instruction. I often recommend that schools spend a year or more assessing and strengthening Tier I or core instruction. This will, in turn, reduce the number of students who require additional instruction and interventions. Schools may then focus their efforts on providing targeted and intensive instruction for those students. Chapter 2 introduces research-based instructional and intervention strategies appropriate for use in all tiers.

These strategies are effective when used in a plan of systematic, explicit, and direct instruction. They should be implemented with fidelity and their impact should be assessed through ongoing progress monitoring.

Chapter 3. Framework for Instructional Intervention With Diverse Learners

Catherine Collier

When implemented properly, RTI has the potential to provide improved instruction for and to reduce disproportionate special education placement of culturally and linguistically diverse (CLD) students. However, educators must be careful to fully address the specific needs encountered as a result of this diversity. Chapter 3 provides an overview of many of these specific factors and offers practical advice for addressing them. The author proposes a multi-dimensional view of the RTI process in which interventions and strategies are layered to provide a more comprehensive approach to meeting the needs of CLD students.

Chapter 4. Using Progress Monitoring Data

Susan L. Hall

Assessment in and of itself will not increase student achievement. However, assessment data used to make informed instructional decisions has the potential to significantly impact student learning and behavior. Progress monitoring is the backbone of RTI, giving teachers a wealth of information—yet many schools find themselves "data rich, information poor" because educators have not learned how to use the data to impact learning. Chapter 4 clearly demonstrates the process of data-based decision making and adjusting instruction based on student needs.

Chapter 5. Leadership Perspectives on RTI

Evelyn S. Johnson, Lori Smith, and Monica L. Harris

Leading RTI process development and implementation in a school, district, or province can be a daunting task. In order for the process to be truly effective, educational leaders must develop in their staff a culture that supports all aspects of RTI. Leaders must provide ongoing, job-embedded professional learning and ensure high-quality core instruction for all students. They must develop a structure that provides time and resources for targeted interventions, use and teach their staff to use data to drive instruction, ensure that all aspects of the process are implemented with fidelity—and the list goes on. In Chapter 5, the authors provide step-by-step guidance for educational leaders involved in the RTI implementation process by answering some of the most common questions they will face.

Chapter 6. The Reading Brain and Literacy Instruction

William N. Bender and Martha J. Larkin

There is a large body of research on the RTI process, and the vast majority focuses on reading. Although many educators have become quite knowledgeable about teaching reading, few understand the physical processes of learning to read. In Chapter 6, the authors provide an overview of research on how the brain and central nervous system process literacy and reading. Without getting too technical, they illustrate how teachers may adjust reading instruction for students to maximize the brain and central nervous system functioning.

Chapter 7. Mathematics Intervention Overview

Paul J. Riccomini and Bradley S. Witzel

Although RTI was originally designed as a tiered reading model, it has quickly evolved as an effective means for addressing math deficits. However, the research base for math interventions is significantly less than that for reading. In Chapter 7, the authors draw from recommendations of the National Mathematics Advisory Panel and the best available research to outline effective math interventions for Tiers 2 and 3.

Chapter 8. Classroom Interventions and Individual Behavior Plans

Bob Algozzine, Ann P. Daunic, and Stephen W. Smith

RTI is a multifaceted approach to school improvement. In addition to addressing academic deficiencies, RTI is highly effective in reducing problem behaviors for students at all grade levels. Schools have implemented successful behavioral RTI models through positive behavior interventions and supports (PBIS) for over a decade. The behavioral framework mirrors the academic model in its essential components; interventions and instruction must be research-based, data driven, and implemented with fidelity. Chapter 8 provides an overview of these components in the behavioral framework and focuses specifically on interventions and assessment for Tiers 2 and 3, including information on screening and progress monitoring tools, individualized behavior intervention plans, and functional behavioral assessment.

Chapter 9. Fidelity of Implementation

Daryl F. Mellard and Evelyn S. Johnson

Chapter 9 addresses the final but perhaps most important of our three essential components for effective RTI—fidelity of implementation. Many schools have put great effort into choosing appropriate assessment tools and effective interventions, but have failed to develop a plan for assuring that the process is implemented as it is designed. Effective schools must monitor many areas, including core instruction, interventions, assessment, and process implementation itself. I think of this component of RTI as "progress monitoring for the school." Without it, we cannot be sure that student data and outcomes are valid or reliable. In this chapter, the authors propose a three dimensional model for monitoring fidelity of implementation. Using this model will give educators assurance that RTI is working as it was designed and researched.

About the Editor

Cara F. Shores received a BA in English from Jacksonville State University and MEd and EdS degrees in special education from the University of West Georgia. She taught special education in both pullout and inclusion classrooms at the elementary and middle school levels. Cara has served as a building-level administrator, system SST and 504 coordinator, and director of special education. In 2000 she served as the principal author of the Georgia DOE Student Support Team Resource Manual. She also served as a consultant on several federally funded projects for inclusion. As president of Wesley Educational Services, Cara presents to school personnel across the United States and Canada. She is a feature presenter for the Council for Exceptional Children. She is the author of *Positive Outcomes: Utilizing Student Support Teams as a Tool for School Improvement*. She is coauthor of *Response to Intervention: A Practical Guide for Every Teacher* and *Using RTI for School Improvement: Raising Every Student's Achievement Scores*.

About the Contributors

Bob Algozzine is a professor in the Department of Educational Leadership at the University of North Carolina, Charlotte, and project co-director of the U.S. Department of Education-Supported Behavior and Reading Improvement Center. With twenty-five years of research experience and extensive, firsthand knowledge of teaching students classified as seriously emotionally disturbed, he is a uniquely qualified staff developer, conference speaker, and teacher of behavior management and effective teaching. He is active in special education practice as a partner and collaborator with professionals in the Charlotte-Mecklenburg schools in North Carolina and as an editor of several journals focused on special education. He has written more than 250 manuscripts on special education topics, including many books and textbooks on how to manage emotional- and social-behavior problems.

William N. Bender is an international leader who focuses on practical instructional tactics with an emphasis on response to intervention (RTI) and differentiated instruction in general education classes across the grade levels. In particular, Dr. Bender has written more books on RTI than any other author in the world, two of which are best sellers. He has now completed seven books on various aspects of RTI, as well as a professional development videotape on that topic. He completes between forty and fifty workshops yearly in the United States, Canada, and the Caribbean. In the fall of 2010, he was selected to work with the Ministry of Education in Bermuda to establish their nationwide RTI framework. One of his recent books, *Beyond the RTI Pyramid*, was a 2010 finalist for the Distinguished Achievement Award for Excellence in Educational Publishing.

Dr. Bender uses practical strategies and easy humor to make his workshops an enjoyable experience for all, and he is frequently asked to return to the same school or district for additional workshops. He consistently receives positive reviews of his professional development workshops for educators across the grade levels. Dr. Bender believes his job is to inform educators of innovative, up-to-date tactics for the classroom, rooted in current research, in an enjoyable workshop experience. He is able to convey this information in a humorous, motivating fashion.

Dr. Bender began his education career teaching in a junior high school resource classroom, working with adolescents with behavioral disorders and learning disabilities. He earned his PhD in special education from the University of North Carolina and has taught in leading universities around the nation, including Rutgers University and the University of Georgia. He is now consulting and writing full-time and has published over sixty research articles and twenty books in education.

Kim Chester began her career as a general education teacher in an inclusive classroom, where for many years she implemented effective principles of co-teaching and differentiating instruction to meet the diverse needs of her students. After her youngest child was born with cerebral palsy, she went back to school to receive her MEd in special education from Kennesaw State University. Currently, she works as a parent mentor in her local school system, as a region AYP consultant, and as an educational consultant for Wesley Educational Services. In addition, Mrs. Chester serves on various committees, including the Governor's Council on Developmental Disabilities in Georgia. She offers her range of perspectives to educators, parents, and administrators. Mrs. Chester enjoys working with students and teachers in classroom settings, providing practical strategies for raising student achievement through inclusion, co-teaching, differentiated instruction, behavior management, and RTI.

Catherine Collier is a specialist in the emerging field of bilingual/cross-cultural special education, and she has worked directly with a small cadre of nationally recognized professionals in establishing this field of study. She has extensive experience as a classroom teacher with nonnative English learners as well as teacher preparation and research. She taught as a bilingual special educator with culturally diverse learners in Alaska, Arizona, Colorado, and New Mexico. Dr. Collier is currently on the faculty of Western Washington University, the director of a national professional development program funded by the Federal Office of English Language Acquisition. There is a current interview with Dr. Collier featured at the Colorín Colorado website (http://www.colorincolorado.com).

Ann P. Daunic is an Associate Scholar in the Department of Special Education, School Psychology, and Early Childhood Studies at the University of Florida. For the past 12 years, she has directed applied research projects focused on the prevention of problem behaviors through school- and classroom-based interventions, including conflict resolution, peer mediation, and instruction in social problem solving. Her interest in preventive interventions for students at risk for school failure reflects an academic background in psychology and her experience as a college counselor for economically and educationally disadvantaged students from the New York City metropolitan area. She has also served as a private high school administrator and guidance counselor, collaborating with teachers and parents to address the social and instructional needs of students with behavioral and academic difficulties. She is currently Director of the Prevention Research Project, a four-year study funded by the Institute of Education Sciences to evaluate the efficacy of a social problem-solving curriculum for fourth- and fifth-grade students. Associated research interests include merging social-emotional and academic learning and the role of social cognition in the self-regulation of emotions and behavior.

Susan L. Hall, EdD, is a consultant specializing in teacher training and early reading. She is founder and president of an educational consulting and professional development company called 95 Percent Group, Inc. The company provides consulting and teacher training to districts and schools in response to intervention (RTI) in early reading. 95 Percent Group specializes in how to use early literacy screening data to place students in groups for tiers of intervention, as well as instructional strategies to address specific skill deficits. Susan is a nationally certified trainer of *DIBELS* and *LETRS*. She is author of *I've DIBEL'd, Now What?* and *Implementing Response to Intervention: A Principal's Guide.* She is coauthor with Louisa Moats of two books, *Straight Talk About Reading* and *Parenting a Struggling Reader,* as well as *LETRS Module 7: Teaching Phonics, Word Study, and the Alphabetic Principle,* Second Edition. Susan can be reached at shall@95percentgroup.com.

Monica L. Harris, PhD, is an Assistant Professor at Grand Valley State University (GVSU) in the College of Education. She began her career in education at the secondary level and has experience teaching adolescents in general and special education settings as well as developing and implementing programs for students who struggle academically or who are at risk for school failure. Prior to joining the faculty at GVSU, she received her doctoral degree in Special Education from the University of Kansas, where her research focused on strategy instruction and adolescent literacy. Dr. Harris is part of the Strategic Instruction Model (SIM) Professional Developer's Network and works with school districts to implement tiered intervention using research-based instructional strategies. Currently, her research interests include developing instructional strategies for use in academically diverse classrooms, teacher preparation, and collaborative teaching models.

Evelyn S. Johnson, EdD, is an Associate Professor of Special Education at Boise State University (BSU) and the coauthor of *RTI: A Practitioner's Guide to Implementing Response to Intervention.* She began her career in Washington in 1994 as a special education teacher, and then at the University of Washington, Seattle, where her research focused on the inclusion of students with disabilities in accountability systems. Dr. Johnson's work on assessment for students with disabilities has included research on accommodations and alternate assessments as well as research on screening for reading problems. Prior to joining the faculty at BSU, she worked as a research associate for the National Research Center on Learning Disabilities (NRCLD), where she developed numerous technical assistance products to assist state and local educational agencies on RTI and learning disability identification–related issues. Currently, her research focuses on RTI implementation at the secondary levels.

Martha J. Larkin taught public school students in general education and special education at the elementary, middle, and secondary levels for several years. She then earned her PhD from the University of Alabama in 1999 and began a career in higher education. She has authored and coauthored 19 journal articles, 14 book and monograph chapters, and 6 research reports and commissioned papers in education and special education. She specializes in instructional strategies, particularly for students with learning disabilities. Her specific teaching and research interests include scaffolded instruction, content enhancement, learning strategies, graphic organizers, and grading rubrics. She especially enjoys pursuing these interests in the areas of reading, writing, and mathematics. She may be contacted at mlarkin@westga.edu.

Daryl F. Mellard, PhD (University of Kansas) began his career in school psychology. Since 1982, Dr. Mellard has been a research associate within the Center for Research on Learning and the Division of Adult Studies. He is the director of the Division of Adult Studies, which includes a professional staff of 12 and approximately 35 student research assistants. The Division's work examines policies and practices that limit the abilities of adults with disabilities to fully participate in society's everyday activities.

He has been the principal investigator of research and evaluation studies. Dr. Mellard's current projects address assessment and services to children and youth with learning disabilities, reading comprehension, and adult literacy. Dr. Mellard is one of the principal investigators with the National Research Center on Learning Disabilities (NRCLD) (nrcld.org) that examined the identification of learning disabilities, including the application of responsiveness to intervention. Dr. Mellard directed the NRCLD staff in their review of RTI as implemented in numerous elementary school settings. Dr. Mellard also directed research on social, education, and employment issues for adults with disabilities. These projects involved consumers, employers, and staff in community and technical colleges, independent living centers, vocational rehabilitation, One-Stop Career Centers, and adult education and literacy programs.

Additionally, as a service to the state of Kansas, Dr. Mellard served as a co-chair to the Kansas Coalition on Adult Literacy and Learning Disabilities. This work group was formed to coordinate the efforts of education, corrections, rehabilitation, human resources, and businesses in meeting the needs and legal requirements of individuals with disabilities. Contributing to his views on adults with disabilities and their services, for the past six years Dr. Mellard has served as an officer on a board of directors' for the local independent living center.

Paul J. Riccomini, PhD, began his career as a dual-certified general education mathematics teacher of students with learning disabilities, emotional and behavioral disabilities, and gifted and talented students in Grades 7–12 in inclusive classrooms. His teaching experiences required a strong content knowledge in mathematics and the development and maintenance of strong collaborative relationships with both general and special educators. He earned his doctorate in special education from The Pennsylvania State University and his master's degree in education and Bachelor of Arts in mathematics at Edinboro University of Pennsylvania. Currently, he is an Associate Professor of Special Education at Clemson University. His research focus is on effective instructional approaches, strategies, and assessments for students who are low achievers and/or students with learning disabilities in mathematics. He has written several research and practitioner articles related to effective strategies for teaching mathematics to students who struggle and has coauthored two math intervention programs targeting fractions and integers. As a former middle and high school general education and special education mathematics teacher, Dr. Riccomini knows firsthand the challenges and difficulties teachers experience every day when working with struggling students, a motivation for writing this book. You can e-mail Dr. Riccomini at pjr146@clemson.edu.

Lori Smith, PhD, is principal at Cheyenne Mountain Junior High in Colorado Springs, Colorado. She has served in public education for fifteen years, nine of which have been in school administration. She began her career as a high school biology and chemistry teacher in 1994 in Colorado. Her work and systematic implementation of RTI at Cheyenne Mountain has led to several state-level presentations, publications, and consultations on RTI implementation. Ms. Smith's commitment to action research on RTI at the secondary level was inspired by the support of Dr. Evelyn Johnson while completing her doctoral degree in Education Leadership and Administration.

Stephen W. Smith is a Professor in the Department of Special Education at the University of Florida (UF). Prior to receiving his PhD in Special Education from the University of Kansas, he was a teacher of special education students for eight years. Dr. Smith teaches graduate courses in the area of emotional and behavioral disorders and research in special education at UF and has conducted multiple federally funded investigations of effective behavior management techniques, including the study of social conflict and the effects of schoolwide peer mediation programs. As the Principal Investigator of a large-scale prevention science research grant funded by the U.S. Department of Education, Institute of Education Sciences (IES), Dr. Smith is investigating the effects of a universal cognitive-behavioral intervention in the form of a social problem-solving curriculum to reduce student aggression and chronic classroom disruption. He has presented his findings and recommendations at numerous state, regional, national, and international professional conferences. While at UF, Dr. Smith has received three teaching awards and a University Research Award, and he has served twice as a UF Research Foundation Professor. He is a member of the IES Social and Behavioral Education Scientific Research Review Panel and is a member of the Executive Board of the Division for Research, Council for Exceptional Children.

Bradley S. Witzel, PhD, is an experienced and decorated teacher of students with disabilities and at-risk concerns. He has worked as a classroom teacher and before that as a paraeducator in inclusive and self-contained settings. Dr. Witzel received his BS in psychology from James Madison University and his master's degree in education and his PhD in special education from the University of Florida. He currently serves as an associate professor, coordinator of the three special education programs, and assistive department chair of curriculum and instruction at Winthrop University in Rock Hill, South Carolina, where he recently received the 2009 Winthrop Graduate Faculty Award. In higher education, Dr. Witzel has taught undergraduate and graduate courses in special and general education methods as well as a variety of other courses from transition to behavior support. He has written several research and practitioner articles, books, and book chapters on mathematics education and interventions, and served as a reviewer of the Final Report from the National Mathematics Advisory Panel. Recently he coauthored an IES practice guide on response to intervention in mathematics. You can e-mail Dr. Witzel at witzelb@winthrop.edu.

1

Response to Intervention

William N. Bender and Cara F. Shores

With the passage of the Individuals with Disabilities Education Improvement Act (IDEA), the federal government officially allowed students to be classified as learning disabled based on documentation of how well they respond to interventions—a procedure commonly referred to as RTI (Bradley, Danielson, & Doolittle, 2005; Fuchs & Fuchs, 2005; Gersten & Dimino, 2006; Marston, 2005; Mastropieri & Scruggs, 2005; Scruggs & Mastropieri, 2002). IDEA 2004 specifies that, for the purpose of determining learning disability (LD) eligibility, a school district may implement a procedure that involves documentation of how a child responds to scientific, research-based interventions as part of its evaluation procedures.

Although the earliest research on the RTI process began in the 1960s, it has only been in the past decade or so that the process has gained significant momentum among researchers and practitioners as a plausible means of identifying learning and/or reading disabilities. Even so, the process in general terms has been untested for use in determining eligibility, or deciding how students are identified for learning disability services. With that stated, ample evidence exists for use of RTI as a progress-monitoring tool for students with or without disabilities (Fuchs & Fuchs, 2005, 2006; Marston, Muyskens, Lau, & Canter, 2003; Vaughn, Linan-Thompson, & Hickman, 2003; Vellutino et al., 1996).

VALID IDENTIFICATION OF LEARNING DISABILITIES

The exploration of RTI as an approach to LD eligibility determination resulted from the general dissatisfaction with the previous approaches for documentation of a learning disability. In particular, many in the field have expressed dissatisfaction with the discrepancy procedure that documents a disability by demonstrating a large difference between a child's cognitive level (using IQ scores) and his or her achievement. Since the late 1990s, many policymakers have indicated that the discrepancy procedure results in over-identification of students with learning disabilities, and thus, that the procedure seemed to be somewhat inexact in documenting exactly who manifested a learning disability and who did not.

Reflection 1.1	Your Experience With Discrepancies

As an educator, you may have had experiences in documenting a discrepancy for a child suspected of having a learning disability that was less than positive. Have you ever experienced a situation where you were sure, based on reversal errors (e.g., a child reverses letters or words), oral reading errors, or spelling problems, that a child exhibited a learning disability, but the discrepancy was not quite "large enough" to have that student qualified as disabled? What other difficulties have you experienced with implementation of the discrepancy criteria?

The construct for LD was controversial when first included in the Federal Education of the Handicapped Act in 1975, and the controversy continued through the passage of the Individuals with Disabilities Education Act of 1997. Much of the debate stemmed from the use of discrepancies between IQ and achievement as the definitive factor in the definition of Specific Learning Disability (Reschly, Hosp, & Schmied, 2003).

Prior to IDEA of 2004, Specific Learning Disability was defined as:

A disorder in one of more of the basic psychological process involved in understanding or in using language, spoken or written, that may manifest itself in an imperfect ability to listen, think, speak, read, write, spell, or to do mathematical calculations, including conditions such as perceptual disabilities, brain injury, minimal brain dysfunction, dyslexia, and developmental aphasia.

The term does not include learning problems that are primarily the result of visual, hearing, or motor disabilities, of mental retardation, of emotional disturbance, or of environmental, cultural, or economic disadvantage. (U.S. Office of Education, 1977)

In short, the seven areas of Specific Learning Disabilities are listening, thinking, speaking, reading, writing, spelling, and doing mathematical calculations. In addition to delineating these aspects of a learning disability, the law also outlined classification criteria, or rules, which would be used to determine LD eligibility. These criteria did not include low achievement and severe discrepancy, but the criteria did mention basic psychological processes, which is the foundation of Specific Learning Disability. Thus, this definition placed the major emphasis on the severe discrepancy between IQ and achievement, but neither criterion was specifically stated in the definition. In a report submitted to the U.S. Department of Education, Office of Special Education Programs, Reschly, Hosp, and Schmied (2003) identified this inconsistency as a major flaw in the LD construct. They noted that "as definitions and classification criteria have less consistency, increasing problems emerge about meaning and eligibility" (p. 3).

Research has revealed that the severe discrepancy formula as a definition for LD has poor reliability and validity when predicting student achievement (Fletcher, Denton, & Francis, 2005; Siegel, 1989; Vellutino, Scanlon, Small, & Fanuele, 2006; Ysseldyke, 2005). The model is often called a "wait to fail" approach because it is difficult to apply until students are in third grade or beyond (Reschly et al., 2003), because students must be exposed to some level of curricular content in order to have a valid measure of their achievement and calculate a discrepancy between IQ and achievement. Further, over-identification of students with learning disability has increased the overall costs of special education (Fuchs & Fuchs, 2006). When special education was first identified as a national priority, estimates of the prevalence of learning disabilities indicated that perhaps 2% of students in public schools would be classified as learning disabled. Today, well in excess of 5% of students in public schools are so classified, and that number seems to increase each year. According to a 2003 national survey, prevalence varies widely throughout the states, ranging from a low of 2.96% in Kentucky to a high of 9.46% in Rhode Island (Reschly et al., 2003). The discrepancy across states seems to be attributable to another problem with the definition, which is a lack of uniformity between state eligibility criteria. The results of the aforementioned survey revealed state-to-state differences in the requirements for IQ, psychological process disorders, achievement domains, exclusion criteria, and methods for determining discrepancy. Based on these discrepancies, a child receiving specialized services in one state may be deemed ineligible for services if they move across the state line.

Other problems with the LD definition have been noted as well. For example, children may be diagnosed as disabled in reading based on evaluation instruments that have poor validity. Further, evaluation and application of diagnostic criteria in the LD definition provide no guidance for instruction. In addition, the severe discrepancy model does not distinguish between reading deficits caused by poor instruction versus reading deficits caused by biologically based deficits (Vellutino et al., 2006).

Clearly, the need for clarification and revision of the definition and eligibility procedures for documenting learning disabilities is apparent. Through the discussion and debates of expert researchers and educators, response to intervention has risen to the top of the myriad of options for determining LD eligibility. However, many practitioners have not had direct experience with RTI because this option for eligibility is so recent. Further, few states have devised methods for implementation of this option, as the new federal regulations went into effect in August 2006.

WHY DID RTI EVOLVE?

In 1982, a National Research Council Study (Heller, Holtzman, & Messick, 1982) outlined three criteria on which special education classification should be based. The first criterion involves determining if the quality of instruction received in the general education environment is sufficient for adequate learning. The second criterion examines whether the special education program is appropriate and of value in improving student outcomes. Finally, the third criterion is that the evaluation process must be valid and meaningful. When all three criteria are achieved, special education placement is considered valid (Vaughn & Fuchs, 2003).

The study by Heller and colleagues (1982) began the momentum for use of responsiveness to instruction in eligibility determinations. This process had been used in two earlier studies (Bergan, 1977; Deno & Mirkin, 1977) that involved similar methodologies; one explored behavioral issues and the other focused on academics. In these studies, a definition of the problem was clearly established and measurable goals were developed based on the student's functioning level. An intervention plan was developed utilizing research-based interventions. Progress was monitored through curriculum-based assessment tools. Finally, decisions regarding continuation or dismissal of interventions were based on achievement of goals and benchmarks.

Over the next two decades, RTI would be heavily debated and researched. Numerous organizations, discussion panels, roundtables, and summits were convened to bring together experts from the field to make recommendations for policy changes (see Table 1.1). In 2001, President George W. Bush established the Commission on Excellence in Special Education (2002) to study special education issues and make recommendations

Table 1.1 Research and Policy Reports Supporting Response to Intervention

Reporting Organization	Date Published	Content of Report
National Institute for Child Health and Development (NIHCD) Studies	Ongoing	Concluded that IQ achievement discrepancy delays services to children. Supports early intervention services as provided through RTI.
National Reading Panel	2000	Outlined major components of reading.
National Research Council Panel on Minority Overrepresentation	2002	Emphasized importance of early identification and intervention for poor and minority children and youth. Made recommendations for LD eligibility criteria.
National Summit on Learning Disabilities	2001	Recommended Response to Intervention as the "most promising" method of LD identification.
President's Commission on Excellence in Special Education	2001	Recommended a focus on results and prevention in LD eligibility determination.

SOURCE: Batsche et al. (2006), Fuchs et al. (2005).

concerning how services might be improved. That commission issued a report that recommended early intervention and assessment practices that were closely linked to instruction. In summation, the commission strongly suggested changing LD eligibility criteria from a discrepancy model to a response to intervention model, which documents how a student suspected of having a learning disability responds to appropriate instruction. This RTI model is described in detail in the following section.

In 2002, the National Research Center on Learning Disabilities issued the *Common Ground Report*, which identified fourteen recommendations regarding identification, eligibility, and intervention for learning disabilities. The report was the product of leaders from eight national organizations coming together to form a consensus on their philosophies regarding LD. Marston (2005) compared the consensus statements to three sound RTI projects in order to determine if the RTI process fulfilled the requirements outlined in the *Common Ground Report*. He determined that RTI positively corresponded to each of the statements, making the process a viable option for LD determination. The consensus statements are listed in Table 1.2.

Table 1.2 Consensus Statements From the *Common Ground Report* of the National Research Center on Learning Disabilities (2002)

- Identification should include a student-centered, comprehensive evaluation and problem-solving approach that ensures students who have a specific learning disability are efficiently identified.
- The field should continue to advocate for the use of scientifically based practices. However, in areas where an adequate research base does not exist, data should be gathered on the success of promising practices.
- Regular education must assume active responsibility for delivery of high-quality instruction, research-based interventions, and prompt identification of individuals at risk while collaborating with special education and related services personnel.
- Schools and educators must have access to information about scientifically based practices and promising practices that have been validated in the settings where they are to be implemented.
- The ability-achievement discrepancy formula should not be used for determining eligibility.
- Students with specific learning disabilities require intensive, iterative (recursive), explicit scientifically based instruction that is monitored on an ongoing basis to achieve academic success.
- Students with specific learning disabilities require a continuum of intervention options through regular and special education across all grades and ages.
- Decisions on eligibility must be made through an interdisciplinary team, using informed clinical judgment, directed by relevant data, and based on student needs and strengths.
- Interventions must be timely and matched to the specific learning and behavioral needs of the student.
- An intervention is most effective when it is implemented consistently, with fidelity to its design, and at a sufficient level of intensity and duration.
- Based on an individualized evaluation and continuous progress monitoring, a student who has been identified as having a specific learning disability may need different levels of special education and related services under IDEA at various times during the school experience.

Reflection 1.2 **Who Determines Policy on LD Definition?**

As described previously, several national study groups have determined that RTI is an effective way to identify students with a learning disability. Both the Commission on Excellence in Education and the National Research Center on Learning Disabilities have weighed in and supported the RTI concept. However, this begs the question of who determines policy on LD definitions. One frequently overlooked fact is that each individual state, via rules and regulations from the state department of education, effectively sets the LD definition and the procedures whereby eligibility determinations may be made. Thus, one critical question for practitioners is: Has your state department of education begun the process of adjusting their rules, regulations, and procedures to accommodate the new rules and regulations that became effective in August 2006? The website for those federal rules and regulations is: www.ed.gov/idea.

WHAT IS RTI?

Response to Intervention is, simply put, a process of implementing high-quality, scientifically validated instructional practices based on learner needs, monitoring student progress, and adjusting instruction based on the student's response. When a student's response is dramatically inferior to that of his peers, the student may be determined to have a learning disability (Fuchs, 2003). The assumption is that failure to respond to otherwise effective instruction indicates the possible presence of a disabling condition. Interventions are most often divided into tiers of instruction. Although the RTI model seems relatively simple and straightforward, the actual implementation of the process requires much consideration and planning of the specific intricacies to make it valid, reliable, and feasible.

The two studies that formed the early research support for RTI (Bergan, 1977; Deno & Mirkin, 1977) were discussed previously. These studies varied in their RTI procedures; those variations have evolved into the problem-solving RTI model and the standard protocol RTI approach. It is important to understand both approaches in order to determine the most effective means of implementation.

In his research, Bergan (1977) utilized a problem-solving approach to address behavioral issues among students in special education. In this process, the behavioral problem was first defined and then measured as accurately as possible. The student's functioning and performance gap in comparison to peers was then established. The intervention team applied a problem-solving process to interpret the data and establish a goal for the student based on the performance of his or her peers. Next, the team designed an intervention plan based on scientifically validated practices for behavior change. Interventions designed specifically for that student were implemented over a period of time and progress was monitored frequently. Data collected from the ongoing progress monitoring was then evaluated and results were, again, compared to peer performance. Finally, the team used the data to make programming decisions for the student (Batsche, et al., 2006). Thus, the team-based "problem-solving approach" evolved based on this general design.

Deno and Mirkin (1977) implemented a different approach in their research. They utilized curriculum-based measurement, a technique that has been proven as an effective method for assessing a pupil's academic progress over time. They then developed an intervention plan to remediate certain reading difficulties among students with learning disabilities. In the growing RTI literature, this method became known as the "standard treatment protocol."

Although there are numerous similarities between the approaches used in these studies, there are some very important differences. Deno and

Mirkin utilized curriculum-based measures to establish benchmarks for student achievement. In this model, each student was essentially compared to his or her own prior performance. This is different from Bergan's problem-solving approach, which compares a pupil's performance to his or her peers. Further, the curriculum-based measures in the standard protocol approach were administered quite often, allowing for a constant adjustment of instruction based on student response. The team determined whether to discontinue, continue, adjust, or intensify instruction based on the student's responsiveness to the adjusted instruction (Kukic, Tilly, & Michelson, 2006).

Reflection 1.3	Your Use of Curriculum-Based Measurement

As you can tell from these initial studies on RTI, the standard treatment protocol is more heavily dependent on curriculum-based measurement than the problem-solving approach, although both incorporate curriculum-based measurement. What is your previous experience with curriculum-based measurement on a weekly, biweekly, or daily basis? Are you currently using such a progress-monitoring tool to follow students' academic growth in your class, or will you need to learn new skills in order to implement curriculum-based measurement?

Thus, from these original studies, two distinct RTI models emerged; the problem-solving model and the standard protocol model. Although the models exhibit similar structure, the processes involved in developing and evaluating the impact or efficacy of the educational interventions are quite different. In essence, the problem-solving approach involves the implementation of interventions designed for individual student needs. The standard protocol approach relies on interventions designed for small groups of students experiencing the same academic problem (e.g., reading comprehension). Both approaches require research-based interventions, ongoing progress monitoring, and measures to assure fidelity and integrity of the intervention and assessment (National Research Center on Learning Disabilities, 2005). In the remainder of this chapter, we will explore examples of each model, noting strengths and weaknesses for both.

THE PROBLEM-SOLVING APPROACH TO RTI

As previously stated, the problem-solving model involves individualized decision making and intervention implementation for each student. Problem-solving teams at the school or system level evaluate student data and make decisions about the need for interventions, the interventions to be used, and the amount of time allotted for each intervention (McCook, 2006). The problem-solving model has been replicated and refined in several school systems, including Minneapolis Public Schools and the Heartland Area Educational Agency in Iowa.

The Minneapolis Public Schools began formal implementation of the problem-solving model in 1992 (Marston, Muyskens, Lau, & Canter, 2003). Their problem-solving model is a sequential pattern of steps divided into three tiers or stages. They are:

Stage 1. Classroom Interventions: This stage is implemented by classroom teachers in general education classrooms. Teachers identify students who are experiencing difficulties, implement instructional strategies or modifications based on individual student needs, and begin to monitor the student's progress. Teachers gather information regarding strengths and specific weaknesses, previous strategies attempted and outcomes, any available screening data, student health, and other information from parents. If the teacher determines the intervention is not successful, the student is referred to Stage 2.

Stage 2. Problem-Solving Team Interventions: Student information is reviewed by a multidisciplinary team, which may include school psychologists, general education and special education teachers, reading specialists, and school administrators. The team considers whether other risk factors (language, poverty, cultural factors) are attributing to or causing the student's lack of progress. Interventions are reviewed and adjusted to more specifically address student needs. Teachers continue to monitor progress and adjust instruction. If teachers determine the student is not sufficiently responding to instruction, the student is referred to Stage 3.

Stage 3. Special Education Referral and Initiation of Due Process Procedures: The school district obtains parental consent and begins evaluation procedures for the student. The evaluation consists of a review of all information available on the student from Stages 1 and 2, including data on the student's response to interventions, direct observation, and the formulation of a means of obtaining cognitive, achievement, and adaptive behavior functioning. The team utilizes all available information to determine eligibility while considering the possible impact of risk factors such as culture, language, and socioeconomic status (Marston et al., 2003).

In 2002, the Minneapolis School District (approximately one hundred total schools) had implemented the problem-solving model in all K–8 schools and was in the training phase for all secondary schools. Outcome data revealed that the prevalence of students with high-incidence disabilities remained constant (7%) before and after implementation. Further, the achievement level of these students on the Minnesota Basic Standards Tests and the Minnesota State Special Education Goals was similar to that of students placed in special education using more traditional methods. Finally, the number of students referred to Stage 3 and placed in special education did not increase (Marston et al., 2003), nor was any decrease in placement noted. Instead, the placement rate remained stable at approximately 7% for the areas of LD and mild mental impairment.

A second example of the problem-solving model was implemented by the Heartland Area Educational Agency. That agency serves approximately 24% of students in the Iowa Public Schools. In 1990, the agency began implementation of a four-tiered problem-solving model. The transition to the problem-solving model involved a shift from traditional special education and general education resources to a seamless model of resource allocation. Similar to the Minnesota Public Schools problem-solving model, Heartland's model involved instruction and assessment at an individual student level (Tilley, 2003).

Tilley (2003) identified several "operational challenges" involved with the four-tiered, individually based system. These challenges included the fact that it is often not feasible to work with student problems at an individual level on a large scale. The resources required make the instructional process somewhat inefficient, especially when working with mild educational problems among large numbers of students. In the past three years, Heartland has shifted to a three-tiered model using the following tiers:

Tier One: Core Instructional Curriculum (all students involved)

Tier Two: Core Instruction and Supplemental Instructional Resources (students who need additional assistance—group or individual assistance)

Tier Three: Core Instructional and Intensive Resources (students who need intensive interventions and specialized resources on an individual basis)

Heartland defines their problem-solving model as "a process that includes an objective definition of student behavior problems or academic difficulties, systematic analysis of the student's problem and implementation of a planned systematic set of interventions" (Grimes & Kurns, 2003). Heartland incorporated "science into practice" by applying the scientific method in the decision-making process (Tilley, 2003). This process was applied at each intervention tier, utilizing four components (see following box).

Define the problem: What is the problem? Why is it happening?
The team looks at the gap between expected and actual student behavior or performance. Appropriate assessment and data analysis are used to distinguish specific problems and to attempt to rule out inappropriate instruction as the cause for this gap.

Develop a plan: What is going to be done about the problem?
Interventions are formulated based on student weaknesses and needs. Research-based strategies are key elements of the plan.

Implement the plan: Is the plan being implemented as intended?
The intervention is implemented as designed. Ongoing progress monitoring is used to evaluate intervention effectiveness.

Evaluate: Did the plan work as intended?
Data gathered throughout the implementation period are evaluated to determine the next course of action (Grimes & Kurns, 2003).

The multidisciplinary team utilizes this ongoing process to make appropriate decisions regarding instructional programming. Intensive support is provided through the Heartland Agency to each school involved in the project. This support most frequently takes the form of additional personnel such as school psychologists, educational consultants, social workers, and/or speech-language pathologists. Students who progress through each tier without making acceptable progress are considered for possible special education eligibility and placement (Jankowski, 2003).

Another important aspect of Heartland's model is teacher training. Teachers in all participating schools receive intensive training in research-based strategies and assessment. In addition, Heartland provides training on problem solving, team building, data collection, and data interpretation. Ongoing training and support have proven to be essential components of the model (Grimes & Kurns, 2003).

The Heartland Agency reports a significant reduction in special education placement rates among kindergarten through third graders. After implementation of the Heartland Early Literacy Project in coordination with the problem-solving model, thirty-nine participating schools reported the following results for the years 1999–2004 (Tilley, 2003):

- Forty-one percent reduction in special education initial placements in kindergarten
- Thirty-four percent reduction in special education initial placements in first grade

- Twenty-five percent reduction in special education initial placements in second grade
- Nineteen percent reduction in special education initial placements in third grade

As you might note, the reduction percentage of students eligible for special education did decline. However, we should note that in the Heartland Agency example, that reduction percentage was noted among students referred for all categories of special education, not merely learning disabilities.

THE STANDARD PROTOCOL RTI MODEL

The standard protocol model utilizes a set of standard research-based interventions usually implemented in two, three, or four tiers or levels. In contrast to the problem-solving model, the interventions occur in a natural progression from tier to tier, and are similar for all students experiencing the same learning problems rather than being specially designed for each individual student. There is a large body of research using standard protocol. In this section, we will explore several studies performed by leading researchers in the RTI field.

McMaster, Fuchs, Fuchs, and Compton (2003) implemented a standard protocol RTI to identify reading problems in eight metropolitan Nashville schools. Students in first-grade classrooms were taught reading using a standard curriculum and the usual reading materials. Students were then assessed using a "Rapid Letter Naming" test. The eight lowest performing students in each classroom were placed in groups where they were instructed with one of two research-based strategies. These two strategies were Peer-Assisted Learning Strategies (PALS), or "PALS + Fluency." First-grade PALS reading (Fuchs et al., 2001) is a peer-assisted instructional process whereby students tutor each other in a reciprocal fashion for some brief period each day. Developed by researchers at Vanderbilt University, PALS focuses on phonological awareness, beginning decoding, word recognition, and fluency. "PALS + Fluency" has an added focus on reading fluency and comprehension (McMaster et al., 2003, p. 9).

In this study, students received ongoing progress monitoring using nonword fluency probes from the Dynamic Indicators of Basic Early Literacy Skills (DIBELS; Good & Kaminski, 2001) and Dolch word probes. After seven weeks of instruction, students were classified as nonresponders if they scored 0.5 standard deviation below average readers on several criteria. Nonresponders were then placed in smaller groups where they received more intensive PALS, modified PALS, or tutoring for a period of thirteen weeks. Modified PALS places three modifications on the PALS design: fewer sounds and words are introduced at once and students work at their functioning level, the student serving as the "coach" models the sounds and words, and phonological awareness and decoding skills are emphasized more (McMaster et al., 2003, p. 9). In the PALS and modified PALS groups, interventions were provided by peers, as the program design dictates. In the tutoring groups, intervention was provided by a trained adult. Again, progress was monitored for each student biweekly. The study explored issues such as appropriate identification criteria and effective instructional strategies.

One of the most comprehensive studies of the standard treatment protocol for RTI was conducted by Vellutino et al. (2006) in suburban and rural schools in New York. This five-year longitudinal study explored the impact of kindergarten and first-grade interventions for children identified as at risk for reading disabilities. The initial sample of 1,373 children was assessed on letter-name knowledge at the beginning of kindergarten. Results of those assessments indicated that approximately 30% of the children were at risk for reading difficulties. Those at-risk students were then divided equally into treatment and control groups. The treatment group members were provided with a small-group (two or three children) early literacy intervention program throughout their kindergarten year. The intervention was provided by a certified teacher who had been trained on that curriculum by project staff. Students were pulled from the general education classroom for two thirty-minute sessions each week. Progress was monitored three times during the school year (December, March, and June). Initial results indicated a significant improvement in reading ability for the treatment group.

During the following year, researchers reassessed all students who had been members of the kindergarten treatment and control groups. Based on this assessment, 50% of the treatment group participants qualified as poor readers whereas 60% of the control group members were considered to be poor readers. All students identified as poor readers in first grade were either given individual tutoring by project teachers or the remediation normally provided by the school in the first-grade classroom. Progress was monitored for all students through the completion of their third-grade year. Results of the study revealed that of the students receiving kindergarten-only interventions or both kindergarten and first-grade interventions, 84% performed in the average range on reading measures by the end of third grade. This is a dramatic turnaround among these poor readers. Perhaps the most important finding of this study is the impact of early intervention for preventing reading disabilities.

Both of these studies involved identification of reading problems in children in third grade or younger. However, the standard treatment protocol model for RTI has also been used to prevent and identify mathematics disabilities. Fuchs et al., (2005) assessed the mathematics performance of children in forty-one first-grade classrooms (ten schools) using weekly curriculum-based measurement. The assessment tool consisted of twenty-five items related to math skills taught in the first-grade curriculum. Curriculum-based measurement scores were taken frequently and averaged across three to five weeks; based on those average scores, children who averaged less than eleven correct math problems were considered to be at risk for a mathematics disability.

These students were then placed into groups of two or three where they received tutoring and computer practice for a total of forty minutes, three times each week. An educational intervention involving tutoring based on the concrete-representational-abstract method for math instruction (Butler, Miller, Crehan, Babbitt, & Pierce, 2003; Cass, Cates, Smith, & Jackson, 2003; Mercer, Jordan, & Miller, 1996) was implemented until every member of the group achieved mastery or until every lesson on the topic had been taught. The method involves using manipulatives to provide for concept understanding. Seventeen topics were covered in up to sixty-six sessions (depending on mastery). Curriculum-based measures continued to be implemented throughout the study. The findings revealed improved performance on computation, concepts and applications, and completion of story problems. In these areas, at-risk students who received intervention outperformed students who received no intervention. Researchers also found that the growth of the at-risk tutored students was, on some measures, equal to or greater than students who were not considered to be at risk. Most important, the study revealed that early intervention in this case reduced the prevalence of math disability by an average of 35%.

In another study involving math performance, Fuchs et al. (2006) explored the effects of a curriculum called "Hot Math" (Fuchs, Fuchs, Prentice, Burch, & Paulsen, 2002) among third-grade students. Tier One involved Hot Math whole-class instruction in forty general education classrooms located in thirteen schools. Instruction was implemented two or three times each week for sixteen weeks, with each session lasting twenty-five to forty minutes. Students who scored lowest after this intervention were assigned to Tier Two Hot Math tutoring. This intervention occurred three times each week in twenty- to thirty-minute sessions for thirteen weeks. Groups composed of two to four students received this instruction together; a student was considered to be unresponsive to instruction if his or her daily performance was one standard deviation below the performance levels of the norm scores in the assessment. Thus, in this study, a student's performance was based on multiple measures and varied depending on how many tiers students participated in. Overall, the study revealed vast improvement on all measures for the

Table 1.3   Strengths and Weaknesses of Problem-Solving and Standard Protocol RTIs

Model	Strengths	Weaknesses
Problem-Solving Model	• Decisions based on individual student needs • Allows more flexibility in choices of interventions and allocation of resources	• Dealing with learner problems at an individual level can become time consuming • Requires teachers and team members to have vast knowledge and expertise in research-based strategies
Standard Protocol Model	• Clear scientific process in literature for strategies and assessment • Standard interventions in place and readily available to students in need • Structured progression between tiers	• Less flexibility with choice of interventions (one size doesn't fit all) • May require additional staff, depending on available resources

majority of students receiving any level of intervention. Unresponsiveness in problem solving for students receiving only traditional math instruction was an alarming 86%–100%. Unresponsiveness for students receiving both tiers of intervention was 12%–26%. This study illustrated that the RTI model had a substantial impact on reducing the number of children at risk for math disability in third grade.

FINAL THOUGHTS

With the release of final IDEA regulations in August 2006, it is expected that many, if not all, states will incorporate some form of RTI into their policies and procedures. However, those regulations do not propose or recommend any specific RTI model. In fact, those regulations do not require implementation of any RTI procedure at all. Rather, those regulations allow RTI as an eligibility procedure for documentation of learning disabilities. The relevant section of those regulations is presented in the following box (see www.ed.gov/idea and look under "Changes in Initial Evaluation or Reevaluation"). According to that source, the IDEA legislation of 2004 includes the following provision.

Establishes procedures for evaluating a child suspected of having a specific learning disability.

Notwithstanding Section 607(b), when determining whether a child has a specific learning disability as defined in Section 602:

An LEA shall not be required to take into consideration whether a child has a severe discrepancy between achievement and intellectual ability in oral expression, listening comprehension, written expression, basic reading skill, reading comprehension, mathematical calculation, or mathematical reasoning.

An LEA may use a process that determines if the child responds to scientific, research-based intervention as a part of the evaluation procedures.

(614(b)(6))

As you can see, this provision eliminates the requirement for a discrepancy calculation, but it does not explicitly prohibit the use of discrepancies. Further, this provision gives no guidance on which type of RTI—standard treatment protocol or problem-solving model—should be implemented.

Although the research base on RTI is broad in some areas, such as reading instruction and interventions for young children, there are many unanswered questions about implementation of RTI. Educators are left with the dilemma of working out the specifics for efficient, cost-effective implementation while providing the desired benefit of early intervention and appropriate disability identification. The remainder of this book will address these issues and provide guidance for effective implementation.

For planning purposes, it may be beneficial for a school or school district to examine current instructional procedures. Appendix A presents a "Needs Assessment" that focuses on many aspects of RTI that are discussed in subsequent chapters. This form may be used as is or adapted as school district personnel deem necessary to assist in your planning as you move into RTI.

Determining Appropriate Research-Based Interventions

Cara F. Shores and Kim Chester

Anew phenomenon is occurring in education in which the "art" of teaching is becoming the "science" of teaching (Marzano, Pickering, & Pollock, 2001). Teaching should not just be about the fun and creative activities—it should also be about the planned systematic research approach that increases learning. We believe that school improvement efforts should be based not solely on intuition, but rather on experience *and* research-based practices. At the core of effective teaching is the classroom teacher. In fact, recent research on teaching shows that the most important factor affecting student achievement is the classroom teacher (Wright, Horn, & Sanders, 1997). For this reason, in this chapter we will focus on specific research-based strategies that teachers can implement in their classrooms throughout all tiers of instruction in order to maximize their impact on achievement.

As discussed in Chapter 1, research-based strategies are required by our nation's federal education laws: the Individuals with Disabilities Education Improvement Act of 2004 (IDEA 2004) and the No Child Left Behind Act of 2001 (NCLB). In particular, NCLB states that only strategies and methods proven effective by scientifically based research should be included in school reform programs (Comprehensive School Reform Program Office, 2002). IDEA 2004 also references the use of research-based strategies, specifically as it relates to the identification of students who are learning disabled and as it relates to providing Early Intervening Services to students at risk for failure (U.S. Department of Education, 2006).

There is an ongoing debate among researchers and practitioners concerning an appropriate definition for research-based strategy. NCLB uses the term "scientifically based instructional strategies" in its requirements for their use in targeted assistance schools. The act defines "scientifically based research" to mean research that involves the application of rigorous, systematic, and objective procedures to obtain reliable and valid knowledge relevant to education activities and programs and includes research that

- employs systematic, empirical methods that draw on observation or experiment;
- involves rigorous data analyses that are adequate to test the stated hypotheses and justify the general conclusions drawn;
- relies on measurements or observational methods that provide reliable and valid data across evaluators and observers, across multiple measurements and observations, and across studies by the same or different investigators;
- is evaluated using experimental or quasi-experimental designs in which individuals, entities, programs, or activities are assigned to different conditions and with appropriate controls to evaluate the effects of the condition of interest, with a preference for random-assignment experiments, or other designs to the extent that those designs contain within-condition or across-condition controls;
- ensures that experimental studies are presented in sufficient detail and clarity to allow for replication or, at a minimum, offer the opportunity to build systematically on their findings; and
- has been accepted by a peer-reviewed journal or approved by a panel of independent experts through a comparably rigorous, objective, and scientific review (NCLB, sec. 9101).

In essence, the law requires that programs and interventions implemented in schools meet this high standard through quality of evidence, quantity of evidence, reliability, validity, and ease of replication. In 2004, Congress adopted this same definition for scientifically based research in IDEA (U.S. Department of Education, 2006; sec. 300.35). Therefore, RTI involves determining a student's response to scientific, research-based interventions that meet this standard.

As schools seek to implement the RTI process, we see interventions of varying types in use. For our purpose, we have divided these interventions into four distinct categories: research-validated curriculum, research-based supplemental materials, research-based practices, and research-based learning strategies.

In most research literature, research-validated curriculum refers to the state and/or local curriculum, including textbooks and structured programs that are in place to teach the curriculum. Most states have moved to curricula based on national standards. They provide state-approved textbook lists from which local districts may choose. These materials become the core curriculum and are used to teach students in general education classrooms.

Supplemental materials are often used for Tier 2 or Tier 3 interventions. They should align with the core curriculum (Vaughn & Roberts, 2007) and provide more intensive instruction in one or more skills. These materials must also meet the scientifically based research (SBR) requirements. They may be in a printed format, a computer software format, a combination of print/software, or kits.

We find that many schools are seeking out this type of intervention. There are some distinct advantages to using a published program. For example, products can be chosen for their ability to target specific skills, such as alphabetics or reading comprehension. They usually provide sequential lessons with specific guidance for the teacher, sometimes even going to the point of being scripted. When this guidance is followed carefully, fidelity of instruction improves significantly over less structured interventions. With proper training, paraprofessionals and other non-certified persons such as tutors may provide the instruction (L. S. Fuchs & Fuchs, 2007; Vaughn & Roberts, 2007).

Computer-assisted instruction (CAI) is being implemented more frequently to address individual student needs. In order to become successful adult learners, students must learn to work independently. One effective method of promoting independent learning is with the computer. Computers are typically engaging for students and can free the teacher to provide intensive instruction to other students in small group settings. It is very important, however, to use quality computer programs to meet individualized student needs; the computer is not intended to be merely a babysitter.

Computer-assisted instruction is used for drill and practice, tutorials, and simulations (Cotton, 1991). Educators are using CAI as stand-alone computer learning or as a supplement to teacher-directed instruction. Stennett (1985) found that well-designed and well-implemented CAI produced significant improvements in achievement when used *as a supplement* to traditional instruction rather than independently of teacher-directed instruction. Multiple research studies show that students who use CAI have a faster rate of learning and longer retention of information than with conventional instruction alone (Cotton, 1991). CAI offers more objectivity, appropriate pacing, opportunities for feedback, individualized learning, and engagement. It is important to match students' needs to appropriate CAI by utilizing classroom data from assessments.

Using purchased materials for interventions, despite its advantages, has some disadvantages. Firstly, using purchased materials is cost-prohibitive for some schools and districts. Because students exhibit a wide variety of skill deficits, it is difficult to provide one or more programs to address all needs.

Additionally, it cannot be assumed that all products on the market meet NCLB/IDEA requirements for scientifically based research. In reality, the extent to which these products meet this standard varies widely. For example, some publishers have valid and reliable internal research but have no independent review of their products. Others have research that is poorly designed, which essentially limits reliability and validity. There are some that have a strong research base, often with development through a research university and replication in large school systems. The dilemma for educators is trying to determine which products meet the standards and which do not. They cannot take for granted that the products they are considering for purchase meet the requirements.

Since 2004, publishers have begun making considerable efforts to establish this research base for their products or to make known the research that they have. In an effort to make their products marketable, some companies compare their materials to National Standards or the recommendations of the National Reading Panel. Others may provide student achievement data from districts that have used their program for some time. Still, most publishers do not have research results that meet the NCLB/IDEA standards.

In an effort to assist schools in finding research-based strategies, the U.S. Department of Education established the What Works Clearinghouse (WWC) through the Institute for Education Sciences. The What Works Clearinghouse provides reviews of research on a variety of scientific research–based interventions, including published materials. The reviews include a rating system, which delineates, on a scale of positive to negative, the amount of effect on student achievement that was documented in the research studies. The information is presented in easily interpreted charts and additional narrative information. It is important to note that the WWC considers evidence only from studies that meet the NCLB/IDEA requirements. Research studies of less rigor and individual system data outside of a research study are not considered in the ratings. (The WWC can be accessed at http://ies.ed.gov/ncee/wwc.)

In addition, the Florida Center for Reading Research has evaluated many reading programs currently on the market at the request of schools in their state. (The results of their evaluations are available at www.fcrr .org/FCRRReports/.) There are other organizations that make similar recommendations concerning research-based strategies and interventions— several of them are listed in Resource A of this book. When looking at various evaluation sites, we consider only ratings done by U.S., regional, or state departments of education or leading research universities. The information should always include the standard of research considered and the basis on which recommendations are made.

We also recommend that educators wishing to purchase materials contact the publisher and ask for their research base. As we mentioned earlier, most publishers are working very hard to provide this information. Many times, the information is available on the company's website. If not, you may call the publisher and ask that they provide you with the information.

Our third type of intervention involves research-based practices. These are overarching concepts that are considered best practice for Tier 1 classroom instruction. They are broad concepts, not specific enough to pinpoint and address targeted deficits. The Access Center, developed by the U.S. Office of Special Education Programs, provides valuable information and teaching modules on many of these practices. The Center was part of a grant whose funding ended in 2007; however, the website is still maintained, at www.k8accesscenter.org.

Our last type of intervention involves research-based learning strategies, appropriate across grade levels and content areas for addressing specific skill deficits often found in students with poor achievement. In implementing the RTI process, many schools are choosing to focus on the use of these instructional strategies to provide Tier 2 and Tier 3 interventions. These types of strategies often have a strong research base that meets the NCLB/IDEA standards (L. S. Fuchs et al., 2003; L. S. Fuchs et al., 2004; Saenz, Fuchs, & Fuchs, 2005).

These types of interventions have some advantages over purchased programs, beginning with their cost-effectiveness. Most involve minimal investment and are taught through materials already available in the school, such as the basal textbook. They may be very beneficial in addressing specific skill deficits, such as inability to glean information from text. They are often most effective when taught systematically to students in intervention tiers, then embedded into the general education instruction. This provides generalization of the skill to multiple content areas.

However, just as with published materials, there are disadvantages to their use. The person who is teaching the intervention must do so in a systematic way through modeling, coaching, guided practice, independent practice, and application to the curriculum. This requires a deep understanding of the strategy itself and how it is best used in content instruction. These strategies, although they have a definite structure, often do not have guidance materials such as teacher guides or scripts.

Therefore, fidelity of instruction may not be as strong as with supplemental materials or scripted programs. When these learning strategies are being used, extra steps must be taken to ensure fidelity. We recommend that, prior to using this type of instructional strategy, teachers receive explicit instruction in its effective use. They may need ongoing guidance from instructional coaches or persons who are considered experts in the strategy.

We believe there is benefit to incorporating both programs and learning strategies in RTI intervention options. Some students will benefit most from a program specifically designed to teach their deficit skills, as in the areas of alphabetics or phonics. Other students need to be taught metacognitive strategies that will increase their learning in the general curriculum. The decision for the type of intervention to be used should be based on the needs of the student.

Most educators agree that research-based practices are more valid methods of instruction than general teaching practices. However, identifying multiple strategies, implementing the strategies with instructional fidelity, and training staff members to use them is often a challenge for schools. For this reason, we believe targeted professional development is critical for successful school improvement. In an effort to accomplish this for a variety of interventions, it is helpful to incorporate a systematic staff development plan that provides for training in small increments into the overall school improvement plan (Eaker, DuFour, & DuFour, 2002).

Best practices should be employed for all instruction, including individualized strategies. Once strategies have been selected, they must be employed with the same intensity and structure as recommended in the research. It is important to remember that modeling and demonstration of key concepts are critical for students to obtain the explicit instruction that they need in order to learn. Students also need opportunities to practice, apply, and receive descriptive feedback. Flexible grouping may be needed for various interventions.

Effective approaches to instruction require a commitment from administrators and use of all resources, including parents. The system of supports that is required includes utilizing every person in the building and establishing a flexible schedule for meeting students' needs. Once this system is established, schools may develop a vast bank of interventions available to address a wide variety of students' needs.

In this chapter, we will not discuss published textbooks or supplemental materials, due to the large number available and the complexity of each program. Instead, our focus will be to provide you with information on a variety of research-based practices and learning strategies, the last two categories that we outlined above. We have chosen to highlight strategies that are applicable across grade levels and content areas. As we discuss interventions throughout this chapter, keep in mind that this is just a sampling of many possible strategies and that these are good practices for all students. The determination of a particular strategy and location for delivery of services will depend on the student's needs both behaviorally and academically, as well as the structure of your school's Response to Intervention model.

TIER 1: BEST PRACTICES IN TEACHING

We begin by examining practices that may be incorporated into Tier 1 instruction. These practices are not considered instructional strategies; instead, they are ways to structure the general education classroom to promote learning for all. These factors must be in place in order to create a solid foundation for effective teaching and learning.

School-Wide Behavior Management

In the 2000 *Executive Summary on Youth Violence*, the U.S. Surgeon General reported an escalating rate of disruptive behavior. As we visit schools on a regular basis, it is clear that the unruly behaviors are impeding student learning. For this reason, teachers frequently request assistance with behavior management. To address these concerns, we will present practical fundamental approaches that should be evident in all settings within the school.

Educators are in need of preventive and positive, rather than reactive and aversive, approaches to behavior. School-wide behavior management provides the support and foundation for promoting appropriate behaviors of all students throughout the building (OSEP Technical Assistance Center on Positive Behavioral Interventions, 2007). School-wide positive behavior supports focus on three levels of strategies to improve learning for all: primary or Tier 1 (school-wide procedures), secondary or Tier 2 (classroom procedures), and tertiary or Tier 3 (individual procedures).

The foundation of effective behavior management can be found at the primary level of supports, which is intended for all students and staff and is in effect in all settings of the school. These strategies should be effective for at least 80 percent of the school population. If more than 20 percent of the school population is requiring secondary supports, the school-wide behavior plan should be strengthened. The National Technical Assistance Center on Positive Behavioral Interventions and Supports outlines seven components that should be evident and effective for a comprehensive school-wide system of discipline:

1. An agreed-upon and common approach to discipline,
2. a positive statement of purpose,
3. a small number of positively stated expectations for all students and staff,
4. procedures for teaching these expectations to students,
5. a continuum of procedures for encouraging displays and maintenance of these expectations,
6. a continuum of procedures for discouraging displays of rule-violating behavior, and
7. procedures for monitoring and evaluating the effectiveness of the discipline system on a regular and frequent basis (OSEP, 2007).

In order to increase support and longevity, every adult in the school should have input as the foundational plan is being created and implemented. The final product should be executed with sincerity by all members of the school, including all staff, students, and parents.

Classroom Behavior Management

Having an effective school-wide behavior plan is an advantage to classroom teachers, because consistency and support are created when they mirror each other. However, some schools are not implementing comprehensive procedures, leaving teachers to independently create their own classroom behavior plan in a well-structured, proactive, and supportive manner.

In many of our workshops, classroom management has been a topic of discussion and concern based on its impact on student learning. In poorly managed classrooms, teachers cannot teach and students cannot learn (Marzano, 2003). One of the first large-scale systematic studies of classroom management was completed in 1970 by Jacob Kounin (Marzano, 2003). He found that effective classroom management had four critical components: "withitness," smoothness and momentum during presentations, clear expectations, and variety and challenge during seatwork (Kounin, 1970; Marzano, 2003). Let us examine each of these more closely.

Withitness

"Withitness" is being aware perceptually and cognitively of what is taking place in the classroom. To accomplish this, teachers must have full view of every child in the classroom and be able to attend to multiple tasks at once. Along those same lines, Wolfgang (2004) found that teachers who expressed their awareness to the class benefited from increased engagement and decreased misconduct from their students. Teachers must make their students feel they have "eyes in the back of their head" by being aware of behaviors and handling them proactively, appropriately, and immediately.

Smoothness and Momentum

Smoothness and momentum in the classroom requires specific planning and practice. Much time is wasted when transitions are not smooth. Expectations and procedures for minimizing transition time must be explicitly stated and practiced. *CHAMPs: A Proactive and Positive Approach to Classroom Management* by Randy Sprick (Sprick, Garrison, & Howard, 1998) is a practical tool for specifically stating expectations and minimizing transition time. CHAMPs is an acronym for "conversation, help, activity, movement, and participation," which clarifies expectations for students at all times of the day. During seatwork, the teacher displays pictures for each of the areas listed above which might include students working quietly (conversation), raising their hand for assistance (help), completing work at their desk (activity), no movement in the classroom (movement), and students actively engaged (participation). Equally important to smooth transitions is keeping the momentum with appropriate pacing. Downtime should be kept to a minimum. Teachers should keep progressing through the lesson at a steady pace to promote student engagement.

Clear Expectations

Clear expectations begin on the first day of school, with specific rules and procedures. These must be visibly posted, actively discussed, and often revisited. "Rules" and "procedures" differ in purpose: Rules are general expectations, while procedures are specific expectations for particular behaviors (Marzano, 2003). For instance, a general rule would be to respect others, while a procedure would define expectations for obtaining assistance in class. Both rules and procedures are significant components of an effectively managed classroom.

Variety and Challenge

Variety and challenge are important to keep students focused and engaged. When students become bored or are not challenged, inappropriate behaviors often emerge. Students may create their own variations to a task, work with very little thought, or create their own excitement in the form of misbehavior (Kounin, 1970). To minimize inappropriate behaviors, teachers should provide activity and instruction that challenge students at their level of learning. In addition, teachers can provide variety through flexible grouping and varied styles of teaching and learning. Since the early 1970s, many resources have been developed to improve classroom management. Resource A provides a list of resources for proactive discipline and positive behavior supports.

Often, teachers say they cannot differentiate their lessons because their students cannot transition well and have difficulty with the variances differentiation brings. We urge teachers to address the root of the problem: The real issue is not differentiation but rather behavior. Therefore, teachers should address the problem behaviorally in order to incorporate necessary teaching strategies. Teachers must directly teach expectations for transition times as well as instructional times. Once behavior management is addressed, teachers can effectively begin to implement strategies of differentiation to meet students' needs.

Differentiated Instruction

"Differentiated instruction" is a teaching theory based on the belief that instruction should vary and be adapted to meet the individual needs of students. Specifically, this means providing many avenues in which students of varying abilities, interests, or learning styles can learn the content. In addition, differentiation provides greater student responsibility and ownership for learning, as well as opportunity to work collaboratively with peers.

Initially, differentiated instruction was designed and implemented in the general education classroom for gifted students. It was developed to address concerns that these children were not being appropriately challenged. As classrooms became increasingly diverse, differentiated instruction was seen as an effective method for meeting all students' needs by adapting the content, process, product, and learning environment for students based on individual readiness, interest, and learning profile.

For a classroom to truly be considered a differentiated classroom, it must include several key characteristics (Tomlinson, 1999). Teachers must have a clear understanding of essential concepts in the curriculum as well as their students' unique differences. Teachers use their understanding of students' differences to determine effective methods for delivering content. In order to do this, the teacher must integrate assessment and instruction. The results from assessment will guide decision making and allow the teacher to adjust content, process, product, or learning environment to support students in their readiness level, interest, or learning profile. As the teacher makes adjustments, the students participate in respectful work that is of interest and is appropriately supported through teacher and peer collaboration. The purpose in this is to encourage maximum growth and individual student success. To have a truly differentiated class, teachers must be flexible and willing to make necessary instructional decisions.

Differentiation is not one instructional strategy. It is composed of many research-based theories and practices. A key element of differentiation requires teachers to look at students' readiness levels to instruct and support students slightly above their functioning level in order to appropriately challenge and advance learning. Vygotsky (1978) researched this process and termed it the Zone of Proximal Development. More recent research supports this process as well (Fleer, 1992; Jacobs, 2001).

As a teacher begins to differentiate, he or she cannot implement every aspect at once. It is most effective to systematically differentiate in a manner that is beneficial to the students and manageable to the teacher. We recommend that teachers begin with one area (content, process, or product) or by differentiating one unit and then building the process in future units. In our discussion of differentiated instruction, we will discuss pre-instruction assessment, flexible grouping, active practice and feedback, tiered lessons, anchor activities, and "think-alouds."

Pre-Instruction Assessment

Pre-assessments are used to determine what students know about a topic before it is taught. As teachers begin the process of differentiation, we encourage them to incorporate pre-assessments from the beginning. Specifically, teachers should evaluate pre-assessment data regularly to determine flexible group memberships and to verify student strengths and needs. By utilizing pre-assessments, teachers have a means of showing student progress throughout instruction. Methods commonly used for pre-assessments include teacher-prepared pre-tests, KWL charts, demonstration, discussion, show of hands, observations, and checklists.

Flexible Grouping

Flexible grouping occurs when an assessment or instruction reveals the need for review, re-teaching, practice, or enrichment. These groups must be temporary and allow students to receive appropriate instruction at all levels. Groupings can be heterogeneous or homogenous. These are specifically based on readiness, interest, reading level, skill level, background knowledge, or social skills. Heterogeneous groups are suitable for critical thinking activities, open-ended discussions, and hands-on experiments. Homogenous groupings are appropriate for drill and practice, math computation, studying for tests, and answering recall questions (Jones, Pierce, & Hunter, 1989).

Practice and Feedback

Practice and feedback are effective outcomes of flexible grouping and are found to be highly effective. The Center for the Improvement of Early Reading Achievement (2001) states that the effectiveness of small group instruction may exceed individual or whole group instruction because children often benefit from listening to their peers respond and receiving feedback from the teacher. Students are more likely to participate in small groups, leading to more interaction and engagement. As students work together, higher-order cognitive processes are practiced, leading to more advanced outcomes. In summary, combining forces can produce a better product. For small group instruction to be effective, the educator must provide organization and clarity of activity through explicit directions.

Tiered Instruction

"Tiered instruction" is a specific differentiated instruction strategy used to teach one concept while meeting the different learning needs in a group (Tomlinson, 2001). It is an instructional framework that we find easy to implement with some planning and one that allows all students to be taught at their zone of proximal development. Tiered instruction is best implemented when pre-assessment reveals multiple learning levels within the class. In tiered instruction, assignments, lessons, and strategies can be tiered based on students' learning profiles, readiness levels, and interests. Tiering can be applied with varied adjustments to the challenge level, complexity, resources, outcomes, processes, or products (Heacox, 2002). All children benefit from tiered instruction, as each student is appropriately challenged and focused on essential learning concepts.

The first step in planning for tiered instruction is to examine the concepts or standards and assess students' learning profiles, readiness levels, and interests in that area. From the assessment information, teachers should choose an activity or project that is focused on the key concepts in the standard and create different instructional groups with appropriate scaffolding (supports). Tiered instruction will take place as the teacher adjusts the activity to provide for different levels of difficulty or complexity of thought.

Planning for tiered instruction begins as the teacher reviews the standard and determines what *all* students should know at the end of the lesson or unit. This ensures that instruction is focused on essential concepts that are critical for every child to understand. Next, the teacher determines what additional information or what higher level of thought processes will be used to instruct the next higher group. This may be thought of as "What do I want *most* of my students to know?" Finally, the teacher looks at the *few* students in the class who have already mastered or perhaps exceeded the standard. She then develops an activity for this group, again relying on complexity of thought or extension of knowledge. To effectively differentiate, the teacher must plan instruction that exceeds the bare minimum and reaches students in the "most" and "few" categories of learning. Within these levels, students are appropriately challenged. Figure 2.1 provides an example of a planning rubric that may be used for planning a tiered lesson. Again, this offers structure for differentiating instruction in the general education classroom.

Figure 2.1   Tiered Instruction Planning Guide

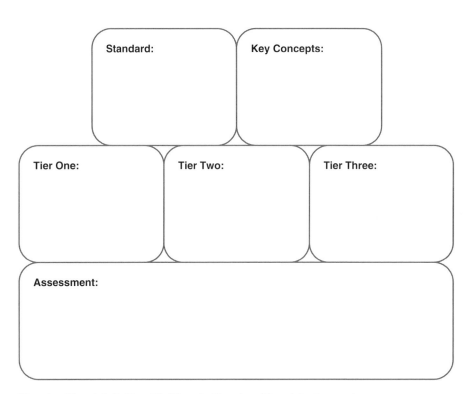

Planning Tiered Activities: Six Ways to Structure Tiered Assignments

- Challenge (Bloom's Taxonomy)
- Complexity (Introductory to Abstract)
- Resources (Reading Levels, Types of Terminology)
- Outcomes (Various Outcomes With Same Resources)
- Process (Various Ways of Learning With the Same Outcome)
- Product (Multiple Intelligences)

Anchor Activities

"Anchor activities" (Tomlinson, 1999) are essential in a differentiated classroom because students will most certainly complete assignments at different times. Anchor activities guide students from one activity to another without wasted time. This allows teachers to work with individuals or small groups of students who need more explicit teacher-directed instruction. Anchor activities are effective methods for keeping students engaged in content-related material. Silent reading, journals, vocabulary practice, math problem of the day, learning centers, spelling practice, science trivia, and website of the week are all examples of anchor activities. In order to make the most effective use of anchor activities, teachers must establish clear expectations for student behavior and performance. Checklists, anecdotal records, student conferences, learning journals, rubrics, and peer review are all methods of assessing progress within anchor activities (Tomlinson, 1999).

Think-Alouds

A "think-aloud" is a differentiated strategy for students who struggle with processing information. Thinking aloud has been found to make students' silent knowledge more explicit (Smith & Wedman, 1988). This process involves describing thought processes aloud as a problem is solved or a concept learned. Think-alouds are a form of explicit instruction as the educator models cognitive and meta-cognitive processes that good readers use to construct meaning and monitor comprehension. Students should practice think-aloud procedures as a class, in partners, and then independently. Throughout this process, students should begin to monitor their own comprehension and self-correct errors (Davey, 1983).

In order to utilize think-alouds, teachers must select a passage and preview the material with a student perspective. Educators should take note of any difficult concepts or unknown words in order to model appropriate thought processes. As the educator reads the passage aloud, the students follow along silently and listen for how meaning is constructed. Teachers should make predictions, explain mental pictures, share analogies that link prior knowledge with new information, express confusing points (monitoring comprehension), and demonstrate fix-up strategies to address areas of difficulty. It is important to provide practice opportunities for students to apply what they have observed.

Consider this example of a think-aloud, in which the teacher reads the following short passage:

> The children were filled with excitement as they opened the gate and entered Sarah's birthday party. They couldn't believe their

eyes! Balloons, streamers, confetti, presents, and sweet treats completely transformed the backyard to a party wonderland. It seemed the birds and crickets were even singing "Happy Birthday." Before long, the children realized that this was no ordinary party. Every child had a present! They had come to celebrate a friend's birthday, but Sarah had a surprise for them.

Teacher think-aloud:

- I predict the friends will have their own personal birthday cakes and more presents than Christmas morning.
- I can see the balloons, streamers, confetti, presents, and sweet treats.
- I imagine hearing the birds and crickets singing "Happy Birthday."
- I have had many birthday parties, so I can relate to the excitement of having a birthday.
- I don't really understand why Sarah wanted to surprise her friends. I am going to keep reading to see what she has in store.

Graphic Organizers

Graphic organizers are effective differentiation strategies that affect student achievement in the classroom by providing a "big picture" view of concepts and by helping to organize the relationships between concepts. Organizers are especially helpful in representing abstract information in concrete forms. Commonly used graphic organizers include webs or concept maps, sequence chains, flowcharts, and Venn diagrams. *Before instruction*, organizers can be used to activate prior knowledge and provide a conceptual framework for new information. *During instruction*, students use graphic organizers to process the information. *After instruction*, organizers are used for summarizing, elaborating, organizing, structuring, and assessing learning. It is important to model new graphic organizers and provide guided practice before expecting students to complete them independently (Jones et al., 1989).

Let us now look at a classroom example in which the teacher incorporates various differentiated instruction strategies into her classroom practices.

Ms. Chapman begins a unit on citizenship by giving a brief pre-assessment. This pre-assessment is in the form of a ticket out the door, a single piece of paper with student's name and answers to the following prompts: What is a citizen? What is an immigrant? How is your family heritage related to these terms? Based on the student responses, Ms. Chapman divides the class into ability groups to address these fundamental concepts. The activities are tiered for three ability groups based on students' levels of understanding and need for direct instruction. Group number 1 needs the most support; therefore, the teacher provides direct explicit instruction for learning the differences between immigrants and citizens. They use graphic organizers to illustrate reasons a person would come to our country as an immigrant and the benefits of being a citizen. Group 2 researches and presents the life of famous citizens and immigrants. Group 2 has moderate teacher assistance in the form of daily discussions and structure through rubrics and checklists. Group 3 has a student-directed activity as they trace family heritage and create an exhibit to display how their heritage relates to citizens and immigrants. Group 3 receives a rubric and mini-check in stages to be sure they are progressing properly. As all students work on their projects, anchor activities are used to keep them engaged when they complete assignments or need assistance. Ms. Chapman establishes various anchor activities for this unit of study. They include daily learning journals in which students summarize the most important concepts learned that day. These journals also contain peer reviews of the effectiveness of their group. Books at various reading levels pertaining to citizenship and immigration are provided in the room. For students who cannot read these texts independently, Ms. Chapman has recorded not only the text but also a think-aloud to guide students through small sections of the text. While reading the books, students record their progress in a reading log, along with any questions or comments the students have as they read the books. Throughout this unit, each child is participating in effective differentiated instruction.

Differentiated instruction is critical at all levels of instruction, elementary through high school. In order to meet the needs of a diverse group of students, educators must continually assess students' progress toward learning goals. These assessments will guide the teacher in making instructional decisions for increasing student achievement. Deliberately using students' background knowledge, interests, and learning profiles to differentiate content, process, product, and learning environment within the classroom will enable the teacher to meet individual needs.

TIERS 2 AND ABOVE: INTERVENTIONS TO MEET SMALL GROUP OR INDIVIDUAL LEARNING NEEDS

Interventions used in Tiers 2 and 3 are designed for students who have not shown progress with strategies in Tier 1. These interventions are targeted to meet specific student needs and should be implemented in combination with Tier 1 strategies in order to enhance and supplement the comprehensive curriculum. Interventions should be taught through a systematic, structured plan and monitored to document progress in order to make instructional decisions that increase learning.

Research-based interventions have a high probability of increasing performance (D. Fuchs & Fuchs, 2005). As stated earlier, in an effort to directly affect student achievement in the classroom and provide immediate support to teachers, we have narrowed our discussion to research-based *instructional strategies*, rather than research-based *curricular programs*. These instructional strategies should be used in conjunction with a research-validated curriculum, whether core or supplemental. The following summary of strategies is not by any means an exhaustive list. This is merely a sampling of strategies and resources that are available to educators as they search for interventions to meet individual student needs.

Behavior Management

As discussed previously in this chapter, it is beneficial to have a sound, proactive, positive, and consistent disciplinary system at all levels of the school. Once this is in place, we begin looking for more intense strategies for students who do not respond adequately. We have found that the individualized supports are more effective when coupled with a strong behavioral management foundation. Certainly, teachers should still implement positive, proactive, and consistent procedures as seen in Tier 1, but with added intensity based on individual student needs. Behavior Monitoring Charts, positive behavior support plans with reinforcement, verbal/visual cuing, social skills training, visualizations, and mentoring are a few of the general strategies designed to meet individual or small group behavior needs. It is critical to match each student's behavior to a strategy based on specific behavior assessments. Research-based behavior interventions generally fall under the broad theoretical categories of Applied Behavior Analysis and Social Learning Theory.

Applied Behavior Analysis (ABA) is commonly implemented in schools. In ABA, the functional relationships between antecedents, behaviors, and consequences are examined to determine the function of the problem behavior (Alberto & Troutman, 2006). When the function is identified, replacement behaviors can be made to the inappropriate behavior to serve the same function.

Consider the analogy depicted in Figure 2.2. Payton is continually oversleeping and being late to school. The problem or behavior (B) is not being tardy but rather not getting up when the alarm clock sounds. Being tardy is the consequence (C). The antecedent (A) that occurs just before Payton falls back to sleep is that he hits the "snooze" button, resulting in waking up late and ultimately being tardy. An appropriate plan of action would be to directly affect the behavior by adjusting the antecedent (what occurs just before the behavior). In order to do this, Payton decides to move the alarm clock across the room so that he must get up to turn off the alarm clock. By doing this, he wakes up enough to make a conscious decision to stay awake, get ready, and be on time to school.

Within ABA, educators consider how the consequence rewards the behavior in question. We know behaviors will continue to occur as long as they are being reinforced. Often, it is difficult to see how the consequence is rewarding the child, as illustrated in the following example: A child yells out in class, the other children laugh, and the teacher removes the child to In-School Suspension (ISS). The child's behavior is actually reinforced in two ways in this scenario. First, the child receives attention from peers, and second, the child is allowed to avoid the task at hand. In order to break this cycle, the child's need for attention and avoidance of task should be examined by the teacher. It could be that the child truly needs attention but does not know how to obtain it in an appropriate manner. This may require the teacher to "catch" the child behaving appropriately, so she can provide the needed attention. The child may require more intense social skills training. As for the behavior of task avoidance, the educator must analyze whether the child *can* in fact complete the task but refuses to or whether the child cannot complete the task. The interventions will differ based on the reason the child wants to evade the assignment. If the child cannot perform the task, the teacher will address the behavior academically. If the child has the ability to but will not perform the task, the

Figure 2.2   ABC Scenario

Antecedent	**B**ehavior	**C**onsequence
Hits snooze on alarm clock located by the bed	Falls back to sleep	Late for school
Action Plan: Change location of clock away from bed		
Gets out of bed to turn off alarm clock	Awake enough to stay up	On time for school

teacher will need to address it behaviorally, through the established behavior management system for that child. This will more than likely include reinforcement for appropriate behavior. It is this type of systematic evaluation and manipulation of antecedent, consequence, and behavior that research has proven effective in behavior change.

In contrast to Applied Behavior Analysis, Social Learning Theory emphasizes the importance of learning from others by modeling, imitating, and observing (Bandura, 1977). Within this theory, it is believed that not all types of learning are affected by direct reinforcement. Rather, people learn from observing others and then modeling expected behaviors through role-play. Many children know intellectually what to do, but they are unable or have never been asked to physically do it.

To teach appropriate behaviors, modeling and role-play have been highly effective in schools. Consider the following scenario. Mr. Lee has reviewed classroom rules and procedures regularly. He noticed that a few students were not following his most valued rule: Respect others and yourself. He spent much time discussing the disrespectful behaviors and had the students repeat the rule back to him. It appeared they understood the meaning of the rule. Mr. Lee even employed a T chart in which the class discussed what respect looks like on the left-hand side and what it sounds like on the right-hand side. This seemed to help a few of the students, but Mr. Lee noticed the behaviors were still evident at times. He took this small group of students and began to role-play, allowing each child to explicitly model specific behaviors found on the T chart. Each child was able to change roles and experience what true respect looks like, sounds like, and even feels like.

From these overriding theories, numerous strategies have evolved. Marzano (2003) has done extensive analysis of research-based strategies in the classroom. We will highlight two specific strategies that have been found to be highly effective in the classroom. These are self-monitoring and cognitive-based strategies. The self-monitoring strategies require students to be aware of their own behavior, record targeted behaviors, and compare their behavior with goals predetermined by the teacher and student. If the goals are reached, the student is rewarded. When using this process, it is important to meet with both the child and his or her parents to clearly define expectations and procedures for the strategy. Various forms and checklists can be used for recording purposes. Marking cards and charts or moving counters are simple ways of recording behaviors as well. Gradually, the record-keeping and rewards are diminished as appropriate until the student can perform the behavior without keeping a record and meeting with the teacher.

Cognitive-based strategies fall under the categories of social skills training and problem solving (Marzano, 2003). These strategies equip students with a means for dealing with social situations. The following four steps are explicit and systematic steps for assisting students who need to increase self-control (Marzano, 2003, pp. 88–89):

1. Notice when you are becoming angry, annoyed, frustrated, or overwhelmed, and stop whatever you are doing.
2. Ask yourself, "What are the different ways I can respond to this situation?"
3. Think about the consequences for each of your options.
4. Select the action that has the potential for the most positive consequences for you and others.

It is important to explicitly discuss the purpose and details of the strategy with the student and his or her parent. After the teacher has modeled the strategy steps, the child should have ample opportunity to practice the agreed-upon protocol before trying it in the classroom. Lastly, a cue to remind the student to use the steps may be necessary initially.

The behavioral strategies presented here are all considered cognitive strategies in that they cause students to actively think about and problem solve about their behavior. Cognitive strategies, however, are not solely for behavior management. Many are used for academic purposes, as you will see in the next section.

Cognitive Strategy Instruction (CSI)

Many struggling students have difficulty regulating their own learning. Cognitive strategy instruction (CSI) provides support for learners as they discover individual strategies allowing them to access knowledge and extend to higher-level understanding. Visualization, verbalization, making associations, chunking, questioning, scanning, underlining, accessing cues, and mnemonics are examples of specific cognitive strategies for learning and remembering. The focus in CSI should be on not only the specific strategies but also the implementation process. The implementation process is systematic and explicit. It involves teaching prerequisite skills that must be used within the strategy, describing with cues, teaching incremental steps, modeling, verbally rehearsing, practicing with assistance, practicing independently, and then generalizing to other settings. The University of Nebraska at Lincoln has compiled various cognitive strategies that can be accessed at www.unl.edu/csi.

Consider the following example of a child, Haley, who requires cognitive strategy instruction to understand and retain information. Visualization was used to assist Haley with spelling irregular words (words that did not follow general spelling rules). After several weeks of modeling and guided practice, the teacher began to provide more independent practice and asked Haley how she could remember the *ow* in *crown*. The teacher knew this could be difficult because the class had just been studying words that had the same *ow* sound but were spelled differently, such as b*ou*nd. Haley thought for a moment and said, "It's easy. I can see a crown on top of a queen's head in the shape of a *w*." Haley visualized the *w* shape to cue herself that the *ow* sound was made with a *w* and not a *u*. On her spelling test that week, Haley paused when the word *crown* was called out, made a gesture toward her head as a cue to herself, then wrote the word correctly. Later, with no teacher prompt, Haley expressed that she remembered the *oo* in *door* by visualizing two knobs on a single door. The teacher could see that Haley had effectively made it through the implementation process for visualizing and was now generalizing the steps to new situations on her own. The progress was documented and shared with Haley's parents, who began using similar strategies with her as they worked on homework.

Strategic Instruction Model

For more than thirty years, the University of Kansas Center for Research on Learning (2008) has conducted research on strategies designed to address the varied needs of diverse learners. The majority of the research was conducted in middle and high school settings. The Strategic Instruction Model (SIM) is a model that incorporates a variety of research-based strategies to be used with content area subject matter. The purpose of SIM is to promote effective teaching and learning within the classroom by focusing on what is important, what can be taught to help students learn, and how to effectively teach students (University of Kansas Center for Research on Learning, 2008).

Strategic Instruction Model strategies are typically taught to small groups of students that range from six to twelve children. A strategy can often be taught and mastered within three to four weeks, with one hour of instruction per day. Within each strategy, there is an eight-stage instructional methodology that must be carefully followed to ensure that students master and generalize the strategy. Two types of interventions are addressed within this model: teacher-focused interventions and student-focused interventions.

The teacher-focused interventions address how teachers present the content. Specifically, Content Enhancement Routines are explicit teaching procedures that assist the teacher in organizing and presenting the information. This systematic and graphic process aids the learner in comprehension and retention of critical content objectives. The routines include instructional procedures for *Planning and Leading Learning, Exploring Text, Topics & Details, Teaching Concepts,* and *Increasing Performance.*

The student-focused interventions provide specific skills and approaches needed for learning. These models were developed and researched across various settings and with general and special education teachers. Specifically, the Learning Strategies Curriculum addresses students' needs in the areas of *Reading, Storing & Remembering Information, Expressing Information, Demonstrating Competence, Social Interaction, Motivations,* and *Math.*

The Strategic Instruction Model is certainly systematic and explicit as it addresses the many varied needs of learners across all settings. Each strategy has impressive data to show the increase in student achievement. The benefit lies within the structure and support each research-based intervention holds. The limitation is in the accessibility of the model. In order to utilize the Strategic Instruction Model, teachers must receive intensive training from certified members of the International Training Network. The training typically occurs throughout the year and gives teachers the opportunity to master individual strategies through implementation and problem solving. While this model requires a commitment of time and professional development resources, we feel the proven gain in terms of amount, rate, and retention of learning is well worth it.

Math

Concrete, Representational, Abstract (CRA)

Many students struggle in the area of math. This is often because students are asked to learn math concepts in abstract form. It is important to begin math instruction with the appropriate base of understanding, which often requires a concrete approach to learning. Concrete, Representational, Abstract (CRA), a three-part instructional strategy used in mathematics to promote student learning and retention, specifically defines the steps to teaching in this manner.

CRA's three phases build upon each other and are implemented to provide a conceptual structure for meaningful connections to be made. The concrete stage, or Stage 1, is the "doing" stage, in which educators model with manipulatives (The Access Center, 2004). These materials can include colored chips, cubes, base 10 blocks, pattern blocks, and fraction blocks. Visual, tactile, and kinesthetic experiences should be considered. Stage 2, also known as the representational stage, is the "seeing" stage, in which the concrete models are transformed into pictorial representations (The Access Center, 2004). This includes drawing pictures or using stamps to illustrate the concepts. The last and final phase, Stage 3, is the abstract "symbolic" stage, in which abstract symbols are utilized (The Access Center, 2004). These mathematical symbols include numbers, letters, and signs (e.g., 2, 6, $3x$, +, −). The premise for CRA is that students should learn the concepts before learning "rules." Students who use concrete manipulatives develop more precise and comprehensive mental representation that leads to increased motivation and on-task behavior, understanding, and application of these concepts (Harrison & Harrison, 1986). CRA is most effective when used for understanding concepts in early number relations, place value, computation, fraction, decimals, measurement, geometry, money, percentage, number bases, word problems, probability, and statistics (The Access Center, 2004). Figure 2.3 depicts a progression from concrete (with chips) to representational (with the number line) and then finally to abstract (with numbers).

Figure 2.3   Concrete, Representational, Abstract (CRA)

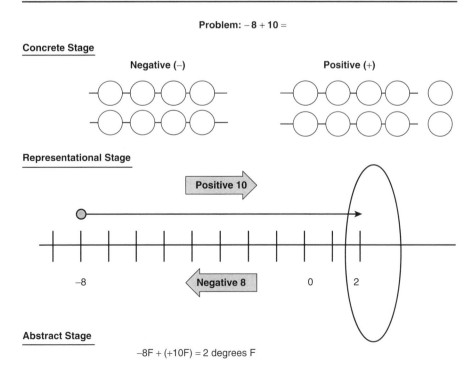

Problem: $-8 + 10 =$

Concrete Stage

Negative (−)   Positive (+)

Representational Stage

Positive 10

−8   Negative 8   0   2

Abstract Stage

−8F + (+10F) = 2 degrees F

Schema-Based Instruction

Problem solving is a critical skill that often confounds struggling learners. It involves combining knowledge, skills, and strategies in application to new problems. The National Council of Teachers of Mathematics places problem solving as a central theme in the *Principles and Standards for School Mathematics* (2000).

Schema-based instruction has been found to improve math word problem skills for elementary and middle school students (Jitendra, 2002; Miller, 1998). Placing word problems into categories before choosing a method to solve them is especially helpful for low-achieving students (Jitendra et al., 2007). According to the concept of schema-based instruction, most addition and subtraction problems fall into three major categories or types. These problems involve a change, a grouping, or a comparison. The first step in schema-based instruction is to identify the problem type and then translate the problem from words into a meaningful graphic representation (Jitendra, 2002).

Explicit modeling, guided practice, and feedback are essential during the stages of implementation. Furthermore, teachers should scaffold instruction by providing written rules as students are learning the procedures. Students should not be asked to use schema-based instruction independently until they have received direct instruction, scaffolding, and practice in first identifying the sets and then solving the problems through explicit guidance (Jitendra, 2002). Figures 2.4 through 2.6 illustrate addition and subtraction schema-based problem types with a graphic representation. Examples in these figures are for basic computation skills

Figure 2.4 The Change Set

The first problem type is the "change" set, which involves a change from the beginning set that results in the ending set. Consider the following example of a change set.

Haley had 12 ladybugs (beginning). Then, 3 ladybugs (change set) flew away. How many ladybugs does Haley have now (ending)?

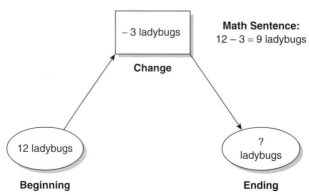

SOURCE: Jitendra, A. (2002). Teaching students math problem-solving through graphic representation. *TEACHING Exceptional Children, 34*(4), 34–38.

Figure 2.5   The Group Set

The second problem type is the group set. It does not involve a change of object amounts. Rather, it involves understanding part-whole relationships and knowing that the sum of the parts equals the whole (Jitendra, 2002). To illustrate this type of word problem, consider the following.

Wesley received 6 gift cards for his birthday. He used 2 from his favorite game store. How many gift cards were left?

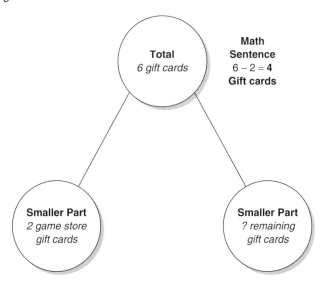

SOURCE: Jitendra, A. (2002). Teaching students math problem-solving through graphic representation. *TEACHING Exceptional Children, 34*(4), 34–38.

Figure 2.6   The Compare Set

The third problem type is the "compare" set, in which two sets have the same unit of measurement. Students focus on the phrase more than or less than to compare these sets (Jitendra, 2002). Consider the following example.

Payton kicked 16 goals (referent set) during the soccer season. Anna kicked 8 fewer (difference set) goals than Payton. How many goals did Anna kick (compare set) during the soccer season?

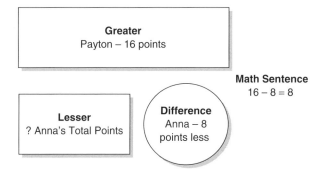

SOURCE: Jitendra, A. (2002). Teaching students math problem-solving through graphic representation. *TEACHING Exceptional Children, 34*(4), 34–38.

typically seen at the elementary level. Additional problem types for multiplication and division can be found in *Teaching Mathematics to Middle School Students with Learning Difficulties*, edited by M. Montague and A. K. Jitendra (2006).

General Content Strategies for Analyzing Information

In their book *Classroom Instruction that Works*, Robert Marzano and colleagues (Marzano, Marzano, & Pickering, 2001) summarized extensive research to present concise information about research-based interventions. They highlighted nine strategies that have high probability of enhancing student achievement for all students in all subject areas at all grade levels. Of these nine, we have chosen to highlight the top two instructional strategies that showed the largest effect size. These are *Identifying similarities and differences* and *Summarizing and note taking*. Specifically, we include these strategies for middle and high school students who struggle with comprehension and gleaning information from text. Either the teacher or the student, depending on the level of support needed, can lead either strategy. When students require explicit teacher support and focus, teachers lead the strategy. As students become proficient at using teacher-directed strategies, students can begin to lead these strategies themselves, which allows for more creativity to work and think. Teachers, however, should continue to guide and monitor students. Graphic organizers are also useful in each of these strategies, to aid students in understanding and visualizing. For specific instructions on implementing each of these strategies, see Marzano et al., 2001.

Identifying Similarities and Differences

Marzano et al. (2001, pp. 13–28) emphasize that identifying similarities and differences might be the "core" of all learning, because it enhances students' understanding of and ability to use knowledge. Identifying similarities and differences is appropriate for any content area in which students are asked to analyze concepts. Seeing similarities and differences is a fundamental cognitive process (Gentner & Markman, 1994). Breaking concepts into similar and dissimilar characteristics increases understanding and ability to solve complex problems by exploring the concepts in a simplified manner. Teachers should explicitly teach similarities and differences through discussion and inquiry. Students' understanding and ability to use knowledge is enhanced when they are guided through the process of identifying similarities and differences and then are provided the opportunity to identify these independently. Identifying similarities and differences involves comparing, classifying, creating metaphors, and

Figure 2.7 Comparison Graphic Organizer (Alternate Form of Venn Diagram)

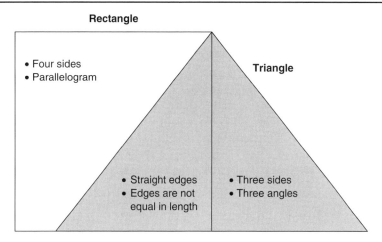

creating analogies. In these methods, students must analyze similarities and differences between concepts.

Comparing. Effective comparison requires recognition of significant characteristics that will improve students' understanding of similarities and differences between the compared items. Consider the following scenario. Students are asked to compare the West and Northeast regions of the United States. It would be insignificant to focus on family members who live in each region as a defining characteristic. More significant characteristics would include a comparison of climate or topography within these regions. When using the strategy of comparing, teachers should provide a comparison task that includes elements being compared, as well as characteristics to compare. Teachers assess students' descriptions of how items are similar or different in relation to the given characteristics. Two graphic organizers are typically used for comparison: the Venn diagram and the comparison matrix. Figure 2.7 provides an example of a comparison graphic organizer.

Figure 2.8 Example of Classification Chart

Herbivores	Omnivores	Carnivores
Eat plant material	Eat plants and meat	Eat meat
Sheep	Chickens	Wolves
Horses	Humans	Cheetahs
Rabbits	Chimpanzees	Dragonflies
Snails		Eagles

Classifying. Classifying requires organizing elements into groups based on their similarities. Classifying is shown in many real-world settings, such as grocery stores. Some students may need more structured tasks, in which teachers define the elements and the classifications for the elements. Figure 2.8 provides an example of a classification chart.

Creating Metaphors. Metaphors are used to experience and understand one thing in terms of another (Lakoff & Johnson, 1980). Socrates used the following metaphor: "Education is the kindling of a flame, not the filling of a vessel." In his metaphor, he depicts the similarity of education to lighting a flame as opposed to just filling a vessel. Teachers often use metaphors in casual conversation, such as "My class is a zoo!" Creating metaphors involves an implied comparison between two essentially unlike things: a classroom and a zoo. These are used to provide strong images and connect to background knowledge. Metaphors are used to give concreteness, clarify the unknown, express the subjective, and assist thought (Weaver, 1967). When using metaphors, teachers should go from the known to the unknown and from the concrete to the abstract. Teachers construct images and models of teaching based upon their prior knowledge and experiences (Johnson, 1987). The level of support provided by the teacher will depend on the student's level of understanding. The teacher may explicitly guide students in how the items are alike at the abstract level. Once students understand the process, the teacher may provide the first element and necessary background knowledge to complete the second element of the metaphor. Graphic organizers assist students in visualizing the abstract pattern between the two elements. Figure 2.9 provides an illustration of metaphors.

Creating Analogies. Creating analogies involves identifying relationships between concepts (Marzano et al., 2001). This involves making associations and discovering similarities between two unrelated elements. Specifically, students relate their background knowledge to unknown concepts.

Figure 2.9   Metaphors

Life **Element 1**	*Is a*	*Teacher* **Element 2**
Literal Pattern: Physical, mental, and spiritual experiences that represent existence	Abstract Relationship: *Life experiences are lessons that teach us along the way.*	Literal Pattern: Educates students

A teacher-directed analogy may be a complete analogy, such as *plane* is to *air* as *boat* is to *water* (plane:air::boat:water), where the teacher ascribes a known relationship to newly introduced elements. The teacher could also leave the very last element out of the analogy, such as *mason* is to *stone* as *carpenter* is to _____ (mason:stone::carpenter:_____). In a student-directed analogy, the teacher supplies the initial elements and the student invents the last two elements of the analogy, demonstrating understanding of how the teacher-supplied elements are related. To illustrate this strategy, consider *water* is to *liquid* as _____ is to _____ (water:liquid::_____:_____). Teachers can assess students' understanding of a concept through their analogies.

Summarizing Strategies

Summarizing and note taking are two of the most useful academic skills students can have (Marzano et al., 2001, pp. 29–48). Note taking is important for middle and high school students across all content areas. Students' comprehension is improved as they analyze content to find the most essential information and rephrase it in a way that makes sense to them. Synthesizing, a higher-order thinking skill, is closely related to summarizing because students must learn to analyze information, identify key concepts, and define extraneous information (Hidi & Anderson, 1987). Students must have skills in analyzing the information at a deep level in order to substitute, delete, and keep information as well as have an awareness of the basic structure of the presented information.

Teaching students to recognize various text structures is essential to summarizing and comprehending what is read or heard (Armbruster & Anderson, 1987). Six different text structure summary frames direct student attention to specific content by using a series of questions. Students should be asked to question what is unclear, clarify those questions, and predict what will happen next in the text. We will briefly discuss specific strategies for summarization: reciprocal teaching, rule-based strategy, summary frames, and note taking. Again, for a full explanation of these strategies, see Marzano et al. (2001).

Reciprocal Teaching. Reciprocal teaching (Marzano et al., 2001; Oczkus, 2005; Palincsar & Brown, 1984; Promising Practices Network, 2005) is a dialogue between teachers and students in regard to content reading in all subject areas. The specific purpose of reciprocal teaching is to bring meaning to small portions of text. Reciprocal teaching is one of the most effective summarizing strategies available to teachers to analyze information at a deep level (Rosenshine & Meister, 1994). It was initially intended to coach poor readers to use reading strategies employed by good readers to improve reading comprehension. Small groups of three to four students are effective for providing practice and receiving feedback. During this strategy, students interact with the text to construct meaning by using prior knowledge, experiences, and text information to predict, clarify, question, and summarize.

- *Predicting* consists of an educated guess. Guessing what may happen next gives a purpose for continuing to read and obtain information. Students should use the information they already have, as well as information obtained from headings, subheadings, and questions to effectively predict.

- *Clarifying* consists of explaining concepts and defining words, which allows students to focus attention on the text. This step often leads to re-reading the material, reading ahead, or asking questions; therefore, it should be incorporated during reading.

- *Questioning* leads to asking questions that can be answered by the text. Students must first identify what is important enough to question, then test their understanding with those questions.

- *Summarizing* is merely having the students put the information in their own words. Students must identify, paraphrase, and incorporate the important information from the text in their own words. This is typically done after predicting, clarifying, and questioning. In addition, text can be summarized in a group or individually.

As with most strategies, the teacher must provide modeling and support to students as they learn how to implement the reciprocal teaching strategy. Eventually, the students become proficient in this strategy and require minimal teacher support. Figure 2.10 provides an example of teaching practices for reciprocal teaching.

The "Rule-Based" Strategy (Marzano et al., 2001). The rule-based summary strategy has a set of rules or steps that a student must take to generate a summary (Brown, Campione, & Day, 1981). Merely having these rules posted will not teach the students how to summarize. It is essential that teachers explicitly present these rules through strategies such as modeling and think-alouds. The rules include (Marzano et al., 2001, p. 32):

- Delete trivial material that is unnecessary to understanding.
- Delete redundant material.
- Substitute superordinate terms for lists (flowers for daisies, tulips, and roses).
- Select a topic sentence, or invent one if it is missing.

Figure 2.10   Teaching Practices for Reciprocal Teaching

- Use any combination of the four strategies: predicting, questioning, clarifying, summarizing
- Incorporate best practices with reciprocal teaching:
  - Think-alouds
  - Cooperative learning
  - Scaffolding (modeling, guided practice, feedack)
  - Metacognition
- Before reading
  - Activate prior knowledge
  - Review strategies: predicting, questioning, clarifying, summarizing
  - Predict based on clues from text
  - Set a purpose for reading (clarify unknown words or possible questions)
- During reading
  - Teacher coaches students in predicting, questioning, clarifying, summarizing
  - Clarify words or ideas
  - Ask question about portions of text
  - Predict what is about to happen
  - Summarize text
- After reading
  - Discuss previously made prediction
  - Review strategies used
  - Clarify words or ideas
  - Ask questions to each other (higher-level questions)
- Summarize what was read

SOURCE: Oczkus, L. D. (2005). *Reciprocal teaching strategies at work: Improving reading comprehension, grades 2–6.*

Summary Frames (Marzano et al., 2001). Summary Frames consist of a series of questions provided by the teacher to students. The questions are based on the type of passage being studied. Summary Frames assist students in recognizing text structure. As students complete the Summary Frames individually, as a group, or in pairs, they begin to truly implement effective summarization skills that are essential for learning. After the questions in each Summary Frame have been answered, students use the information to write a summary. Marzano et al. (2001) highlight six types of frames, which include:

- The Narrative Frame
- The Topic-Restriction Illustration Frame
- The Definition Frame

- The Argumentation Frame
- The Problem/Solution Frame
- The Conversation Frame

Figure 2.11 provides an example of a narrative Summary Frame.

Note-Taking Strategies

Note-taking skills correlate with summarizing skills in that they both require students to determine what is most important. Marzano et al., (2001) describe four generalizations from Beecher's research (1988). The first generalization is that verbatim note taking is the least effective way to take notes (Bretzing & Kulhary, 1979). In verbatim note taking, efforts center on writing every word, not synthesizing or analyzing the information. The second generalization states that notes should be a work in progress. Scheduled time and teacher support should be a part of the routine for students to revisit, revise, and update notes. The third generalization is that notes should be used as study guides for tests. Marzano et al., (2001) continue by saying the utilization of well-designed notes to prepare for exams or other summative assessments can be highly effective. Lastly, less is not more when it comes to note taking. Research shows that there is a significant connection between the amount of notes taken and student achievement (Marzano et al., 2001; Nye, Crooks, Powlie, & Tripp, 1984).

We will conclude by discussing classroom practice in note taking. Teacher-prepared notes are explicit models of what the teacher finds important and precise models of how to structure notes (Marzano et al., 2001). Teachers should prepare notes in both linguistic and nonlinguistic formats, which include idea webs, sketches, and outlines (Nye et al., 1984). Each of these has distinct advantages for different learning styles.

Figure 2.11   Narrative Frame Summary Questions

Who are the main characters and what distinguished them from others?

When and where did the story take place? What were the circumstances?

What prompted the action in the story?

How did the characters express their feelings?

What did the main characters decide to do? Did they set a goal, and if so, what was it?

How did the main characters try to accomplish their goal(s)?

What were the consequences?

SOURCE: Marzano et al., 2001, p. 35

Informal outlines use indentations to indicate importance, and webbing uses a larger circle to depict importance with a line connecting circles to show relationships. Webbing limits the amount of information that can be recorded. To receive the benefit of both, a combination of both note-taking formats can be used. In the combination technique, the left column is reserved for informal outlines, the right is for webbing, and the bottom portion is for summarizing (Marzano et al., 2001). This method incorporates key attributes of effective note taking.

Summarizing and note taking are critical to student understanding. Explicit teacher guidance is essential as students learn to effectively summarize and record critical information. Teachers should continue to support and encourage consistent implementation while students become more independent and effective with this strategy. Figure 2.12 is an example of a note-taking guide.

Figure 2.12   Combination Note-Taking Guide

Outline Notes:	Webbing:
Summarization:	

SOURCE: Marzano, R., Pickering, D., & Pollock, J. (2001). *Classroom instruction that works: Research-based strategies for increasing student achievement.* Alexandria, VA: McREL.

> ## Partnering With Parents
>
> Parents should know specific strategies being implemented with their child across all tiers. Parents can be active team participants as strategies are being discussed, and they at least need to be notified of chosen strategies. Not only should parents know the strategies, they should also know the timeline of implementation. Strategies and materials for use at home should be considered during school intervention meetings. Be sure to consider parent expertise and ability to perform specific strategies. If parents are unable to aid students with particular approaches, consider computer-based programs or checklists to assist the parent. Many research-based strategies, such as those found in Marzano et al. (2001) can be implemented at home with a little teacher guidance.

SUMMARY

Educators are required to implement research-based strategies more than ever before, to guarantee quality instruction. Response to Intervention is designed to increase effectiveness of these strategies by requiring the research base for Tier 2 and above. The strategies described in this chapter have been found to be effective for students across many grade levels and content areas. We feel that these strategies are best implemented with a team approach; no longer can one person meet the varied needs of students. It truly does take the team to research, implement, and evaluate the effectiveness of these strategies. Lastly, these strategies are most effective when they are implemented in positive, supportive environments in which all of the child's strengths and needs are acknowledged and systematically addressed. It is important to remember that the interventions presented here for Tiers 2 and 3 must be implemented within a well-designed RTI plan.

We realize many educators and administrators are immersed in the day-to-day challenges of education, which leaves little time to sort through the research. Fortunately, there are many resources available to guide schools in the process of identifying research-based strategies. Resource A of this book is provided to guide educators, schools, and systems as they begin to meet students' needs with research-based practices.

Framework for Instructional Intervention With Diverse Learners

3

Catherine Collier

> *The biggest mistake of past centuries in teaching has been to treat all children as if they were variants of the same individual, and thus to feel justified in teaching them the same subjects in the same ways.*
>
> —Howard Gardner (in Siegel & Shaughnessy, 1994)

Culturally and linguistically diverse (CLD) students, including those who are learning English as an additional language, face tremendous challenges in our schools as do the educators who teach them. Students must overcome culture shock, acquire basic communicative competence in English, master academic language for each subject area, deal with shifts in family roles and language use in the dominant culture, and negotiate problematic concerns of identity in a social climate that is often hostile to difference. Teachers face the challenge of finding ways to ensure the academic success of these students whose educational backgrounds, home cultures, and languages are, in the majority of cases, different from their own. Most teachers are not prepared, by either their experiences or their teacher-preparation programs, to respond to the diversity they find in public schools. Although significant advances have been made in our understanding of effective teaching for CLD students, the transfer of the research to practice remains scant. This is particularly true for English language learners (ELL) with learning and behavior problems and has been magnified by the introduction of response to intervention models in most school districts in the United States.

The use of response to intervention (RTI) as an alternative means of identifying students with specific learning disabilities was made part of the 2004 reauthorization of the Individuals With Disabilities Education Improvement Act. Although RTI is not mandated, states are authorized to choose a more effective way to identify specific learning and behavior disabilities than the older discrepancy and checklist screening (Bradley, Danielson, & Doolittle, 2005). Because of this legislation, many states have quickly begun to move toward implementation of some form of response to intervention.

WHAT IS RESPONSE TO INTERVENTION?

RTI is the current paradigm for the instructional intervention process discussed as part of problem solving. As currently practiced in the majority of school districts, it goes beyond a focus on learning disabilities to problem solving for various learning and behavior issues arising in the classroom setting. RTI is usually described as a multistep approach to providing services to struggling students. Bender and Shores (2007) cite research related to this model going back to the 1960s, but the RTI process remains new for most teachers and parents. E. Johnson, Mellard, Fuchs, and McKnight (2006) define the RTI process as a student-centered assessment model using problem-solving and research-based methods to identify and address learning difficulties in children. Teachers provide instruction and interventions to these challenged and challenging students at increasing levels of intensity. They also monitor the progress students make at each intervention level and use the assessment results to decide whether the students need additional instruction or intervention in general education or referral to special education.

Although few education professionals disagree with the general concept of RTI and the theories behind it, some fear the implementation of RTI as currently carried out may shortchange children with disabilities as well as those with diverse language needs (Tomsho, 2007). As noted by Tomsho, the push for RTI is the latest chapter in a long-running battle over just how far schools should go to educate disabled and challenged students in regular classrooms. Some educators think RTI could boost mainstreaming to unprecedented levels by shifting resources away from separate special education programs and requiring regular-education teachers to tackle tougher learning challenges in their classrooms.

In many places, RTI is being directed at children with specific learning disabilities (SLD). Created under federal law, this fast-growing category includes dyslexia and other processing disorders that are manifested in an imperfect ability to listen, think, speak, read, write, spell, or do mathematical calculations. SLD students account for approximately 46% of the nation's 6.1 million special education students, up from less than a quarter in the 1970s. Finally, the number of students identified for SLD services has increased 200% since 1977, creating concern in the field about misdiagnoses (Vaughn, Linan-Thompson, & Hickman, 2003), such as false positives including overidentification of students with high IQs and average achievement, and false negatives such as underidentification of students with lower IQs and below-average achievement (Kavale, 2005; Semrud-Clikeman, 2005). Meanwhile, there are no standards for what the RTI process should look like or how long the various tiers of intervention should last.

RTI supporters call the traditional SLD identification of discrepancy between achievement and ability a wait-to-fail approach. They maintain that many children now in special education are simply victims of poor instruction and wouldn't need expensive special education services if they had received extra help as soon as their problems surfaced.

Under RTI, children are generally considered for special education only if they don't respond to a gradually intensifying series of closely monitored interventions. As noted by Reschly (2005), RTI is both more humane and more cost-effective to screen for problems early and intervene at younger ages than it is to attempt to treat problems after they are firmly established. Many of us who work with CLD students with various learning and behavior problems have welcomed the move away from prereferral protocols toward intensive problem solving as more responsive to our students' diverse learning needs.

Thus, RTI is commonly seen as a process that involves problem solving, progress monitoring, and ongoing evaluation of children's responsiveness to instruction and/or evidence-based interventions as a guide for instructional and eligibility decisions. The greatest benefits of RTI for limited English proficient and CLD students may come from its utility as a framework for guiding service delivery for those with unmet needs. The 2004 reauthorization of the Individuals with Disabilities Education Act (IDEA) provides a legal basis for RTI. IDEA ensures educational services to children with disabilities on a national level and regulates how states and public agencies administer these services to more than 6.5 million children with disabilities in the United States (U.S. Department of Education, n.d.). With the reauthorization, the law now reads that schools can "use a process which determines if a child responds to a scientific, research-based intervention" as a mechanism for identifying (and subsequently serving) those with learning and behavior problems, including ELLs and those with specific learning disabilities. RTI models have several components in common. Bradley et al. (2005) and Bender and Shores (2007) identify several core components including high-quality classroom instruction, universal screening, continuous progress monitoring, research-based interventions, and fidelity or integrity of instructional intervention. RTI uses tiers of instructional intervention for struggling students, relies on a strong core curriculum and instruction prior to intervening with individual students, incorporates problem solving to determine interventions for students, requires regular monitoring of students, and can be used to predict at-risk students and to intervene with all students who have academic and behavioral difficulties.

RTI models differ in the number of tiers or levels, who is responsible for delivery of the interventions, and whether the process is viewed as a problem-solving process that is an end in itself or as a standard protocol (i.e., a prereferral) leading to a formal evaluation for eligibility. Sometimes the process itself serves as the eligibility evaluation (Fuchs, Mock, Morgan, & Young, 2003).

An additional shift in the current application of RTI and other problem-solving models is the expansion of the model to include progress monitoring of response to instruction (RTII) as well as intervention. These RTI and RTII models are becoming more popular as the limits of RTI are being felt, particularly in districts with large emerging numbers of CLD learners.

Current RTI and RTII models are based on three or four tiers. Generally, in all models, both three and four tiers, at Tier 1, general education teachers provide instruction within the core curriculum to all students in the school. In RTI and RTII models, progress monitoring begins with measuring how students are doing in response to the general content core curriculum with particular attention paid to students identified at entry as at-risk or coming from CLD backgrounds. It is assumed that about 80% of students in a school will be successful in the benchmarked curriculum and will not need intensive further assistance (Philip Chinn, personal correspondence, August 2004). In some models, differentiation of instruction including language support is included as part of Tier 1, particularly where dual-language and two-way bilingual transition models are implemented. In others, specific differentiation for learning and behavior, particularly language transition and behavior adaptation support for students experiencing culture shock, is provided in Tier 2 (both Kansas and Pennsylvania have variations of this model). In all multitier models, Tier 2 is generally seen as the point at which focused, small group assistance begins, based on some emerging need identified through the progress monitoring done during Tier 1 instruction and intervention. It is here that reading specialists, English as a second language (ESL) instructors, and other content area assistance may be provided to struggling students in small group pullout or push in situations. In most schools with bilingual transitional or dual-language programs, English literacy development (ELD) is not seen as a specific intervention but as an essential core curriculum component of Tier 1. Emerging issues such as unusual delays in language acquisition or unresolved culture shock and transition issues would call for moving the student into a more focused Tier 2 setting for intervention.

Figure 3.1 Example of the Three-Tier Model illustrates the basic three-tier RTI or RTII model and the percentage of students considered appropriate to be served at that level. Most state programs have some sort of version of this basic model. However, there is great variation in these applications.

Figure 3.1   Example of the Three-Tier Model

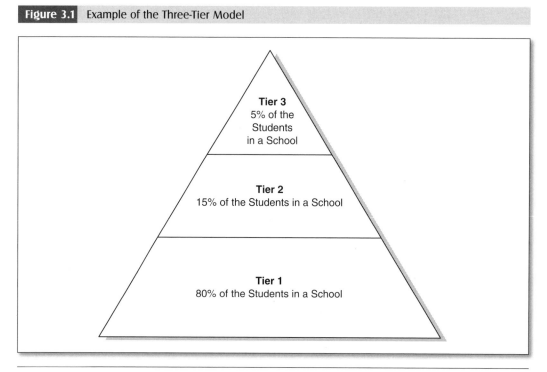

Adapted from National Association of State Directors of Special Education (2005).

In other programs, there are more levels or tiers within each tier although the common is three or four tiers. In both the four-tier and three-tier models, when students fail to respond to small group and intense, individualized interventions, they are referred for special education. Special education teachers may help develop interventions and/or plan assessments for students receiving instruction and interventions in Tiers 1 and 2. They may not provide instruction to students until Tier 3 or 4, when the student could be referred and identified for special education. In the four-tier model, Tier 4 is generally seen as the most individualized and intensive level of instruction and intervention and usually includes students on individualized education plans (IEP) and other special education or related service provisions.

Figure 3.2 Example of the Four-Tier Model illustrates a four-tier RTII problem-solving model for CLD students. As students are served at the various tiers, the intensity of intervention and instruction increases as illustrated by the arrows going up the left side of the pyramid. As services move up the pyramid and intensity increases, the number of students served at each tier decreases. This is shown by the arrows going up the right side of the pyramid. In some school districts, students will be moved up until their needs are met and then moved back down to the lower tier to solidify this problem resolution. Not all students return entirely to Tier 1 but need to continue some form of Tier 2 differentiation their entire school career.

Some advocates of the problem-solving approach disagree with illustrating repeated response to instruction and intervention with a triangle, which seems to imply movement in only one direction. They prefer to use a circle to show that movement of the student and intervention process is continuous. This is shown in Figure 3.3 Continuous Problem-Solving Model.

Figure 3.2 Example of the Four-Tier Model

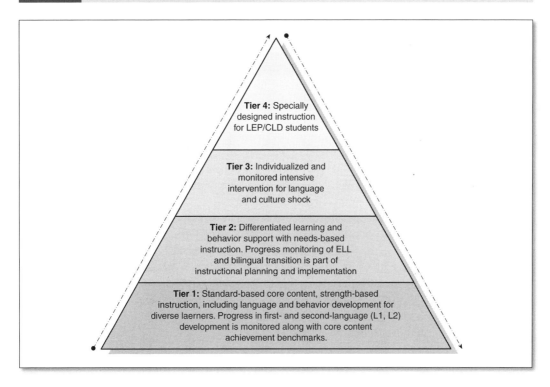

Tier 4: Specially designed instruction for LEP/CLD students

Tier 3: Individualized and monitored intensive intervention for language and culture shock

Tier 2: Differentiated learning and behavior support with needs-based instruction. Progress monitoring of ELL and bilingual transition is part of instructional planning and implementation

Tier 1: Standard-based core content, strength-based instruction, including language and behavior development for diverse laerners. Progress in first- and second-language (L1, L2) development is monitored along with core content achievement benchmarks.

Figure 3.3 Continuous Problem-Solving Model

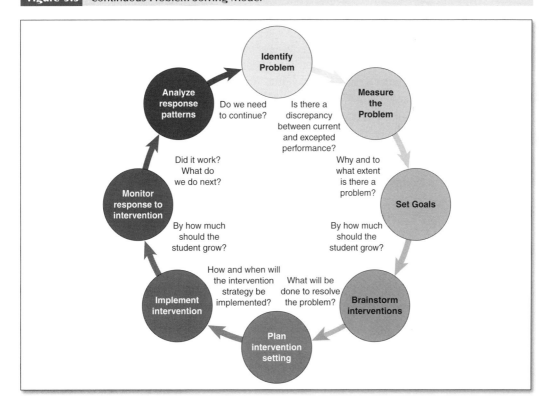

Identify Problem

Measure the Problem

Analyze response patterns

Do we need to continue?   Is there a discrepancy between current and excepted performance?

Did it work? What do we do next?   Why and to what extent is there a problem?

Monitor response to intervention

Set Goals

By how much should the student grow?   By how much should the student grow?

How and when will the intervention strategy be implemented?   What will be done to resolve the problem?

Implement intervention

Brainstorm interventions

Plan intervention setting

The difference between the process depicted in the triangles (Figures 3.1 and 3.2) versus the circles (Figure 3.3) highlights an issue in the use of these models with diverse learners mentioned earlier (i.e., the idea of a standard protocol or set of prescribed steps to follow in resolving one or more learning or behavior problems versus a problem-solving model that works to resolve a continuing series of problems with no end point as part of the process). Teachers have told me of their frustration with specific aspects of both models when working with challenging CLD students.

Typically, in the RTI standard protocol, lists of interventions and instructional procedures are provided to classroom personnel to follow until the student meets target benchmarks of response to the prescribed activities. Often, a specific timeline is given in which a response is to be achieved. These are often expansions from a previously implemented prereferral process and classroom personnel are given specific workbooks or reading kits, checklists, or other guidelines to follow in the application of prescribed numbers and types of interventions to use. The materials and procedures are designed to address specific learning disability areas of concern. I have heard teachers call this "RTI in a box" along with their common frustration in following a fixed set of procedures that they see as inappropriate or ineffective with CLD learners. The strategies presented in this book are specifically designed to work "out of the box" for school personnel frustrated with prepackaged RTI interventions and provide teachers with expanded, research-based RTI and RTII options.

Although less frequent, I have also had teachers express dissatisfaction with the circular, continuous problem-solving model when used with CLD students with learning and behavior problems. On the one hand, problem solving can be out of the box and focus on actual presenting problems, including a variety of language transition and behavior adaptation issues. However, teachers have expressed frustration with what appears to be recycling or a never-ending cycle of problem solving. They have told me their ELL/CLD students with continuing learning and behavior problems never get out of the circle of problem solving into service resolution. Therefore, I recommend a blend of dynamic problem solving in a tiered RTII model and not a static triangle.

• The way I propose looking at problem solving for ELL/CLD students is to think of a pyramid of instruction and intervention comprised of many specific strategy blocks: a three-dimensional RTII structure without a fixed number of tiers per se. Each block represents a specific strategy cluster or approach designed to build on the strengths or address the needs of an individual ELL/CLD student, and each level represents a degree of intensity of focus. As various instructional and strategic approaches are used with each individual student, they fill in that particular tier of the pyramid. The complete pyramid of resiliency and intervention strategies model is illustrated in Figure 3.4 Pyramid of Resiliency, Instruction, Strategies, Intervention, and Monitoring (PRISIM) for diverse learners (C. Collier, 2009).

Figure 3.4	Pyramid of Resiliency, Instruction, Strategies, and Intervention Monitoring

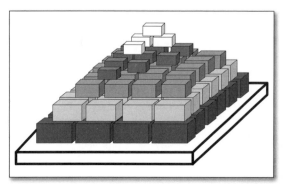

• The principal elements of PRISIM are the myriad strategies that comprise the building blocks. This book contains my current recommended set of strategies with the research base necessary under today's RTI/RTII structures. As new problems with diverse learners arise, I recommend teachers keep their strategy and intervention toolboxes open, as new approaches will become necessary.

• A pyramid is only as strong as its foundation, so the more comprehensive and complete the information gathering, teacher preparation, curricula, and system support can be, the stronger and more effective the instructional program of the school will be for ELL/CLD students, including those with special needs. The foundation of personnel, system, curricula, and comprehensive data provide a solid foundation on which the building blocks of learning are firmly established. Each block represents a cluster of strategies, core content, and settings that may be differentiated for specific strengths and/or needs of learners.

A teacher may end up using all of these strategies, but differentiate them for different student needs and issues. The instructional strategy set at Tier 1 in the PRISIM version of the RTII model will be comprehensive and geared to the larger group process and based on facilitating resiliency and learning readiness of all students. As teachers see that some students need more intensive differentiation and present some unresolved learning or behavior problems, they may move the instructional focus to smaller group interventions for particular ELL/CLD students. At Tier 2 of the PRISIM version of the RTII model, teachers may use several different approaches, of which many will be successful for the majority of ELL/CLD students. However, some of the more challenging ELL/CLD students will need even more individualization and some students will require assistance from other education personnel. At this point, students may be moved into more intensive problem solving, whether this is termed Tier 3 of an RTI or RTII model or whether it is an individualized application in the continuous problem-solving model. At these more structured points in problem-solving or tiered intervention, the student is more tightly monitored with more intensity in individual intervention.

During this entire RTI or RTII process, it is extremely important that specific cultural and linguistic issues be addressed as well as the specific learning and behavior that are part of the teacher's concern. Before school personnel can move to formally evaluate and consider placement in special education services, they must document that the presenting problems are not principally because of language and culture issues. They must document that the primary cause of the presenting problem is not because of the student's English proficiency or level of culture shock. Language and culture issues will always be part of serving an ELL/CLD student, but under the reauthorized IDEA of 2004, the team must document the extent to which these are part of the presenting problem and that they are not the most significant determining factor.

Asking the Right Questions

These issues frequently appear in school settings as questions asked by concerned school personnel. "He has been here for more than two years, so isn't his lack of academic achievement a sign of a possible disability?" "Is this communication problem a language difference or is it a language disability?" "She was born here, so can't we rule out culture shock and language development issues?" Although illustrative of the good intentions and heartfelt concern about these students by education professionals, it is more productive to ask what information do we need and how will we use it.

What Information Do We Need?

The information to be gathered answers specific questions critical to separating difference from disability (SDD) considerations.

- **Education:** Has the student been in school before? Are there gaps in the student's education experiences? Sufficient intensity of instruction?

- **Home language**: Are languages other than English spoken in the student's home? What languages other than English does the student speak? Is the student maintaining an ability to communicate with his or her family members?
- **Language proficiency**: What is the student's language proficiency and literacy? Is the student developing the home language at a normal rate?
- **English**: Does the student need assistance with learning English? Is the student acquiring English at a normal rate?
- **Achievement:** What is the student's level and rate of academic achievement? Is this normal for the general student population in your district/school? Specific population of the student?
- **Behavior**: Is the student's emotional stability developmentally and culturally appropriate? Are there individual or family circumstances that may explain the observed behavior?
- **Adaptation:** What is the student's level of acculturation? Is the student at risk for culture shock? Is the student adapting to our school at a normal rate?

How Should We Use the Information?

Information about students is not valuable if it is not instructionally meaningful and does not lead to a course of action for the student's benefit.

- **Education**: Prior experience in school, whether in the United States or another country, facilitates transitional instructional models. Thus, knowing that the student has received schooling elsewhere tells school personnel they can focus on transition from one academic language foundation to English academic language (V. P. Collier & Thomas, 2007). If the student has never had a formal education experience, school personnel must start by building an understanding of school culture, rules, expectations, and basic school interaction language in the student's most proficient language before transitioning to English.

SDD concern: If the student shows little progress with adapting to school expectations and continues to struggle with acquiring school interaction language in the home language, he may have an undiagnosed disability and a full evaluation may be needed.

- **Home language:** Students who are raised in homes where English is infrequently or only one of the languages used come to us with unique strengths that can become the foundation of instruction. Research shows that they have cognitive and linguistic capacities that can facilitate learning (Baca & Cervantes, 2003). Additionally, psychological well-being is built on quality family communication and interactions (Padilla, Padilla, Morales, Olmedo, & Ramirez, 1979).

SDD concern: If the student has not acquired a developmentally appropriate proficiency in a language other than English, it may be because of family circumstances or the presence of an undiagnosed disability. In either case, this can delay English acquisition. A structured, intensive intervention in the primary home language would show whether the student has the ability to develop language and communication. If the student's communication does not improve under intervention, then a referral for a full evaluation might be warranted.

- **Language and literacy**: The student's proficiency and background in a language other than English assists in deciding the most effective instructional communicative models. It is critical to assess to the extent possible the student's proficiency in her home language/communication mode. As there are not standardized tests available for every language or communication mode, alternative measures are frequently needed (Baca & Cervantes, 2003). These can be structured sampling and observation, interview, interactive inventories, and other analytic tools (Hoover, Baca, & Klingner, 2007).

SDD concern: A student may score low on a standardized test in the home language because he has never received instruction in the language and has only an oral proficiency. Thus, low primary language and low English may look like there is some language disability. A structured intensive intervention in the primary language including basic literacy readiness would serve to profile the student's proficiency and establish whether the low score is learning based rather than something else. If the student makes little or no progress in the RTI or RTII, a referral for a full evaluation may become necessary.

- **Communication:** The student's language proficiency in English is directly related to eligibility and entry level for ESL instruction. There are many tools available for determining whether a student needs assistance with learning English (Baca & Cervantes, 2003). For initial services in English language learning for limited English proficient (LEP) speakers, school personnel should select instruments that are quick, nonbiased, and focus on speaking and listening skills. Including a literacy screening would be instructionally meaningful only for students who have received prior instruction in English.

SDD concern: Some students speak enough English to not qualify for ELL/LEP services but have such a limited classroom language foundation that they look like students with learning disabilities. Thus, English screening for ELL/LEP services must include screening for cognitive academic language proficiency and not just social language. A structured, intensive intervention in English including basic phonemic awareness, phonics, vocabulary, fluency, comprehension, and other reading and writing readiness would serve two purposes: (1) profile the ELL/LEP student's proficiency and (2) establish whether the low score is learning based rather than something else. If the student makes little or no progress in the RTI or RTII, a referral for a full evaluation is necessary. Additionally, if the child has a disability, is receiving special education services, and is an ELL/LEP student, the IEP should list the ELL/LEP accommodations as part of related services. This could be bilingual assistance or specially designed assistance in English (Freeman & Freeman, 2007) in the special education setting or some other appropriate monitored intervention with specific objectives related to acquiring English. In many cases, the disabling condition is such that it seriously impacts the acquisition of English, and thus, special education personnel and ELL/LEP personnel must work together on realistic outcomes. These modified language outcomes need to be included in the IEP.

- **Cognition:** All children can learn but they learn at different rates and in different manners. All children can learn but they enter and exit at different points. A challenge of today's standards-based education models is that students who do not fit the scope and sequence of a particular school system are frequently placed in alternative instructional settings that may or may not be appropriate to their needs (Baca & Cervantes, 2003).

SDD concern: If a student is not meeting the benchmarks established by a school system even when given learning support, she may be referred to special education as having a learning disability of some sort. Sometimes special education is the only instructional alternative available in the building. It is not appropriate to place students who do not have a disability in special education even when it is the best alternative instructional setting available. Programs should be restructured to include differentiated instructional environments where any student can enter a lesson at his or her entry point and learn to the maximum of his or her abilities. A structured intensive intervention in fundamental learning strategies would establish whether the low score is learning based rather than something else. If the student makes little or no progress in the RTI or RTII, a referral for a full evaluation may be necessary.

- **Behavior:** Family and community events can be a contributing factor, and it is critical to effective instruction to explore both school and nonschool environments and their relationship to the student's presenting problem. Whether the behavior problem is because of an innate disorder, biochemical dysfunction, or a temporary response to trauma or disruption in the student's home or school environment, the student needs effective and immediate intervention and assistance.

SDD concern: Although the student needs assistance with managing or controlling his behavior, special education is not the appropriate placement if the etiology of the problem is culture shock or an event or chronic stressors in the student's home or school environment (C. Collier, Brice, & Oades-Sese, 2007). An intensive instructional intervention that facilitates self-monitoring and control in a supportive and safe environment should always be implemented first. If the problem does not appear to decrease in frequency or intensity, or if the student makes little or no progress, a referral for a full evaluation might become necessary.

- **Adaptation:** The level and rate of acculturation and accompanying degree of culture shock must be addressed in the instructional environment. All students must adapt to the school environment regardless of if they speak English; students who come into your school from homes or communities very different from the school will experience greater degree of culture shock (C. Collier et al., 2007).

SDD concern: The manifestations of culture shock look a lot like learning and behavior disabilities and unaddressed acculturation and adaptation needs can concatenate into serious learning and behavior problems later in the education experience. An intensive instructional intervention that mitigates culture shock and facilitates adaptation and language transition should always be implemented, particularly for newcomers. Most students will respond within weeks to this intervention. This positive response does not mean that culture shock may not reappear, as culture shock is cyclical and a normal part of our adaptation to anything strange to us. However, a positive response to acculturative assistance lets school personnel know that the presenting problems are because of a normal adaptive process, acculturation, which responds over time to instructional intervention. Students should have their level of acculturation measured at entry into your school system and their rate of acculturation monitored annually to assure the student is making normal progress in your school. If the student's rate of acculturation is not within normal range, it is an indication either that the program is not adequately addressing his transition needs or that there may be an undiagnosed disability of some sort that is depressing the rate of acculturation.

Although RTI and RTII are generally thought of as referring to academic intervention, most programs (93.3% according to Berkeley, Bender, Peaster, and Saunders, 2009) also incorporate behavioral intervention in the RTI and RTII model or use a similar multitiered approach to address the behavioral needs of students. All but one of the programs examined by Berkeley et al. use tiered approaches to address behavior in addition to academics. In conclusion, while RTI and RTII are seen as a positive development in assisting all learners, our principle concern is that typical RTI/RTII programs are designed for native English-speaking students with learning and behavior problems and need to be expanded and adapted for use with ELL and CLD students.

Providing Some Context

Up to this point, I have described what is current practice or what research has established as best practice in typical K–12 schools including serving students with various learning and behavior problems. These problem-solving programs can be effective for all learners with specific modifications for use with ELL/CLD students. Problem-solving programs with progress monitoring are particularly helpful with ELL/CLD students when expanded to include instructional

What RTI/RTII for ELL/CLD Students Is and What It Is Not	
RTI/RTII Is	**RTI/RTII Is Not**
An initiative that supports general education school improvement goals for all diverse learners	A stand-alone special education initiative
Intended to help as many CLD students as possible meet proficiency standards without special education	A means for getting more ELL/CLD students into special education
A method to unify general and special education to benefit CLD students through greater continuity of services	A method for increasing or decreasing special education numbers
Focused on effective instruction to enhance CLD student growth	Focused primarily on learning disability determination among CLD students and documented through a checklist

strategies and instructional interventions directly addressing their unique learning and behavior needs (Baca & Cervantes, 2003; C. Collier, 2009). As my goal with this book is to provide direct pragmatic suggestions for implementing instructional interventions in classroom settings with ELL/CLD, I will provide examples from my teaching experience. Specific examples will precede the list of recommended interventions for each RTI/RTII level or tier of instruction and intervention. These recommended interventions are not a substitute for other content intervention that research has shown to be effective with ELL/CLD students but are to be used in conjunction with research-based academic strategies and interventions typically used with all students exhibiting learning and behavior problems. There is nothing magic about these instructional and intervention strategies; they all take extra effort and focus on the part of instructional personnel. Some teachers will be familiar with many of these but may not have thought about using them as part of an intensive, focused instructional strategy or intervention process. They are particularly effective with ELL/CLD students who are in integrated classrooms with non-ELL/CLD students of mixed ability level but are also beneficial in ELL and special education pullout settings.

Prior to becoming a special education teacher, I was a primary teacher and a beginner teacher. Beginner was the term used for students who had never been in school before and who did not speak English. These students were assigned to my classroom until they tested as able to participate in a classroom with their grade-level peers. Thus, I had mixed ages, mixed abilities, and mixed language proficiency in my classroom, and I was responsible for instructing all of my students in the core curriculum detailed in our school's scope and sequence guidelines.

Over the years, specific students with very challenging learning and behavior problems passed through my classroom doors. I will use these students' stories to illustrate the instructional intervention process.

Using Progress Monitoring Data

Susan L. Hall

Deficiencies in phonemic awareness and phonics need to be addressed before they can be fluent third-grade readers. RTI gives the students who need instruction the extra help they need.

—Third-grade teacher

Progress monitoring sometimes is the forgotten cousin of benchmark screening. Yet it is the most important part of the RTI process. Progress monitoring is collecting data on at least one of the indicators given in the benchmark periods yet with alternative forms so students cannot remember the prompts or passages. The problem is that after all the effort is expended to complete the benchmark assessments and launch the initial intervention groups, teachers often believe they have no time left to consider collecting and using progress monitoring data.

IMPORTANCE OF PROGRESS MONITORING DATA

Why is progress monitoring so important? It is the heart of RTI. These are the data that are used to make adjustments in instruction along the way. The progress monitoring data allow the principal, RTI coordinator, and teachers to see what is working and what must be changed. They are the data that tell you how well the student is responding to intervention. Not only do they tell you whether instruction is successful for an individual student, they are a check on the effectiveness of the tiers of instruction for a grade level.

> Why is progress monitoring so important? It is the heart of RTI. These are the data that are used to make adjustments in instruction along the way.

Producing and using progress monitoring data is one of the most important components of RTI, yet it is often the first thing principals let go when the teachers begin to talk about being overwhelmed. The progress monitoring data gathered in October, November, and December are needed to motivate the teachers to continue their intervention group time.

When teachers begin to complain that they are overwhelmed with the extra work of organizing to teach these intervention groups, it is tempting to give up the progress monitoring assessments with the idea that there will be data available once the winter benchmark is completed in January. In kindergarten and first grade, the progress monitoring data will show student improvement by November if the teachers have grouped the students tightly, selected materials or strategies that enable them to teach the skill deficits for each group, and have consistently taught the intervention groups. Progress monitoring is exactly what is needed to demonstrate to teachers that RTI is working.

> Progress monitoring is exactly what is needed to demonstrate to teachers that RTI is working, and it's nearly always the first thing a principal gives up when teachers feel overwhelmed.

It is far better to reduce the frequency of progress monitoring than to give it up altogether. For example, if the teachers are feeling overwhelmed the first several months, progress monitoring can be cut back to monthly instead of every 2 weeks. We do not recommend progress monitoring weekly during the first year of RTI implementation because it's too easy for teachers to criticize the extensive amount of time spent assessing. The staff's understanding of how to use the data is more limited at the beginning of the RTI process, so it is easier to justify having a little less data the first year.

After intervention groups are formed and instruction has started, the RTI coordinator can focus on collecting and planning for the use of progress monitoring data. Most principals establish an assessment calendar before the year begins so all teachers know that giving progress monitoring assessments is expected.

DETERMINING WHICH INDICATORS
TO PROGRESS MONITOR

It is not necessary to progress monitor all the indicators that are collected at the benchmark periods. Select one or two indicators that measure the skills that are the focus of the instruction for each intervention group and progress monitor only on that indicator or indicators for now. For example, imagine a first-grade group at the middle of the year that did not reach the Dynamic Indicators of Basic Early Literacy Skills (DIBELS) benchmark on either Nonsense Word Fluency (NWF) or Oral Reading Fluency (ORF). If the instructional focus of the group is on teaching the alphabetic principle using words that have the consonant–vowel–consonant (CVC) word pattern, the NWF indicator is a more targeted measure of this skill than the ORF. The first-grade ORF passages contain not only words with the CVC pattern but also nonphonetic sight words and words with other patterns such as words with a long vowel, silent *e* pattern. Although it's a good idea to measure ORF maybe once every 4–6 weeks, progress monitoring with the NWF indicator measures when students have mastered the CVC skill and are ready to move on to other word patterns.

In kindergarten and first grade, DIBELS measures subskills of reading such as phonemic awareness (Initial Sound Fluency [ISF] and Phoneme Segmentation Fluency [PSF]) and the alphabetic principle (NWF). Not only are the skills finite, but the measures are sensitive enough to capture small increases in a student's skills after instruction. Therefore, DIBELS measures are useful for progress monitoring in kindergarten and first grade.

Sometimes it is preferable to progress monitor with a measure other than DIBELS or your selected curriculum-based measure (CBM) assessment, especially at the later grade levels. Teachers who are working with an intervention group of students in second grade and beyond, in which the students are reading well below grade level, will not get much information by progress monitoring with the grade-level ORF if the student is reading inaccurately. Progress monitoring with the informal phonics screener provides more useful data than using ORF if the students are receiving intervention in phonics and word study skills. Progress monitoring with an alternative form of the phonics screener reveals when to move the student up to the next group on the phonics continuum. Teachers can progress monitor with ORF periodically, but less frequently, until the student has mastered the types of word patterns expected for a student of his or her grade level.

If students read at least 95% of the words in the passage accurately but are not at benchmark because of poor fluency, then they do not need intervention in phonics and word study. They need instruction, guided practice, and independent practice in reading more fluently at the passage level. Progress monitoring with CBM oral reading passages is very helpful in tracking the rate of progress for the students receiving fluency intervention.

GRAPHING RATES OF PROGRESS

Graphing progress monitoring data is one of the most important ways to use the data. From the point when a student first enters intervention, a graph is prepared and the teacher draws a targetline from the student's initial data point to the expected level of performance. This line shows the teacher the level of growth the student needs to achieve to reach benchmark. This required rate of progress for the student is a constant reminder that the goal is to close the gap and reach benchmark rather than to be satisfied with some progress in the current year.

The progress monitoring targetline graph helps in comparing actual with expected level of progress. Every time the teacher administers a progress monitoring assessment, the new point is added to this graph. Once a minimum of three progress monitoring points have been collected for a student, the teacher can compare the actual data points with the targetline. All data points that fall below the targetline reveal inadequate progress. Comparing the actual with expected performance is critical for determining whether the rate of progress is sufficient.

Principals need these progress monitoring graphs for a number of reasons. The first is to determine whether the delivery model selected by a grade level is effective. This can be assessed at a grade level meeting where each teacher sorts his or her progress monitoring graphs into two piles; one pile includes students progressing above the targetline, and the second pile includes those whose progress monitoring points fall below the targetline. If the majority of the students receiving intervention at a particular grade level are not making a sufficient rate of progress with the intervention instruction provided, there is a systemic problem to address first before tackling any individual teacher or student difficulties.

If the rate of progress for the grade level is insufficient, then some aspect of the intervention needs to change. If groups are meeting only three times a week, then try five times a week for the next 6 weeks and reexamine. Maybe the amount of time per day should increase from 20 to 30 minutes. If the intervention time is limited because the team is relying on the reading teachers to provide all the group instruction, then the principal needs to let the grade-level team know that for students to make more improvement, the classroom teachers also need to meet with intervention groups. Try an approach in which the reading specialist meets daily with the lowest-performing students and the classroom teacher meets with the students whose skills are not quite as far behind. If an adequate amount of instructional time was provided but the progress is insufficient, then explore some other factors. Discuss whether the group size is too large, the instruction is not focused enough, or the curriculum doesn't match the student needs well enough.

DECISIONS THAT REQUIRE PROGRESS MONITORING DATA

Moving Students From Tier II to Tier III

Some experts recommend a system in which teachers schedule periodic data meetings to discuss student progress and to determine movement of students between the tiers. In the University of Texas Center for Reading and Language Arts publication called *The 3-Tier Reading Model*, the recommendation is that students remain in Tier II for 10–12 weeks of instruction at a time. After the first round of Tier II, teachers review progress monitoring data to determine whether the student will receive another round of Tier II instruction or be moved to Tier III.

I recommend the following:

- Start most students in Tier II to see whether it works.
- Place a limited number of students immediately in Tier III if there are sufficient data to believe they will make progress only with the intensity provided in Tier III.
- Keep a student in Tier II long enough to give the instruction a chance to work.
- Move a student from Tier II to Tier III after every adjustment to Tier II has been made and the student's skills still haven't responded adequately.
- Require a minimum of three data points to compare progress with the targetline.
- Increase the frequency of progress monitoring if the student's scores are extremely variable.
- Remain flexible about when to move students.
- View the tiers as gradations along the continuum of intensity rather than only two distinct layers.

When the groups are first formed in the fall, don't be alarmed if there is a brief shake-out period during the first week when a few students need to be moved right away. Occasionally the assessment data do not accurately measure a particular student's skill level because some students are not comfortable in testing situations and others are lucky guessers.

After this initial shifting, the groups probably can remain the same for the first 6–9 weeks. If progress monitoring is assessed every 3 weeks, at week nine the initial benchmark plus three progress monitoring points will be available. If groups began meeting the third week in September, then the sixth week will be around Halloween, and the ninth week will be around Thanksgiving. Many schools more formally reexamine student progress between Halloween and Thanksgiving and then again just after the winter benchmark in January. For a student whose rate of progress is seriously insufficient, it's important not to wait too long before intensifying instruction.

> For a student whose rate of progress is seriously insufficient, it's important not to wait too long before intensifying instruction.

Responding to Inadequate Rates of Progress

If a student's progress is insufficient after the first round of Tier II instruction, it is tempting to move him or her immediately from Tier II to Tier III. Yet many other things can be tried first. Tier III intervention is very costly and should be the last resort.

If a student is not making adequate progress in Tier II, there are a number of alternative approaches. If the student is making progress but the rate of progress is insufficient, first try adding more time. Monitor progress weekly for 3 weeks and look at the graph again. If additional time increases the rate of progress, continue with the added time. If the rate of progress doesn't respond to additional time, then try intensifying the instruction in one of several ways. Options for intensifying instruction include the following:

- Increase the number of student responses in a minute by reducing the group size.
- Increase the number of questions and error corrections the student receives in a minute.
- Increase the scaffolding by breaking the task down more or providing more structure so that the student can be successful.
- Spend more time modeling the "I do" and "We do" guided practice before the student practices independently.

- Increase the number of repetition cycles on each skill before moving on to see whether mastery is achieved with more practice.
- Use a more systematic curriculum so that skills are taught in a pre-scribed manner, with the teacher asking questions and cueing with the same language for each routine.

If the student still doesn't make gains after these efforts to intensify instruction within Tier II, it may be time to move him or her to Tier III.

Determining When a Student Meets Exit Criteria

Once students receiving intervention instruction reach benchmark, it is important to exit them from Tier II or Tier III to make sure they sustain this level using only Tier I instruction and without the extra support of the intervention group. Many schools establish an exit criterion, such as a given number of progress monitoring scores at or above benchmark. The Heartland Group in Iowa recommends four data points above benchmark, and we typically advise three consecutive data points at or above benchmark.

> *Once students receiving intervention instruction reach benchmark, it is important to exit them from Tier II or Tier III to make sure they sustain this level using only Tier I instruction and without the extra support of the intervention group.*

Exiting students who have reached benchmark leaves more staff time and energy to focus on the students who have not responded to instruc-tion so far. Some people call these students "treatment resisters," but this term sounds as if the students aren't cooperative. I prefer to discuss these students as those who have made an insufficient level of progress. The key word is *insufficient* because although most students respond somewhat to intensive intervention instruction, teach-ers should remain focused on getting each student to a sufficient level of progress. *Sufficient* is defined as progress at or above the targetline on the student's progress monitoring graph. If the progress is less than this, then the teaching staff must do everything possible to achieve a sufficient rate of progress. Remember, teachers should be striving for 95% or more of K–3 students reading at grade level. Principals

> *The key word is insufficient because although most students respond somewhat to intensive intervention instruction, teachers should remain focused on getting each student to a sufficient level of progress. Sufficient is defined as progress at or above the targetline on the student's progress monitoring graph.*

help when they continue to articulate the 95% goal yet accept that it may take up to 3 years to get second and third grade to that level. In many schools, more than 90% of kindergarten and first-grade students reach benchmark in the first 2 years of full RTI implementation, and 95% in kindergarten is not unusual even in the first year. Progress in second and third grade depends on first achieving high levels of benchmark in kindergarten and first grade so that fewer and fewer students reach the upper grades behind in their reading skills.

When schools fully implement tight and focused intervention group instruction just after the fall benchmark and consistently teach the groups throughout the year, rapid progress will be achieved. At least a third of the students who enter Tier II in the fall should be exited by the winter benchmark and another third by spring break. No more than one third of the students who began the year in Tier II groups should remain in a group after spring break. Generally, these groups are small, and the time for these groups is extensive.

Teachers sometimes find it difficult to exit their students from intervention groups. This reluctance may occur because these are the students they identified as struggling, and they are worried that the students will slip backwards again when removed from the intervention group. Despite any reluctance, teachers must exit the student once he or she sustains benchmark scores and then watch to make sure that he or she doesn't regress without the support of the intervention group. If a teacher keeps a student in the group without determining whether he or she can sustain the gains without the support of intervention instruction, the student will go on to the next grade-level teacher without the benefit of a closely monitored transition.

It may be easier for teachers to exit students from intervention groups if they continue monitoring the students' progress and watching their scores for at least a month after the exit. That way, if a student slips back, he or she can be placed right back in a group. If the student sustains the gain, then the teacher knows that he or she is ready for the core instruction only. When a school has universal screening of all students at the three benchmark periods per year, teachers can be assured that a student will not go more than 4 months between screenings.

USING PROGRESS MONITORING DATA AT MEETINGS

Far too often schools that implement RTI are swimming in data, yet the staff has no big-picture sense of what the data mean. Much of the time when a principal explores consulting or professional development on RTI, his or her school has been administering the CBM assessments for anywhere from 1 to 5 years. The principal typically comments that the data are not being used to inform instruction and the staff needs help learning to use the data to group students and plan intervention. One of the questions I ask, generally in the first 10 minutes of the conversation, is "Approximately what percentage of your students are at grade-level benchmark for K–3?" Most principals struggle to answer that question. It is critical for a principal to be able to name an approximate number (e.g., somewhere around 60% of the kindergartners benchmarked in DIBELS at the end of last year).

Even schools that are several years into RTI and making exceptional progress in analyzing data to make instructional decisions for each individual student are too often missing the big picture. While sitting in a kindergarten grade-level meeting recently, the team reviewed data showing that 78% of kindergartners were at benchmark in early February. When asked how that compares with last year at this same time, no one had any idea. That's a critical question for goal setting. The reading coach, who could not answer the question, had to get online and look it up. A very simple chart, like the one that follows, was needed to help the teachers consider their goal for the end of the year.

> *Far too often schools that implement RTI are swimming in data, yet the staff has no big-picture sense of what the data mean.*

Percentage of Students at Benchmark

	February	*May*
Last year	66%	89%
This year	78%	Goal needed

With this information available, a goal of 95% at benchmark this year is reasonable.

Preparing Data for Meetings

It is important to have historical and current data available to reference instantly at teacher meetings while the discussions are occurring. The RTI coordinator or coach should have a data notebook and be responsible for updating a duplicate notebook for the principal. This notebook contains copies of key data reports for the current and previous years. In addition to helping establish goals, keeping the data accessible helps avoid the spread of incorrect information.

During a recent first-grade team meeting, one resistant teacher was raising questions about why his grade team needed to implement RTI. His claim was that intervention groups weren't needed because more than 95% of first graders were at benchmark on DIBELS the previous May when baseline data were collected. Because no one at the meeting had the data handy, he swayed his colleagues to wonder why they were being asked to do this extra work.

After the meeting we checked the data, and the first-grade teacher's figure was wrong. Only 72% of students had reached benchmark on ORF and 58% in NWF. Allowing this misperception to go uncorrected during this first-grade team meeting was a huge mistake, and it affected the rest of the teachers in that meeting.

The principal needs to have two types of data readily available:

1. The percentage of students currently at benchmark at each grade level

2. Progress this year compared with the same time last year.

This information is needed not only to establish realistic goals for this year but also to help decide where to concentrate problem-solving time. For example, if the kindergarten students seem to be on track to achieve their goals this year, then it may be possible to explore whether any intervention staff can help with the students in first grade who are not as far along. If there is a dip in the percentage of students at benchmark in the middle of second grade, then that's the place to focus more of the principal's time. The principal should meet with the RTI coordinator and decide which grade-level meetings need his or her attention.

The data even show where to focus instructional attention within a grade level throughout the year. If the data show that nearly all kindergarten students reached benchmark in ISF, then the focus of the intervention groups should shift to the next skill, which is PSF. If the first graders came in with strong phonemic skills from kindergarten, then the focus of the first half of first grade should be on developing their alphabetic principle skills, as measured by the NWF indicator. If most first-grade students reached benchmark in NWF but not in ORF, then the teachers need to examine sight word acquisition and have students spend more time applying their word study skills to text.

Data Meetings With Grade-Level Teams

It is common to hear the term "data meetings" around schools that are implementing RTI. What does a data meeting look like? One type typically occurs with a grade-level team, and the purpose is to evaluate the effectiveness of the overall approach to intervention for the students at that grade level. Another is one in which all the staff that serve an individual below-benchmark student meet to analyze the student's data and discuss whether any changes in his or her intervention plan are needed.

RTI offers an opportunity to convert the discussions that occur at grade-level meetings. Too often the discussion is around administrative topics such as staffing for the field trip or deadlines for report cards. Nearly all such details can be handled via e-mail or through staff mailboxes. The grade-level meetings should be dedicated to talking about curriculum and instruction.

Some schools have changed the name of the meetings to "curriculum collaboration time" to signal that the purpose is for a team of teachers to discuss the curriculum at their grade level. Many schools provide weekly time for teams to collaborate. This is not time for teachers to make individual plans but is intended to be spent discussing curriculum with all the teachers at a grade-level meeting. It is important for the RTI coordinator to attend these meetings to facilitate communication and alignment across grade levels.

The RTI coordinator or reading coach should always bring a data notebook to these meetings. Although in some schools the grade-level team leader plans the agenda for the meeting, the RTI coordinator should have a close relationship with each team leader so that topics related to RTI are discussed at the meetings. At least monthly, the RTI coordinator should have CBM data charts ready in order to discuss the students' progress to date. RTI coordinators can update the charts by receiving the progress monitoring data from each classroom teacher. It is possible to make a fairly accurate estimate of the number of students at benchmark at any point in time from this ongoing data analysis.

After looking at progress to date, the team should discuss how the organizational structure of the intervention groups is working. Are all teachers getting in their full intervention time? Should they review the schedule of the interventionists who come into the classrooms to help teachers with a group? What materials have teachers been using that they believe are particularly effective? Is there a shortage of any materials?

Collaboration time is especially important for teams using the walk-to-intervention model, where there is an established intervention block and students receive intervention from teachers other than their homeroom teachers. As more progress monitoring data are collected, teachers may recommend that particular students in their intervention group be moved up to the next skill on the continuum. Teachers also need to review whether they have students who are not making progress and whether they should be moved down a group.

Sometimes there is a case study time during the grade-level meetings. Each week the schedule rotates, and one teacher has a total of 10 minutes on a student: 5 minutes to provide information about a student about whom they are concerned followed by 5 minutes of group brainstorming on instructional strategies to try with this student. It is helpful if the RTI coordinator provides a format for the discussion so that the teacher supplies only the pertinent data about the student during the first 5 minutes. The idea is to help teachers stay focused on data, pinpoint skill deficit areas, and analyze the success of the curriculum used so far. It is helpful if the RTI coordinator initially models what these discussions should look like so that they don't fall back into discussion about why the student's family life makes it hard for him or her to learn how to read.

The data analysis varies by time of year. At the beginning of the year, the process focuses on placing below-benchmark students in groups, and as the year progresses the discussion shifts to analyzing the progress monitoring scores to determine which students need more intensive instruction. In general, the discussion at the meetings centers around three different purposes:

- Placing below-benchmark students in groups based on skill deficits
- Determining the appropriate instructional strategies or programs for each group to address the skill deficits
- Reviewing progress monitoring data to intensify instruction for some students and to move children between groups

Data Meetings With Individual Teachers

At least every 3 months the principal and RTI coordinator should have one-on-one meetings with each teacher. The focus of these meetings is on the progress of the class overall and the progress of the individual students in the class. Each teacher should bring a data notebook to these meetings. The contents of this notebook should include the following information:

- Error pattern analysis worksheets
- Lists of intervention groups
- Progress monitoring data graphs for each below-benchmark student and each group
- Intervention logs to track attendance, intervention time per week, curriculum used each week, and observation notes on each student

One of the best reports for this meeting is available from the University of Oregon's DIBELS data management system. Similar reports may be available in other reporting systems. A sample appears in Figure B of the Case Study. This report is ideal for meetings with teachers because it shows on a single graph the level of progress at two time periods for all the students in a classroom. The principal can start by acknowledging the excellent progress made by particular students and ask the classroom teacher what she believes has caused the remarkable level of growth. Then the discussion can shift to the students not making sufficient progress.

While discussing the students who have not demonstrated a sufficient rate of progress, the principal can ask the following types of questions:

Current Intervention

- Which skills are below benchmark for this student?
- What is the most important instructional focus for this student at present?
- Which intervention group is the student in?
- What is the instructional focus of this group, and who teaches it?
- How many minutes of intervention is the student receiving per week?
- How many students are in the group with the student?

Identifying the Problem

- Is the entire group making insufficient progress, or only this student?
- How is the student's attendance?
- Would the student benefit from more time in intervention?
- Is the group too large to provide adequate corrective feedback?
- Is the focus of instruction matched to the student's core deficit?
- Does the curriculum used for the group address the student's skill deficits?
- What else have we already tried with this student?
- What other assessment data do you have for this student (e.g., results from an informal phonological or phonics assessment screening)?

Problem Solving

- Is it possible to "double-dose" this student so he or she receives intervention in two groups daily?
- Would it enhance the intervention if the parents are asked to help at home (e.g., work on a list of sight words)?
- Would moving this student to another group provide better results?
- Does this student need a different curriculum?

- What else can we provide that may help this student?
- How can the RTI coordinator help you?

Once a plan is constructed, a follow-up meeting is needed to monitor whether the changes helped. These data meetings with teachers should be focused entirely on the students and what the school community can do to create a plan to help each student reach benchmark. With the RTI coordinator in attendance, keep these discussions focused on the students, not the teacher's performance. The RTI coordinator has to remain a peer coach and cannot be placed in a position of evaluating a classroom teacher's performance.

After examining the progress of the students in a class, teachers should be asked to set a goal for the number of students they believe will reach benchmark by the end of the year. Principals can discuss this during a meeting with each teacher or provide a form to be filled out before or after the data meeting. It is helpful for each teacher to have a goal and then track the class progress toward this goal. Goal setting helps communicate accountability for the students reaching a high reading level.

Principals should be cautious about linking CBM results directly to individual teacher performance appraisals. When DIBELS or other CBM data are referenced in a teacher's performance review, there is a risk that teachers may respond by cheating on student assessments. Although it may be appropriate to say that increasing reading achievement is a goal for teachers, there are very sticky problems to deal with when the DIBELS becomes a threat to them.

Data Meetings With Parents

One of the most powerful examples of how CBM data can have a positive impact on relationships with parents comes from a principal who shared his story with his colleagues. At a quarterly meeting with four elementary principals who were implementing RTI, this principal shared an experience he had about 3 months into the first year of RTI in his school. He was meeting with a parent who was forcefully requesting that her son be moved to a different class because she feared he was not learning to read. After discovering that the parent had not yet discussed her concerns with the teacher, the principal explained that he needed to consult with the teacher about her son. The teacher joined the meeting with her RTI data notebook under her arm. The principal asked the teacher to share information about the student's assessment data and the school's plan to help raise the child's reading level.

The teacher told the parent about her child's DIBELS fall benchmark data and said that her son was receiving intervention in a small group with two other students on specific prereading skills he was lacking. The teacher then opened her data notebook and showed the parent her analysis of the error patterns on the child's DIBELS indicator probes, the focus of instruction for the group in which he was placed, and a brief overview of the type of strategies that were used in this group according to the group's weekly lesson plan. Then she showed the parent her child's progress monitoring chart and expressed that, with his current rate of progress, she fully expected that he would be at benchmark by the midyear DIBELS benchmark assessment. The teacher explained that the student would be exited from the skill group after three consecutive progress monitoring scores at or above benchmark, with progress monitoring for a month after that to make sure that he doesn't slip back.

The principal thanked the teacher and excused her to return to the classroom. The parent then expressed appreciation for what the school was doing to help her child learn to read and withdrew her request that the child be moved to a different class because the teacher obviously knew her child very well and had a plan in place that was working. The principal said that in his many years of administrative leadership, he had rarely seen anything quite as powerful for addressing this type of parent concern. The principal believes that the key to this parent's turnaround was the progress monitoring graphs that enabled the teacher to show in a concrete manner where the child's skills were, where he needed to be to reach benchmark, what the school was doing to help him, and when he was expected to reach the goal.

Communication with parents about RTI helps develop strong home–school relationships. Many schools send letters home at the beginning of RTI implementation to provide an overview of the initiative. The letters often include a parent-friendly description of what the various assessment measures mean. At an administrator workshop, one principal shared her regrets about sending home a letter for a parent's signature to gain permission to place a student in a Tier II intervention group. This permission letter raised many questions and concerns about whether the child was entering a special education procedure. The principal regretted this approach because placement in the group was delayed by several weeks. A better approach may be to explain to parents in the handbook and in communication that the school's curriculum in early reading includes periodic assessments and the use of tiered intervention instruction.

On occasion, concerns have arisen because some parents download the oral reading passages to help their child practice reading the passages. This is an unfortunate misunderstanding of the purpose of the assessment. Parents should want their child to be assessed properly because they may not be selected to receive special help if they reach benchmark levels artificially. It is important to explicitly state to parents that not practicing for the assessment is important because the norms were derived from cold reads.

DATA CHARTS THAT ARE A MUST FOR PRINCIPALS

Earlier in this chapter it was recommended that the principal and RTI coordinator have an administrative RTI data notebook. The contents will be different from the teacher's data notebooks. Resource A, at the end of this book, provides a sample set of reports for this notebook.

5

Leadership Perspectives on RTI

Evelyn S. Johnson, Lori Smith, and Monica L. Harris

OVERVIEW

"Beginning with the end in mind" (Covey, 2004, p. 95) is advice applicable to school leaders starting the process of RTI implementation. As explained in the previous chapter, if a systemic approach to RTI is adopted at the beginning of the implementation process, RTI can become the organizing framework around which secondary schools align their mission, vision, and values with schoolwide programming. More specifically, RTI should become a *system* through which schools work to increase student achievement rather than operating as a piecemeal program operating in isolation. Although RTI implementation may seem like a daunting task for school leaders, it can become a comprehensive framework for meeting the needs of all students. In discussing the *Breaking Ranks* framework of school reform (National Association of Secondary School Principals [NASSP], 1996), Lachat (2001) describes the importance of this type of systemic reform, noting that altering one component of the school system affects other components as well. Therefore, piecemeal change can never be as effective as systemic reform.

The implementation of an RTI model can create a natural process for organizational analysis and evaluation of key school components related to academic achievement and positive behavior support of students. As a school leader, your challenge will be to manage, organize, and prioritize the implementation of systemic change.

School leaders are also charged with the important but difficult task of developing a school culture that is supportive of systemic reform. Change is often viewed as a purely technical challenge—do we have the resources and information to implement this new process? But an increasing amount of literature on school reform and change demonstrates that effective leaders also address the social and cultural values of an organization in order to guide the process of systemic reform (Elmore, 2007). Organizations that fail to consider the social context and personal values of its members *in addition to* addressing the technical aspects of change will likely not be successful in their efforts (Reid, 1987). Therefore, strategic models of RTI implementation address the required "investment in human capital" (Elmore, 2007, p. 2) by ensuring that the necessary conditions for implementation of RTI are in place (Fuchs & Deshler, 2007). As described by Fuchs and Deshler (2007), necessary conditions for RTI implementation include the following:

1. Sustained investments in professional development programs.

2. Engaged administrators who set expectations for adoption and proper implementation.

3. Willingness to stay the course.

4. Willingness to redefine roles and change the school's culture.

5. Providing staff sufficient time to understand the changes, to accommodate changes into their current practices, and to have their questions and concerns addressed.

Throughout this text, we discuss the leader requirements for successful implementation of the various components of RTI. However, building leaders may have questions about the overall process. In this chapter, we present and answer frequently asked questions about the role of the building principal in implementing RTI, drawing on information from building leaders who have been successful in this enterprise.

WHAT IS MY ROLE AS BUILDING LEADER TO IMPLEMENT RTI?

The role of the building leader during the initial launch and continuing development of an RTI model is multifaceted: supervisor, facilitator, and mentor. The building leader's role in RTI reflects the significant changes in responsibilities that secondary principals have faced over the last several decades (Portin, DeArmond, Gundlach, & Schneider, 2003). The most complex of these changes has been the increase in the number of issues for which the principal is responsible, which necessitates a movement toward shared leadership in schools (Portin et al., 2003). Shared leadership, which has been widely discussed as a way for principals to gain consensus among staff based on collaboration, is a means of sharing and transferring leadership responsibilities among administrators, staff, and community members (DuFour, DuFour, Eaker, & Many, 2006; Lashway, 2003; Portin et al., 2003). As discussed in Chapter 1, the PLC framework is an effective means of developing shared leadership.

The use of shared leadership models can be a great support for RTI. Although RTI can be implemented in many ways in a secondary school building, the process must fit the needs, goals, mission, and vision unique to each school. As school and district staff begin to evaluate, analyze, and examine the needs of individual students, the needs at the building level become apparent. Forming an RTI team that participates in all aspects of designing, establishing, and supporting the school's RTI model increases the likelihood of its success. The RTI team becomes its own PLC to work toward continuous school improvement (DuFour et al., 2006). The role of this PLC is the persistent analysis of the status quo and a constant search for better ways to achieve goals and accomplish the purpose of the organization (DuFour et al., 2006, p. 4).

Both the RTI and PLC models are systems-level initiatives that can work together to achieve common goals. For example, each model employs a problem-solving team in the continuous cycle of gathering data about students, developing strategies and ideas to support student learning, implementing these strategies, and analyzing the effect of the changes to determine what worked. Then, if additional changes are needed, the knowledge gained from this cycle is applied to make modifications, and the next cycle of improvement begins (DuFour et al., 2006).

An effective building leader under an RTI model will coordinate the efforts of PLCs (or shared leadership teams). The principal should keep staff focused on the school's goals of improved student outcomes. In addition, the principal will be primarily responsible for managing resources, setting priorities, and coordinating multiple processes such as researching interventions or specific programs for each intervention tier.

HOW DO I START THE PROCESS OF IMPLEMENTATION?

A building leader should focus on three main tasks as a school begins to develop an RTI model: (a) identifying the functions and compositions of the PLCs, (b) conducting a needs assessment, and (c) developing an action plan for year one of implementation. Each of these tasks is explained in more detail.

Identify PLCs

A building leader may want to identify a number of PLCs to begin the process of establishing an RTI model for the school. A problem-solving/data-evaluation team will serve as the core PLC for the process. Other PLCs may include one that develops common assessments in the general education program (see Chapter 7 on progress monitoring) and one that focuses on instructional strategies such as differentiation and universal design. With each PLC, it is important to clearly define the roles of each member and to remain consistent about their responsibilities. This is especially true for the "core team," which has the responsibility for analyzing and evaluating student data to determine appropriate interventions.

The core team should comprise staff who participate in every monthly meeting, who can evaluate the learning needs of students, and who are able to support teachers in the use of effective instructional strategies. PLC members may include district support staff, such as a school psychologist who has expertise in the area of learning disabilities and understanding student needs. The building leader's responsibility at PLC meetings is to create the infrastructure to hold them. This includes planning for resources, scheduling, and supporting staff participation. A teacher from each grade level should participate, though this might be a rotating position; in other words, the same teacher would not have to serve for the entire year but could share the responsibility with grade-level colleagues. Allowing such a rotation can ensure that all staff have the opportunity to participate on the core team to understand how the process works.

Conduct a Needs Assessment

As a school leader, there is no denying that the word "change" can be interpreted by staff as negative and the initial reaction can be one of resistance. The most important tool to prepare an organization for change and alleviate some of that resistance is to assess conditions for change for launching a new initiative (Lachat, 2001). An assessment of current schoolwide practices provides data that a building leader can use to prioritize next steps. A needs assessment also serves as the initial step for involving the entire staff in the process of change. Mellard and Johnson (2008) have developed RTI implementation checklists that include measures for determining the current stage of development of specific RTI components in a school. Our version of their checklists is included in the Appendix. The first task of the PLCs should be to conduct the needs assessment using this checklist.

In addition, all staff and parents should participate in the needs assessment through a comprehensive school survey. This survey should include questions related to academics, school climate, behavior, resources, community relations, and out-of-school programs. Once data from this survey have been compiled, the building leader uses both assessments to identify areas of strength on which the school can build and areas for improvement. A sample survey for parents is included in Figure 5.1.

Figure 5.1   Cheyenne Mountain Junior High Parent Survey

Cheyenne Mountain Junior High Parent Survey

The Building Accreditation Accountability and Advisory Committee (BAAAC) Survey is your chance to let our school receive your feedback on its ability to meet your child's/children's needs. The BAAAC Committee is comprised of parents, school staff, and community members that discuss, review, and evaluate all aspects of our school, including programs, curriculum, and student achievement. Future goals and improvement plans for the junior high will be based on the results of this survey. Your opinion counts! Thank you for taking the time to complete this survey.

Please use the attached Scantron sheet to answer questions 1–51.

1. Student's Grade Level (mark "A" for seventh grade or "B" for eighth grade)

2. Student's Sex (mark "A" for male or "B" for female)

PTO/Other Committees

(Mark "A" for yes or "B" for no.)

3. I read the school newsletter.

4. I would be satisfied with an electronic school newsletter.

5. I would like to serve on the Building Accountability Committee.

6. I am aware of the district/school website and what information to obtain from it.

Curriculum

For questions 7–11, mark "A" for strong agreement with the statement, "B" for agreement with the statement, or "C" for disagreement with the statement. Please comment in the space provided for each "disagreement" answer.

7. Overall, my child is progressing academically as well as expected.

8. My child's individual academic needs, strengths, and weaknesses are recognized and addressed.

9. My child is being challenged academically.

10. My child's daily homework load is appropriate.

11. There is enough variety in the course offerings at the junior high.

Please rate your satisfaction with your student's curriculum in the following academic areas (A = excellent, B = good, C = satisfactory, D = needs improvement, E = not observed).

(Continued)

Figure 5.1 (Continued)

12. Mathematics

13. English

14. Social studies

15. Foreign language

16. Media Center/Library

17. PE

18. Performing Arts (band, choir, drama)

19. Visual Arts (ceramics, 2D/3D design, jewelry, drawing, sculpting)

20. Technology (applications across the curriculum)

21. Science

22. Special education

Comments

_____

_____

_____

_____

Home/School Communications

23. When contacting a CMJH staff member, I most often use the following method(s):
    A. Phone
    B. E-mail
    C. Written communication (note, letter)
    D. Conference

For questions 24–30, mark "A" for strong agreement with the statement, "B" for agreement with the statement, "C" for disagreement with the statement, or "D" if the statement does not apply. Please comment in the space provided for each "disagreement" answer.

24. I am satisfied with the three-week interval of schoolwide student progress reports.

25. I am satisfied with the personal communication I have received from staff about my student.

26. I am satisfied with the parent/teacher conferencing process.

27. I am satisfied with the access to my student's counselor.

28. I am satisfied with the process of obtaining make-up work from teachers.

29. I am satisfied with communication from my child's teachers concerning poor performance or declining grades.

30. I am satisfied with the response time from staff when I communicate with them through e-mail or by phone.

Comments

_____

_____

_____

_____

School Climate

For questions 31–44, mark "A" for strong agreement with the statement, "B" for agreement with the statement, "C" for disagreement with the statement, or "D" if the statement does not apply. Please comment in the space provided for each "disagreement" answer.

31. My child has had a positive academic transition from sixth to seventh grade.

32. My child has had a positive social transition from sixth to seventh grade.

33. My child's older sibling has had a positive academic transition from the junior high to the high school.

34. My child's older sibling has had a positive social transition from the junior high to the high school.

35. I am satisfied with the information provided to prepare my child for the high school.

36. I am satisfied with the disciplinary actions/policies implemented at the junior high.

37. I feel that harassment is addressed appropriately at CMJH.

38. I am aware of the tools that my child has been taught at CMJH to address harassment/bullying.

39. My child enjoys attending school at CMJH.

40. My child feels safe at CMJH.

41. I am satisfied with the school lunch program.

42. My child takes advantage of the before- and after-school time when teachers are available.

43. My child takes advantage of the counselors when social or academic issues arise.

44. My child feels comfortable talking with administration when social or academic issues arise.

(Continued)

Figure 5.1   (Continued)

Comments

_____
_____
_____
_____

Staff

For questions 45–51, mark "A" for strong agreement with the statement, "B" for agreement with the statement, "C" for disagreement with the statement, or "D" if the statement doesn't apply. Please comment in the space provided for each "disagreement" answer.

Staff members listen to my concerns and work cooperatively with me to meet my student's needs:

   45. Administration

   46. Counselors

   47. Office staff

   48. Teachers

   49. Coaches

   50. Maintenance/Custodians

   51. Special education

Comments

_____
_____
_____
_____

Parent name(s) (optional): _____

Develop an Action Plan

At the conclusion of the needs assessment, the principal, assistant principal(s), and core PLC team develop an action plan. Including several staff in creating the plan is consistent with the model of shared leadership and also underscores the collaborative (rather than top-down) nature of the RTI process. A schoolwide action plan should include the following components:

1. A description of the expected benefits, objectives, and purpose of the shift to RTI.

2. A list of indicators that were used to guide the action plan.

3. A projection of expected short-term, incremental gains.

4. A realistic timeline for implementation.

5. A list of roles and responsibilities for staff as they relate to RTI.

6. A plan for regular monitoring to inform the process.

7. A plan for a coordinated professional development process to support implementation.

8. A process for maintaining continuing communication to ensure that staff are involved, understand the process, and have an opportunity to voice concerns. (Lachat, 2001)

WHAT WILL THE PROFESSIONAL DEVELOPMENT NEEDS BE?

Professional Development for the Principal

Principals will require professional development in the PLC framework as well as in the specifics of RTI. In addition, as the implementation process progresses, principals will notice the increased importance of evaluation, both formal and informal. This includes the use of formative and summative assessments for use in all areas of school functioning. At Tier 1, principals will need to learn effective methods to evaluate teacher performance in ways that support RTI implementation and promote collaborative processes. Related to this, principals will need to develop strong knowledge of and facility with instructional strategies such as differentiation so that they can support teachers instructionally. Tier 2 and Tier 3 require knowledge of progress monitoring and the management of that system at the school level.

Professional Development for Staff

As the core team begins the process of discussing RTI implementation, professional development needs should quickly align with areas projected on the needs assessment. For example, if the needs assessment identifies that the school lacks interventions to support student reading, math, or writing, teachers responsible for implementing such interventions will require professional development in these areas. If schools do not already use a process of progress monitoring, professional development will be needed in this area. It will be important to ensure that the professional development is aligned with the systems and interventions the school is using. For example, in a district that uses AIMSweb for progress monitoring, training on that particular system will be important.

It is impossible to recommend a standard sequence of professional development topics here because each building's needs will vary. The important point is that the needs assessment and action plan will help each school determine its unique professional development needs. Principals also might consider requiring that teacher requests to attend professional development opportunities be accompanied by a rationale of how the opportunity supports the school's RTI framework. Alternatively, principals might require staff to develop a longer range, coordinated, professional development plan that supports RTI implementation.

RTI FOCUSES ON ACADEMICS: WHAT ABOUT BEHAVIOR?

As described in Chapter 1, in this book we conceptualize a model of RTI that focuses on academics and behavior. Many secondary schools have a strong focus on academics because of high-stakes accountability and in the past have focused on a punitive approach to behavior. One of the many potential benefits of RTI is that it moves schools away from a "wait-to-fail" model and allows for proactive instruction, early intervention, and prevention. However, the wait-to-fail model applies to more than just academics. Through the use of a PBIS model as a part of the RTI process, schools can develop a *universal* and proactive approach to improve both behavior and academics.

The core RTI team should use the expertise of its team members who regularly practice aspects of behavioral modification to investigate current behavioral models created for schools, such as the PBIS model. These suggestions and models will most likely create an uncomfortable paradigm shift for some staff members. Moving from a reactive to a more proactive approach to discipline requires practices such as clearly defined student expectations that focus on catching students doing something right (the positive, in PBIS). This requires a schoolwide development and adoption of common standards and expectations for student behavior.

The National Technical Assistance Center on PBIS provides comprehensive resources for schools interested in implementing a schoolwide model of positive behavior (see the Resources section of this text). As a starting point, the PBIS center identifies seven main components of an effective PBIS model: (a) a common approach to discipline, (b) a positive statement of purpose, (c) a small number of positively stated expectations for all students, (d) procedures for teaching these expectations, (e) a continuum of procedures for encouraging maintenance of outcomes, (f) a continuum of procedures for discouraging displays of rule-violating behavior, and (g) procedures for monitoring and evaluating the effectiveness of the discipline system on a regular and frequent basis (http://www.pbis.org). In addition, this website offers many resources on PBIS functions within the RTI framework.

WHAT IF WE IDENTIFY TOO MANY KIDS IN NEED OF INTERVENTION?

If too many students are identified as in need of intervention, this suggests that the core program may need adjustment. Recommendations for RTI implementation state that eighty to eighty-five percent of students should make adequate progress with a strong core (Tier 1) program. About fifteen to twenty percent of students will require more intense interventions provided at either Tier 2 or 3. If significantly more than twenty percent of students are identified as in need of intervention, a school's first priority should be improving the Tier 1 program.

Even with a strong core program, managing Tier 2 will likely be one of the most difficult aspects of RTI at the secondary level and will be a continuous struggle even after the system has been in place several years. Several strategies for managing the potentially large number of students in need of intervention are available. The first two are directly related to the effective management of Tier 2. The use of objective screening processes (described in Chapter 4) is a critical first step. Objective data accompanied by clear decision rules should be used to identify students in need of intervention. These decisions cannot be based on teacher referral (without supporting evidence). The results of screening then guide intervention development. Screening helps to identify not only an individual student's needs, but also helps a school plan for school-level resources. For example, reading support is likely an area of concern that will be shared by most students who are identified as in need of academic support. If screening data confirm this, schools should invest in effective, standardized protocols that address reading. More information on interventions is provided in Chapter 6.

A third effective strategy consists of assigning staff to serve as mentors for students who receive Tier 2 or Tier 3 interventions. Because the counseling staff can become overwhelmed with the time requirements of each student's interventions, assigning a teacher mentor who has a strong connection with the student increases the likelihood that the intervention will be successful by ensuring that students do not fall through the cracks. It also helps teachers become familiar with tiered interventions and progress monitoring. Some teachers may require training to fulfill the role of teacher-mentor, but connecting teachers with students in need of support is worth the investment. Teacher-mentors who track specific students also can prevent system "clogs" caused by a bottleneck of students requiring intervention or a breakdown in the progress monitoring system. These minor setbacks will occur, but if they occur too early and too often in the beginning phase of RTI, the result will be the slow death of support for RTI among staff and parents. Sustaining an effective and efficient RTI process within a middle or high school is the most critical role the principal has.

WHAT RESOURCES WILL I NEED TO PROVIDE?

Resources can be organized into three main areas: (a) professional development, (b) materials and equipment, and (c) infrastructure. Professional development is discussed above. Specific resources, including materials and equipment, for each component are discussed in the relevant chapters of this text.

Creating the infrastructure to support RTI will depend largely on issues such as scheduling, assigning roles and responsibilities, and coordinating meetings and other aspects of school functioning under the RTI framework. For example, to ensure that the PLC framework is effective, staff will need regular, dedicated time periods to collaborate and communicate. Some suggestions for allocating time include providing teachers within a grade level (e.g., all ninth-grade teachers) to have some shared time to discuss the students they have in common. This allows them to review data regarding student performance across content areas and interventions (if applicable). In addition, collaborative planning time for teachers within a department (e.g., mathematics) can create opportunities for teachers to collaborate on issues related to instruction and assessment. Although such scheduling is not easy to arrange, without some collaborative time, the process will not work.

WHAT IF I DON'T GET THINGS RIGHT THE FIRST TIME?

Remember that RTI is a dynamic, continuous process. Begin somewhere within the current system. There is no perfect formula for the perfect team meeting with a perfect plan for continuous school improvement. Although a wealth of technical information is available to support RTI implementation, when principals ignore the social context and values of the staff and stakeholder community, change cannot take place (Reid, 1987). In addition, asking staff to make too many changes at once can result in hitting a dysfunction threshold, the point at which people can no longer react to so many changes simultaneously and so avoid change altogether. RTI implementation will be an incremental and iterative process, and the use of DBDM and the PLC frameworks supports continuous review, evaluation, and adjustment.

RTI IMPLEMENTATION IN PRACTICE

Cheyenne Mountain Junior High School began the process of RTI Implementation in the 2004–05 school year. Figure 5.2 depicts a flow chart of how Cheyenne Mountain Junior High School began the process of RTI implementation.

Figure 5.2   Cheyenne Mountain Junior High's RTI Implementation Process

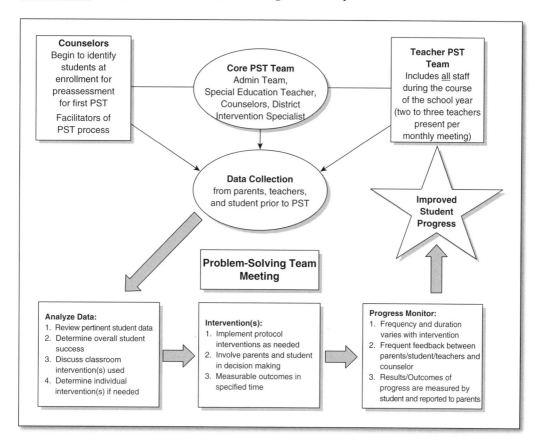

The principal of Cheyenne Mountain followed five main steps to begin the process of implementation. These are dynamic processes and decisions that need to be evaluated annually for effectiveness as related to the RTI process. In addition, other schools may find that a different process is more appropriate depending on the results of their needs assessment.

Step 1: Determine Core Problem-Solving Team

Remember that RTI implementation is more effective when administrative team members are a part of it. If it is important for the teachers to be a part of RTI, then it should also be important for administration. And, it is most effective if the same Core Team is used for each Problem-Solving Team (PST) meeting during the year. You will also need to determine any district specialists that could be a part of the Core Team and/or your special education teachers. A Core Team of five to seven members is optimal plus two to three classroom teachers. Include no more than ten members per meeting or the efficiency of meetings will decrease.

Once the Core Team is determined, include them in the following:

Task #1: Evaluate current practices used to assess student progress within the building, and determine how those current practices could be redesigned to fit within the structures of RTI.

Task #2: Determine how classroom teachers will be involved in the RTI process. The key is to involve them all to build knowledge and consensus about the process. However, in a secondary setting of large staffs, this may only be possible within a multiyear cycle.

Task #3: Determine the schedule (frequency and duration) for PST meetings (e.g., once-a-month meetings, biweekly). These decisions are important because they will be linked to progress-monitoring procedures and the review of intervention effectiveness.

Step 2: Data Collection Procedures

Using the Core Team, determine how data for each student referral into Tier 2 will be collected and managed.

Task #1: Determine individuals that will be responsible for taking initial student referrals and beginning the data collection process.

Task #2: Determine the specific forms that will be used for data collection. Look at what is already available online or from other schools. There is a wide variety of forms that have already been produced, use them! Much valuable time can be wasted on the creation of forms.

Task #3: Determine how and when parents will be involved in the RTI process. It is optimal to begin to include parents when gathering student data. Determine protocols for involving parents at PST meetings.

Step 3: Determine Data Analysis Procedures

Data analysis is the most important part of the process, but it is also the most time-consuming and most difficult to implement. However, it can be accomplished over time with adequate resources and professional development.

Task #1: Agree upon the data that should be collected for an initial referral. This could include information such as student history, summative assessments, formative assessments, and other tests that give an overall depiction of a student's academic performance and abilities.

Task #2: Determine how data will be distributed to the Core Team and classroom teachers involved in upcoming PST meeting. This can be a tricky task! It may take several different attempts to determine what works best for your team. Some possible questions to discuss with team members: Should a summary sheet be constructed and given to each team member before the meeting to aid in efficiency? Should the team collectively discuss the student's information during the PST meeting? How should parents be involved in this process?

Task #3: Determine who will be responsible for creating and presenting the data during PST meetings. This can be a labor-intensive process at the secondary level. Therefore, divide and conquer! One suggestion is to have counselors assigned to each grade level prepare their own grade-level referrals, as they know their own kids best. It is common in the high school setting to have more referrals in the ninth and tenth grades than in the eleventh and twelfth grades. Therefore, give consideration to workloads of the lower grade-level counselors and try to equalize the efforts of all counselors.

Step 4: Developing a Bank of Interventions

At the secondary level, it may not be common for schools to have a strong system of intervention and support. It will be important to determine the specific needs of your students in order to develop an effective bank of interventions.

Task #1: The most dynamic part of the RTI process is the development of interventions. Start small and remember that less is more in the beginning stages of implementation—there are no "silver bullets" where interventions are concerned. Begin evaluating what interventions are already being used in various capacities within the school. Evaluate, divide, and classify each one as either an academic or a behavioral intervention.

Task #2: Determine the greatest areas of need both academically and behaviorally in the building. Identify three to four needs each for behavior and academic interventions. As a team, prioritize needs for both types of interventions. Research possibilities that could be implemented within your building for the following year. Attempt the implementation of no more than two new interventions for each category.

Step 5: Determine Progress Monitoring Tools, Documentation, and Evaluation Procedures

Task #1: Based on the needs and priorities for intervention within the school, research progress-monitoring tools. The tool(s) chosen should frequently assess gains within major academic areas such as reading, writing, or mathematics, in conjunction with the interventions being implemented. This is an opportunity to receive input from district assessment personnel, other schools, or other educational assessment experts. The use of progress monitoring tools may take several years to implement correctly and effectively within the RTI process.

Task #2: Consider implementing readily available curriculum-based measures before investing in larger-scale progress-monitoring tools. This is a simple approach for the classroom teacher to grasp the importance of progress monitoring and its benefits for measuring growth quickly and efficiently.

Task #3: Align professional development with progress monitoring and interventions.

Process Summary

The steps and tasks described to begin RTI implementation within a secondary school will vary according to the unique needs of each building. It is important to remember that RTI is a systemic change that cannot be completed in a year. However, following these guidelines for starting the process will create important conversations about continuous school improvement. It is up to school administration teams and the Core Team to determine the systems and structures that best fit their school to sustain an RTI process.

SUMMARY

Successfully developing and establishing an RTI process requires strong, consistent leadership. The change will be complex, involving numerous moving parts to the system, a tremendous culture shift in the general education program, and an opportunity to integrate numerous practices to include not only what is helpful for students but also what is helpful for teachers. The building principal must understand the system, lead a needs assessment, and develop short-term and long-term goals and procedures to make implementation successful. The principal must keep staff focused on the school's goals of improved student achievement and will have to manage resources if specific populations require a higher intensity or different level of support than others. The principal will lead the integration of systems that allow the school to collect, analyze, and evaluate data at the individual student level, at the classroom level, at the grade level, and at the building level—and then prioritize and act on what should happen next. Most critically, the principal must create a climate of collaboration and shared responsibility.

In recent years, nearly all schoolwide reform initiatives have recognized strong principal support and schoolwide buy-in as key to the reform's success. RTI is no different—strong leadership is necessary if RTI implementation is to be successful.

The Reading Brain and Literacy Instruction

6

William N. Bender and Martha J. Larkin

Strategies Presented in This Chapter Include

- ✓ Big Ideas From Reading Research
- ✓ Several Informal Early Literacy Assessments
- ✓ A Phonics Literacy Checklist
- ✓ DIBELS
- ✓ Ten Tactics for the Brain Compatible Classroom
- ✓ Brain Compatible Research Results for the Classroom Teacher
- ✓ The Basics of RTI in Reading

THE GOOD NEWS IN READING RESEARCH!

Although the initial picture of reading success among students with learning disabilities and other reading difficulties, as presented by the National Reading Panel (NRP), was not overly positive, there is much good news to report (King & Gurian, 2006; National Institute of Child Health and Development [NICHD], 2000; Sousa, 2005). Research on reading instruction has exploded in the past two decades, resulting in major advances in several related areas including the brain and central nervous systems bases for reading, literacy instruction, phonological awareness research, and reading comprehension instructional

---

tactics for students with reading difficulties (Bender, 2008; Bhat, Griffin, & Sindelar, 2003; Chard & Dickson, 1999; Joseph, Noble, & Eden, 2001; Kemp & Eaton, 2007; Rourke, 2005; Sousa, 2005; Sylwester, 2001; Wood & Grigorenko, 2001). Much of this research (e.g., brain functioning during reading) is rather esoteric in nature and generally not readily accessible for the practicing teacher. In fact, a major emphasis of this book is to make this research—and the instructional ideas that are based on it—readily available to every elementary teacher in the classroom.

There is more good news. Because of the passage of the Individuals With Disabilities Education Act (IDEA) of 2004, teachers across the nation now are beginning to implement response to intervention (RTI) procedures that more closely track how struggling students are doing in their reading and early literacy (Bender & Shores, 2007; Bradley, Danielson, & Doolittle, 2007; Fuchs & Fuchs, 2007; Kemp & Eaton, 2007). As teachers "ramp up" their efforts in this regard, reading instruction will improve for many struggling readers as earlier interventions are provided that are specifically targeted to address their reading problems.

Within this growing body of research, three emerging emphases will provide the basis for this text—the emphasis on a holistic view of early literacy instruction (Haager, 2002; McCutchen et al., 2002; Shaker, 2001), the growing literature on brain compatible reading instruction in the classroom (King & Gurian, 2006; Prigge, 2002; Rourke, 2005; Sousa, 2001, 2005; Sylwester, 2001), and the recent RTI mandate (Bradley, Danielson, & Doolittle, 2007; Fuchs & Fuchs, 2007). Each of these emphases is presented below to provide a backdrop for the strategies discussed in this and each subsequent chapter.

BIG IDEAS FROM EARLY LITERACY RESEARCH

As mentioned previously, there has been an explosion of research in the area of reading within the past decade (Bender, 2008; King & Gurian, 2006; Rourke, 2005; Sousa, 2005). As a result, a number of recent research-based conclusions have been developed concerning how reading skills progress among learners without reading difficulties. A number of points about reading instruction from a variety of sources are presented to provide a basis for discussion of the reading strategies and tactics for students with reading problems (Fuchs & Fuchs, 2007; Kame'enui, Carnine, Dixon, Simmons, & Coyne, 2002; NICHD, 2000; Sousa, 2005). These big ideas represent our best understandings of reading difficulties, as well as the best practices in reading instruction for all students today. These seven ideas are

- Reading is not natural.
- There is no "reading" area in the brain.
- Reading disabilities result from both genetic and environmental influences.
- Development of reading skill is complex and long term.
- Students must learn the alphabetic principle and the alphabetic code.
- Phoneme manipulation and phonics are the most effective ways to teach reading.
- Students must develop automaticity with the code.

Reading Is Not Natural

Unlike sight, hearing, cognition, or the development of language, reading is not a natural process. For example, an infant isolated on an island will develop sight, hearing, attention skills, rudimentary numeration and counting skills, and language of some sort, but reading will not develop naturally (Sousa, 2001, 2005). Of course, a human infant isolated on an island probably would not survive, but give us some literary flexibility here! In short, reading skills will not develop unless these skills are specifically taught, so teachers should emphasize them in every aspect of the school curriculum throughout the earliest instruction in kindergarten, as well as the early and middle school years.

There Is No "Reading" Area in the Brain

Although regions of the brain can be associated with sight, hearing, physical movement, or language, there is no single reading area within the brain. Rather, reading involves many more areas of the brain than does language development but must be understood as a function of linguistic capability (Armstrong, 2007). While speech and language seem to be "hardwired in the brain," with specific areas related to these skills, reading is not hardwired in only one or two brain areas (Sousa, 2001). This is one reason that reading skill does not develop naturally.

Reading Disabilities Result From Both Genetic and Environmental Influences

The evidence for a genetic abnormality that may lead to a reading disability has grown stronger over the years (Wood & Grigorenko, 2001), and various research studies have implicated a variety of specific regions within specific chromosomes—particularly chromosomes 1, 2, 6, 13, 14, and 15—as possible genetic problem areas for students with learning disabilities (Raskind, 2001). However, much more research is needed prior to isolating a specific genetic basis for either learning disabilities or reading disabilities. Further, although teachers cannot control genetic influences in a child's life, they can control the environment in which reading instruction occurs, and manipulating that reading environment offers teachers the best option to assist students in developing reading skills. For our purposes, we will concentrate on environmental strategies such as RTI, phonemic instruction, and tactics for enhancing reading comprehension, rather than the growing literature on genetic causes of reading problems for students with learning disabilities. Teachers also would be well-advised to adopt such an emphasis on environmental-instructional bases of reading development.

Development of Reading Skill Is Complex and Long Term

All children speak (or communicate in some fashion) before they read, and speech sounds serve as the basis for reading (Sousa, 2005). A *phoneme* is the briefest discrete sound that can communicate meaning. In total, all the languages in the world include only about 150 phonemes (Sousa, 2005). For the

English language, some researchers report 41 phonemes (NICHD, 2000), whereas others suggest there are 44 discrete phonemes (Sousa, 2001). Reading involves making brain connections between phonemes and *graphemes*, or the squiggly lines on a page that represent printed letters. This transition is very difficult for some 30% of children, and these children develop reading problems to some degree; this group also includes children who are later identified as students with learning disabilities.

Just to confuse matters further, there is no one-to-one relationship between the phonemes and the specific letters in our alphabet. Thus, learning to read is both a complex and a long-term endeavor for all students, and students with learning disabilities in particular (Kame'enui et al., 2002). Teachers in kindergarten through middle school should build reading instruction into every instructional period as a primary and major emphasis, and recent federal and state initiatives are emphasizing that instructional need.

We now know that reading is based on the brain's ability to detect and manipulate phonemes, and that students who have not mastered these prereading skills will have great difficulty in reading (Sousa, 2005). Further, phonemic-based skill is a prerequisite for teaching phonics (which is the pairing phonemic skill and letter recognition), and even as late as middle school, phonemic instruction can be an effective component of reading instruction (Bhat, Griffin, & Sindelar, 2003).

Students Must Learn the Alphabetic Principle and the Alphabetic Code

The *alphabetic principle* involves the fact that most phonemes, and all speech sounds in English, can be represented by letters, and the pairing of speech sounds to printed letters is referred to as phonics instruction. Further, a child's ability to decode unknown words is based on those letter-sound relationships. The *alphabetic code* thus represents the relationships between letters and the sounds they represent. Research has documented that students with learning disabilities must learn the alphabetic principle to read effectively across the grade levels; merely memorizing words and word meanings is not enough for successful reading long term (Kame'enui et al., 2002; Sousa, 2005). Further, the alphabetic principle is not learned merely from exposure to print, but must be specifically taught (Sousa, 2005).

Phoneme Manipulation and Phonics Are the Most Effective Ways to Teach Reading

Although debate has raged for decades over phonics versus sight word instructional techniques, the evidence has clearly shown that an emphasis on phonemic instruction, and phonics (as represented by the alphabetic principle involving discrete sound manipulations and sound-letter relationships), is the most effective instructional method for reading for almost all children with and without reading problems (NICHD, 2000). Elementary and middle school teachers should emphasize the relationships between sounds and letters in every subject area whenever possible.

Students Must Develop Automaticity With the Code

While phoneme manipulation, phonetic decoding, word segmentation, and use of context clues to determine word meaning are all essential skills in early reading, rigorous application of these skills for every letter or word on the page would result in a highly cumbersome reading process. Rather, to develop effective reading skills, students must learn the alphabetic principle and the alphabetic code extremely well, so that the brain processing involved in decoding these letter sounds is "automatic" (Kame'enui et al., 2002)—this is referred to as *automaticity*. In that fashion, the student's brain may process many letters, sounds, or words at one time, and fluent reading is possible. Teachers should build their instruction such that every child with reading problems can attain automaticity in reading. Various reading programs described in subsequent chapters (e.g., Academy of Reading by AutoSkill, or Fast ForWord) focus directly on developing automaticity and fluency in all aspects of reading skill, from phonemic awareness and manipulation up through reading comprehension.

REFLECTIVE EXERCISE 6.1
USING THE BIG IDEAS FROM READING RESEARCH

Pause for a moment and consider the big ideas presented above. Almost all these ideas can suggest instructional activities within the classroom for students with learning disabilities and other reading difficulties, and we encourage you to reflect on how many of these ideas are currently implemented in your class. Remember that, with the growing national emphasis on reading, all teachers in elementary and middle grades should be teaching reading skills and should be building an emphasis on these skills into every lesson plan.

THE EMERGING EMPHASIS ON LITERACY

Within the last decade, an emphasis on early literacy instruction—versus merely an emphasis on reading—has emerged (Armstrong, 2007; McCutchen et al., 2002; Shaker, 2001). Literacy approaches focus not only on the discrete skills in reading such as phonics and reading comprehension (Bos, Mather, Silver-Pacuilla, & Narr, 2000; Patzer & Pettegrew, 1996; Smith, Baker, & Oudeans, 2001), but also on the more holistic set of skills that enhances and supports a student's skill in reading, such as the student's ability to speak, write, and listen effectively, as well as to use these literacy skills in reading and communicating (Winn & Otis-Wilborn, 1999). The emphasis in a literacy approach is on the interrelationship between reading, writing, and language and the interdependence of these systems within the human brain. However, this certainly does not mean that the particulars of phoneme manipulation, phonics, word attack, or comprehension are not taught—they are. Rather, the emphasis is on the end goal of reading—the ability to derive meaning from the written word and to use that skill as a communication tool.

Further, within the literacy emphasis, there is a growing emphasis on assisting struggling readers to improve their literacy skills, rather than merely a focus on remediation of specific and discrete reading deficits (Dayton-Sakari, 1997). In most cases, this results in an emphasis on the phoneme manipulation skills that have not been mastered previously or on instruction on the alphabetic principle. Smith et al. (2001) delineated several components of early literacy instruction that constitute an effective literacy program. Notice the emphasis on discrete skill instruction on letter names and sounds in the following skills.

1. Allocation of time for daily, highly focused literacy instruction

2. Consistent routines for teaching the big ideas of literacy

3. Explicit instruction for new letter names and sounds

4. Daily scaffolded or assisted practice with auditory phoneme detection, segmenting, and blending

5. Immediate corrective feedback

6. Daily application of new knowledge at the phoneme and lettersound levels across multiple and varied literacy contexts

7. Daily reviews

A word of explanation may be in order for several of these skills. First, examples of big ideas in literacy instruction may include things such as teaching the alphabet as code or teaching students that all stories have structure (e.g., character, story problem, climax) and using story structure as a basis for instruction. Next, the term *scaffolded* in Point 4 refers to the supports that a teacher provides to an individual child in assisting that child to improve his or her current reading skill. Typically, scaffolded instruction involves an in-depth, individualized examination of the reading skills, instructional support from the teacher to the child for the next skill to be mastered, and a planned withdrawal of support from the student to ensure that the student masters each successive skill independently (Larkin, 2001).

Research on Literacy Instruction

Consistent with the broader research results reported earlier, research on early literacy instruction has supported a strong phoneme-based instructional approach for students with reading problems (Bender, 2008; Bos et al., 2000; NICHD, 2000; Patzer & Pettegrew, 1996; Smith et al., 2001). The research supports the use of group-based oral reading, or choral reading, as an instructional technique to enhance reading fluency, because reading is dependent upon a student's language ability. Also, choral reading practice is recommended because students often are called upon to read orally in class across the grade levels (NICHD, 2000). This emphasis will be discussed in more detail later in the book.

Next, early instruction in reading should be quite robust; that is, instruction in each area of reading skill should be undertaken with sufficient intensity to assist students in reaching their early reading goals. Research has also shown that, for young readers who lag behind others in kindergarten and first grade, phonological instruction is even more important in their early literacy instruction (AutoSkill, 2004; Kame'enui et al., 2002). In fact, students who miss early phonological instruction always will lag behind in reading, and phonological instruction may be necessary in the late elementary or middle school grades for those students with reading problems.

McCutchen et al. (2002) used an experimental design and studied teachers' awareness of these newly emerging literacy emphases by investigating teachers' instruction and student outcomes in 44 classrooms scattered throughout the western states. These researchers not only assessed teacher knowledge of these literacy skills, but also observed how teachers instructed their students and noted the students' outcomes in phonological awareness, listening comprehension, and word reading. The results indicated that teachers were, in many cases, unaware of this emerging emphasis on phonemic instruction. However, based on a two-week instructional workshop, the teachers in the experimental group quickly grasped the importance of this emphasis, as well as the instructional techniques involved. Those teachers then implemented these practices, and students' reading skills improved rather dramatically in each area.

The good news from this study, as well as other research, is that phonological awareness is a teachable skill—teachers can learn these instructional techniques and students can learn the phonological manipulation skills that will improve their overall reading skill. Many of these instructional techniques are presented in Chapter 2, which concentrates on phonemic instruction, as well as subsequent chapters. Further, these results document that adequate instruction in that area will enhance the reading of students who display subsequent reading disabilities (Kame'enui et al., 2002; Smith et al., 2001). Thus, as teachers become aware of this broader emphasis on early literacy instruction, as well as the need to emphasize the alphabetic principle and phonemic instruction, the prognosis for remediation improves considerably across the grade levels (Bhat, Griffin, & Sindelar, 2003).

Further, phonemic instruction can be managed very effectively in a technology format (AutoSkill, 2004). Various computer-based reading programs have been developed that emphasize a student's ability to detect, compare, and manipulate phonemes, and this will save teachers considerable instructional time.

 REFLECTIVE EXERCISE 6.2
DEVELOPING LITERACY INSTRUCTIONAL SYSTEMS

With the emerging emphasis on literacy in recent years, coupled with the No Child Left Behind legislation from the federal government in 2001, a number of comprehensive literacy programs have been developed. These new literacy programs involve a wide array of skills ranging from early phoneme instruction to reading and writing skills. As one example, you may wish to review the Four Blocks program by Patricia M. Cunningham and Dorothy P. Hall (www.four-blocks.com). The four blocks involve (1) guided reading, (2) self-selected reading,

(3) writing, and (4) working with words. The early research on this project indicated strong initial results in one school in North Carolina. The Four Blocks program is a comprehensive program that involves the entire range of literacy skills.

Word Play and the Development of Early Literacy Skills

With the continuing research efforts in reading, as well as the advent of several newly developed research technologies (described below), we have gained a more complete picture not only of how reading skills develop, but of the dependent relationship between reading and the development of language. A representation of the development of these interrelated skills is presented below.

A List of Early Literacy Skills	
Development of oral language	Birth to 24 months
Phoneme discrimination	Birth to 11 months
Says first words	6 months to 11 months
Follows simple verbal directions	12 months to 17 months
Pronounces first vowels and most consonants	18 months to 24 months
Enjoys having a story read	18 months to 24 months
Awareness of certain letters (such as letters presented in advertising; i.e., *M* stands for McDonald's and *K* for Kellogg's)	24 months to 36 months
Complex phoneme manipulation	48 months to 8 years
Can tell a story	36 to 48 months
Becomes aware of the alphabetic code (i.e., letters stand for specific sounds)	48 months to Grade 1
Begins to read first words	48 months to Grade 1
Can grasp meaning from reading short paragraphs	Grade 1 to Grade 3
Begins to comprehend longer texts	Grade 1 to Grade 3

As you can see, reading is dependent upon the development of language in most children, and children with learning difficulties are no different in terms of these general milestones. However, children at risk for reading failure do progress through these milestones somewhat later than other children. Likewise, children who are hearing impaired do not follow this sequence, but the placement of oral language at the top of this list of skills correctly presents language as a fundamental basis for reading for almost every child.

Also, note that informal reading instruction begins prior to school. In our society, children—including children with learning difficulties in reading—learn that a *K* means breakfast cereal (can't every three-year old grab the cereal from the cabinet under the sink?) and an *M* means McDonald's. Children are surrounded by letters and many pick up the correct meaning of those letters at an early age. Of course, parents are well-advised to engage in word play or letter play whenever young children show an interest in these letters. This can prepare a child for later work in reading. Finally, teachers should make letter play and word play a fun aspect of the classroom from the prekindergarten programs through the elementary grades. This will greatly enhance the reading skills of the students with learning disabilities in the class and will develop reading skills that will stay with those children throughout life.

ASSESSMENTS OF EARLY LITERACY

Using Informal Literacy Checklists

As an example of a comprehensive literacy strategy, teachers may wish to consider using a literacy checklist. Literacy checklists are available from many sources and have been offered by a number of authors in the literature. The skills on the checklists may reflect the entire array of reading skills ranging from early phonemic awareness to higher-order reading comprehension. However, rather than depend on checklists devised by a reading scholar, Winn and Otis-Wilborn (1999) suggest the use of individually developed checklists for monitoring the literacy of individual students. An individually developed checklist allows the teacher to develop individually the items on the checklist and thus to specifically tailor the checklist to the needs and strengths of the student. A sample of such a literacy checklist is presented in Teaching Tip 6.1.

As you can see, this informal literacy checklist encompasses a wider variety of literacy skills, in this case phonemic and phonics skills, than would a traditional reading instructional lesson, and this broader view is the perspective supported by proponents of literacy instruction. Of course, teachers should vary the reading skills on the checklist for each student to reflect specifically those literacy skills that are relevant for that particular student. For some students, the indicators on the checklist would be exclusively comprehension, and for other students a mix of decoding or word attack skills and comprehension skills may be noted. A checklist for comprehension skills that would be useful for elementary and middle school students is presented in Teaching Tip 6.2. Teachers should feel free to alter or adapt these checklists to exclude or include any skills relevant for a particular student.

DIBELS: An Informal Assessment of Basic Literacy

The *Dynamic Indicators of Basic Early Literacy Skills* (DIBELS; Good & Kaminski, 2002) is an informal assessment of early literacy skills that can be obtained from Sopris West (in Longmont, CO). Although we do not intend to discuss large numbers of curricula or assessments in this book, we will present commercial materials that are research based and can enhance reading assessment and instruction for students with learning difficulties. On that basis, we recommend that every teacher of kindergarten through Grade 3 take the time to investigate this informal assessment of early literacy skills.

☞ **TEACHING TIP 6.1**

A Sample Literacy Checklist

Name _____ Date _____ Reading Material _____

   While listening to a child read, the teacher should note below specific examples of the successes and difficulties experienced. Completing this checklist during several reading activities will present a more complete picture of the child's reading skills. The teacher may also complete this checklist at the end of the grading period, as a postinstructional assessment.

1. Attempts to decode unknown words _____
   _____
   _____
   _____

2. Difficulty with initial consonant sounds _____
   _____
   _____
   _____

3. Difficulty with vowels _____
   _____
   _____
   _____

4. Difficulty with consonant blends _____
   _____
   _____
   _____

5. Difficulty with multisyllabic words _____
   _____
   _____
   _____

6. Demonstrates self-correcting _____
   _____
   _____
   _____

7. Demonstrates understanding _____
   _____
   _____
   _____

☞ **TEACHING TIP 6.2**

A Comprehension Checklist for Elementary Textbook Reading

Name _____ Date _____ Reading Material _____

   While listening to a child read from a subject area textbook, the teacher should note below specific examples of the successes and difficulties experienced. Completing this checklist during several reading activities will present a more complete picture of the child's reading skills. The teacher also may complete this checklist at the end of the grading period, as a postinstructional assessment.

1. Reflects on the relationship between the current chapter and previous or subsequent chapters _____
   _____
   _____

2. Reviews chapter headings and subheadings prior to reading _____
   _____
   _____
   _____

3. Reviews vocabulary lists or review questions prior to reading _____
   _____
   _____
   _____

4. Reflects on pictures and picture captions presented in text _____
   _____
   _____
   _____

5. Makes predictions about information which may be found in various sections of the chapter text _____
   _____
   _____

6. Reads the chapter reflectively _____
   _____
   _____
   _____

7. Answers comprehension or review questions after reading with 85% accuracy
   _____
   _____
   _____

DIBELS is a research-based assessment that teachers love because it is quite easy to administer. Individual sections of this assessment take approximately two to three minutes to complete, which makes this assessment a user-friendly approach to early literacy instruction (Langdon, 2004).

DIBELS is based on a number of early indicators of literacy success (Haager, 2002). Its four stepping-stones indicate with a high degree of accuracy which students will display learning difficulties and eventual learning disabilities in reading. For example, by two months into kindergarten, students should master onset recognition—referred to as initial sounds fluency—and that measure becomes a benchmark. Students who do not master initial sounds fluency by several months into kindergarten are quite likely to develop later reading difficulties (Langdon, 2004). Other stepping-stones through the first several years of school, such as those presented below, represent similar benchmarks.

Onset fluency (initial sounds)	Two months into kindergarten
Phoneme segmentation fluency	End of kindergarten
Nonsense words fluency	Middle of Grade 1
Oral reading fluency	End of Grade 1

The DIBELS assess students' performance on these benchmarks and can predict, with a high degree of accuracy, which students will develop subsequent reading problems. This assessment also includes some higher-level reading skills such as oral reading fluency through Grade 3. Other DIBELS measures include word-use fluency and retelling fluency (story retelling frequently is used as an indicator of early reading comprehension). Again, for students who meet these benchmarks on time, reading difficulties are not likely to develop. However, for students who do not master these skills by the times mentioned above, reading problems are quite likely to develop. Thus, for teachers to determine which students are having difficulty or may be likely to have difficulty, DIBELS is quite useful as an information measure of early literacy skill. Further, with the emerging emphasis on RTI across the nation, many states (e.g., Ohio and West Virginia) have chosen to use this instrument as the early screening instrument for all students in kindergarten through Grade 3.

BRAIN COMPATIBLE READING INSTRUCTION

With the growing national emphasis on early literacy in mind, we can turn to the emerging information on how the human brain learns to process information during the reading process. This area of research—commonly known as brain compatible instruction—has emerged only within the past 15 years and is based primarily on improvements in the medical sciences (Bhat, Griffin, & Sindelar, 2003; King & Gurian, 2006; Leonard, 2001; Prigge, 2002; Sousa, 2001, 2005; Sylwester, 2001).

Specifically, several brain measurement techniques have emerged that have added to our understanding of brain functioning. First, much of our increasing understanding of the human brain has come from the development of functional magnetic resonance imaging (fMRI). This is a nonradiological technique—and thus a relatively safe brain-scanning technique—that has allowed scientists to study the performance of human brains while the subject concentrates on different types of learning tasks (Richards, 2001; Sousa, 2005).

The fMRI measures the brain's use of oxygen and glucose during the thinking process, and from that information, physicians can determine which brain areas are most active during various types of educational tasks (Richards, 2001; Sousa, 2005). For example, specialists have now identified brain regions that are specifically associated with various learning activities such as language, math, auditory processing, motor learning, listening to music, or verbally responding to questions in a classroom discussion (Leonard, 2001). Further, a body of research on students with learning disabilities or other reading disorders also has emerged (Sousa, 2001).

As one example of this research, researchers working with Shaywitz at Yale University compared brain functioning of 29 dyslexic readers and 32 nondisabled readers (Shaywitz et al., 1996). Dyslexia readers had great difficulty in reading nonsense rhyming words (e.g., "lete" and "jeat"), whereas normal readers had no such difficulty. Further, using fMRI scans while readers were performing these tasks, these researchers showed that brains of the dyslexic readers were underactivated in the brain region that links print to the brain's language areas, compared to normal readers. However, the brains of the dyslexic readers were overactivated in Broca's area—a brain region associated with spoken language. These researchers suggested that readers with dyslexia were "overcompensating" in Broca's areas for the lack of activation in other areas. Thus, a clear functional difference has been shown between normally reading brains and brains that are challenged by reading.

Another recently developed technique for studying the brain is referred to as PEPSI, which stands for proton echo-planar spectroscopic imaging (Posse, Dager, & Richards, 1997). This technique measures activity in various brain regions by assessing lactate changes in various brain regions, related to a mismatch of the delivery of oxygen to those regions. Richards et al. (1999) compared six dyslexic and seven nondyslexic readers and demonstrated not only differences in brain functioning, but also the brain's ability to modify brain functioning as a result of intensive phonemically based reading instruction.

Many researchers have suggested that the research has developed to a point where specific teaching suggestions may be made (Richards et al., 2000; Shaywitz et al., 1996; Sousa, 2005). Based on this growing understanding of how students with learning difficulties learn, teachers across the nation have begun to restructure their classroom practices based on these brain compatible instruction guidelines (Goldstein & Obrzut, 2001; Leonard, 2001; Sousa, 2005). Although various authors make different recommendations, the ten tactics for a brain compatible instruction classroom, presented in Teaching Tip 6.3, represent some of the accumulated thought in this area; these tactics can enhance your reading instructional practices for all students, in particular students with reading difficulties (Gregory & Chapman, 2002; Prigge, 2002; Richards, 2001; Sousa, 2005).

TEACHING TIP 6.3

Ten Tactics for the Brain Compatible Classroom

1. Provide a safe, comfortable environment. Research on learning has demonstrated that the brain serves as a filter on several levels. The brain selectively focuses on sounds, sights, and other stimuli that threaten our safety, often to the exclusion of other stimuli. A second priority is information resulting in emotional responses, and only as a last priority does the brain process information for new, nonthreatening learning tasks (Sousa, 2001). Thus, students with reading problems must not be distracted by either a sense of danger in their learning environment or emotional threats in the classroom. Unsafe classes and emotional threats or challenges can prevent learning.

2. Provide comfortable furniture. As a part of structuring a comfortable learning environment, many teachers bring house furniture into the classroom and set up reading areas with a sofa and perhaps several comfortable chairs for students with learning difficulties. Lamps also are used in brain compatible classrooms for more home-like lighting, and some research has suggested that lighting closer to the red end of the light spectrum functions like a wake-up call for the brain (Sousa, 2001).

3. Provide water and fruits. Research has shown that the brain requires certain fuels— oxygen, glucose, and water—in order to perform at peak efficiency (Sousa, 2001). Water is essential for the movement of neuron signals through the brain. Research has shown that eating a moderate amount of fruit can boost performance and accuracy of word memory (Sousa, 2001). Thus, in brain compatible classrooms teachers offer students water and dried fruits quite frequently.

4. Require frequent student responses. Students with learning difficulties will learn much more when work output is regularly expected from them, because students generally are much more engaged in the process of learning when they must produce a product of some type (Bender, 2001). Products may include a range of activities such as pictures to demonstrate comprehension of an 1860s Midwestern farm or development of a one-act play to show Washington crossing the Delaware River in the battle of Trenton, New Jersey, during the Revolutionary War.

5. Base instruction on bodily movements when possible. Motor learning takes place in a different area than do higher order thought processes within the brain. Motor learning is based in the cerebellum and motor cortex whereas higher order learning and planning takes place in the frontal lobes of the cerebrum. Thus, motor learning takes place in a more fundamental or *lower* brain area than does learning languages and other *higher* brain functions. Also, the brain considers motor skills more essential to survival, because our evolutionary ancestors often had to run from predators or to hunt for prey. Consequently, motor skills (e.g., swimming, riding a bike), once learned, are remembered much longer than cognitive skills (e.g., foreign language) without a motor basis. This suggests that whenever possible teachers should pair factual memory tasks of higher order with physical movements to assist in memory for students with learning difficulties.

As an example of movement-based learning in an elementary class, the first author developed the following movement-based teaching idea. Students had read a text selection on the functions of a cell wall in protecting the cell. The lesson required an instructional demonstration that represented a cell wall in the processes of protecting the cell from bacteria while letting in various food enzymes. Initially three students stood together facing inward and locked their elbows tightly to represent the cell wall. The teacher then pointed out, "The cell wall is very strong to protect the cell." Next, the teacher selected a bacteria (i.e., another student) to try to break into the cell, with the cell wall holding that bacteria out. The teacher stated, "Cell walls protect the cell from bacteria." Finally, the teacher had a student representing the friendly enzyme move toward the cell wall to gain entrance. The cell wall let her in without delay! The teacher concluded, "Cell walls let in food and friendly enzymes." Elementary students who participate in this motor learning example will never forget this simple demonstration, because movement was used as the basis for comprehending this reading selection on the functions of a cell wall.

6. *Emphasize visual novelty.* The human brain is specifically attuned to seek out novelty and differences in stimuli (Sousa, 2001). In elementary grade reading instruction teachers should use color enhancements, size, and shape enhancements in developing worksheets or material posted in the classroom. However, in order to make this an effective learning tool, teachers should specifically discuss with the students why certain aspects of the material are colored differently and the importance of those colored items. Students with reading disabilities will benefit greatly from color and other novelties in the reading passages. Teachers should consider coloring every topic sentence in paragraphs for students with reading disabilities.

7. *Use chanting, rhymes, and music to increase novelty in learning.* Because music and rhythms are processed in a different area of the brain from language, pairing facts to be learned to a musical melody or a rhythmic chant can enhance memory for reading comprehension. Most adults, upon reflection, can remember the song that was frequently used to memorize the ABCs—the tune to *Twinkle, Twinkle, Little Star*—and many students used that same song for other memory tasks in the higher grades (e.g., multiplication or division math facts).

8. *Increase your wait time.* Different brains process information at different rates, independent of intelligence. Of course, elementary students have learned that teachers often will call on the first one or two students who raise their hand after the teacher has asked a question in class. On average, teachers will wait only two or three seconds before calling on someone for an answer, and this period of time between the question and when an answer is called for is defined as "wait time" (Sousa, 2001). However, the brain research has demonstrated the importance of waiting for a few seconds (perhaps seven to ten seconds) after asking a question, prior to calling on someone for the answer. This increased wait time gives students with reading disabilities, many of whom process information more slowly and deliberately, a longer period of time to consider their answer and hopefully raise their hand to volunteer a response to the teacher's question.

9. *Increase students' choices.* Sylwester (2001) emphasized the use of choices for students. In short, if teachers want their students to make reasonable and informed choices when they are not in the context of the school, teachers must offer choices and coach students in making informed choices within the context of the classroom. Such choices may involve options for demonstrating competence or understanding of a set of facts or other choices among assignments on a particular topic.

(Continued)

TEACHING TIP 6.3 (Continued)

10. *Use students to teach other students.* Teachers should present some information and then pause and let students discuss it and synthesize it (Sousa, 2001). Alternatively, teachers may wish to have students read a short text selection and then discuss it with a peer buddy. One good idea is to have students discuss the information after every five minutes of reading or discussion.

Teachers may say something like the following:

Turn to your learning buddy beside you and take turns explaining the four points I just made and that we just read about. Let me know if you uncover any disagreements in what each of you heard.

The teacher should then move around the room for one to two minutes, listening to the discussions between the students and checking that the students have a correct understanding of the information just presented.

 REFLECTIVE EXERCISE 6.3
MY BRAIN COMPATIBLE TEACHING

Consider the ten tactics for brain compatible instruction described in Teaching Tip 1.3 in terms of your current teaching. The research on brain compatible instruction, while emphasizing many of these tactics, was not the origin for many of these ideas, and you may be currently using many of these tactics in either small group instruction or whole class instruction for students with learning difficulties. Which tactics can you identify as representative of your methods this year? Which would you like to use more often? The emerging research does suggest that the more we use these ideas, the stronger our instruction in reading will be. Which new ideas would you like to try?

A BRAIN-BASED MODEL OF READING

Although no one argues that teachers should become "brain experts," a general insight into the basic brain processes involved in reading does help to understand many types of reading difficulties for students with learning difficulties. As noted previously, reading is a very complex process. We believe that reading instructional strategies for students with learning difficulties should be presented within the context of this broader emphasis on brain compatible instruction. Further, Sousa's model of the reading brain can provide teachers with numerous insights for instruction, as well as a guide for selection of strategies and tactics for students with reading problems who may demonstrate different instructional needs within the class. Sousa (2001) presented this model in his work, *How the Special Needs Brain Learns.* Within Sousa's model of the reading brain, four areas of the brain, working simultaneously, seem to be most heavily involved in reading: the visual cortex, Wernicke's area, the angular gyrus, and Broca's area (Sousa, 2001).

Beginning on the left of the top section of the model of the reading brain in Figure 6.1, the brain perceived the word *dog* via the visual cortex, which is located at the rear of the brain. The actual brain areas are shown on the sketch of the brain in the figure, which presents both the left and right hemisphere of the brain. The visual stimulus *dog* is immediately transferred to several parts of the brain. These include the angular gyrus, which is involved in this process of phoneme interpretation (Joseph et al., 2001). Next both Broca's area and Wernicke's area become involved in interpretation of those phonemic sounds into meaningful sounds, combinations of sounds, and word. Wernicke's area has traditionally been associated with various types of language function, including auditory processing, comprehension of words, and deriving meaning from words (see Joseph et al., 2001; Sousa, 2001).

Next, Broca's area becomes involved in the translation of the sounds into meaningful language. Broca's area has been associated with not only language, but also grammar and syntax, so while Broca's area is involved in the linguistic aspects of reading a one-word stimulus such as *dog*, it is also searching for and identifying meanings for this word, as well as relationships and meanings that relate this word to other previously read words. Thus, Broca's area is believed to be the language area in which meaning is attached to the stimulus word, *dog*.

Notice that, from the outset, several areas of the brain are heavily involved in the process of reading, that is, the process of translating graphemes (letters on the page) into phonemes (sounds). Even when a student is reading silently, this translation into letter sounds takes place in the brain during the initial stages of reading, and mistranslation can take place throughout this system, leading to reading errors. Of course, one must realize that while these four major areas of the brain are involved in noting the word, decoding the word by

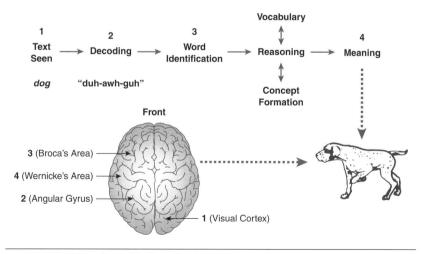

Figure 6.1   Sousa's Model of Reading

SOURCE: Sousa (2001).

sounding it out, and attaching meaning to the word, the eyes and brain continue to scan the page for other words to begin the process all over again. Thus, this word reading process is repeated many times each minute when a student reads, and often the eyes and visual cortex are scanning a word prior to the association of meaning with words read previously. Therefore, the timing of these mental processes becomes involved in reading, and the process becomes even more complex. In fact, with only one or two misread letters or words, the reading process can become very confusing.

 REFLECTIVE EXERCISE 6.4
TEACHING STUDENTS ABOUT THEIR BRAINS

Prigge (2002) suggested that teachers should teach students with learning difficulties about their brains. For example, even young children can be taught the importance of water, appropriate sleep, appropriate diet, and so on, whereas older children can be taught to informally assess their own learning styles and preferences. Knowledge of one's learning styles and preferences can assist students with learning difficulties in understanding how they should study textual material or prepare for exams.

As a guide for instruction about the brain, the ten tactics for brain compatible classrooms could be used initially. Also, many interesting Internet research possibilities could be explored. The website at www.brainconnection.com, for example, provides a series of brain diagrams that can be used as worksheets for identifying various parts of the brain. As an interesting activity, you may wish to develop several lesson plans for instruction on how the brain thinks (or reads) based on this information, Sousa's (2001) model of the reading brain, and the sample worksheets at the website mentioned above.

For students who manifest reading difficulties, reading problems can occur at any point in this highly interactive reading process (Sousa, 2001, 2005). Perhaps because of quick scanning, a child thinks he or she sees the word *bale* instead of the word *tale* in a sentence—the visual cortex has thus introduced an error into this complex process that will, in all probability, lead to a lack of comprehension on the other end. Alternatively, either Wernicke's area or Broca's area could introduce an error with any word read, which will also lead to comprehension problems in the final reading of the text.

With this level of reading complexity in mind, this book will follow the basic processes of the brain noted above, emphasizing specific instructional tactics that may be associated with each major area. First, reading strategies will be presented that assist students in mastering the decoding auditory processing skills that emerge somewhat early in this reading sequence. Specifically, Chapters 2 and 3 present information on phoneme-based instruction and phonics, respectively, two sets of skills that are heavily involved in auditory processing, which takes place in Wernicke's area and the angular gyrus, as noted above. Chapters 4, 5, and 6 present information on vocabulary development, reading fluency, and reading comprehension during reading instruction in the lower grades, and reading comprehension in elementary and middle grades. This comprehension emphasis corresponds to the later involvement of Broca's area in the reading process. Thus, this overall model of the reading brain will serve as an organizer for the remainder of this book of reading strategies in various reading areas.

WHAT THE BRAIN RESEARCH ON READING HAS FOUND

With this model of the reading brain as a basis, several specific results from the emerging brain research on reading can assist teachers in understanding the reading performance of students with reading problems in the lower and middle grades. Also, this brief list of research results emphasizes the contributions of the brain research to reading instruction. These research conclusions by no means represent the extent of understanding from research on the reading brain, but these results are interesting and some may surprise you. Further, these research findings can inform teachers on how we should manage students with reading problems in our classes.

Reading Problems May Be Speech-Timing Problems

Brain research on students with reading problems and learning disabilities has shown that a dysfunction in how the brain processes information concerning letter sounds or speech sounds may lead to reading problems. In fact, when one group of researchers used a computer program to pronounce words more slowly than normal, some children with reading problems were able to advance their reading levels by two years in only four weeks of training (Tallal et al., 1996). Thus, their reading problem was a brain-based, language-timing problem—they needed to hear the words more slowly than usual to process the information, even when they themselves were doing the reading. This would seem to implicate Wernicke's area—the auditory processing area—in the reading problems of some students with reading difficulties. Recently, a number of phonemically based, computer-delivered reading programs have incorporated these findings into a practical reading curriculum by allowing teachers to vary the timing on pronunciation of phonemes and/or syllables while students learn to read. These include programs such as Fast ForWord and Academy of Reading by AutoSkill.

Poor Readers Often *Are* Trying Harder

Have we, as teachers, ever told a student to "try harder" in reading? While encouraging students in their reading efforts is essential, recent brain research suggests that teachers of students with learning difficulties may wish to find another phrase to use. Brain scans have shown more frontal lobe activity in the brains of poor readers than in the brains of good readers. In fact, these data show that poor readers are putting forth additional effort—indeed more effort than good readers—in decoding. For example, many students with reading problems subvocalize (e.g., softly pronounce) what they read to interpret words correctly (Sousa, 2001; Tallal et al., 1996). This work requires extra brain processing and can be shown using fMRI technology among many students with reading difficulties.

This sheds new light on the admonishment from teachers or parents for students with reading problems to "try harder." For poor readers, the automaticity with the alphabetic code that good readers have developed is not yet present; consequently, these poor readers are, in many cases, already trying harder.

A further note is required on this research result. Because of a lack of automaticity with the alphabetic code, the reading problems of many poor readers tend to grow and compound. Thus, students who have not developed automaticity with phonemes, letters, or letter sounds will experience increasing problems in reading throughout the elementary and middle school years.

Letters Can Be Confused Because They Sound Alike

The brain essentially pronounces phonemes associated with specific letters during the early decoding process—transferring phonemes into graphemes—and this process, if not successful, can result in reading problems. While early research in dyslexia concentrated on letter confusion as a visual processing problem (e.g., confusing *b* and *d* because these letters look similar), recent research in dyslexia has implicated the angular gyrus, the location for interpreting letters that sound alike, as the basis for some letter confusion problems. In addition to looking alike, the letters *b* and *d* also sound alike, and if the angular gyrus mistranslates one of these letters in a particular word or text, a reading error will occur. Thus, a problem of the dyslexic reader, which previously was viewed as a visual discrimination problem involving these two mirror image letters, may in fact be an auditory discrimination problem based on the similar sounds they represent. In that context, the term *dyslexia* takes on an entirely new meaning—a language-based reading problem!

Nonlinguistic Deficits May Cause Some Reading Problems

We like to think that most reading problems are caused by language deficits, and language problems do result in reading problems. However, we now know that nonlanguage problems (i.e., nonlinguistic deficits) can also cause reading problems. Wright, Bowen, and Zecker (2000) suggest that auditory problems in the perception of sequential sounds can lead to reading problems. In effect, while reading a passage, the child may be subvocalizing and if certain sounds are held in auditory memory too long, the letters those sounds bring to mind may actually be superimposed over other letters, resulting in considerable reading confusion. This would represent a problem in Wernicke's area involving auditory processing. Further, this type of reading problem will create numerous errors in reading.

Some Reading Interventions Result in Measurable Changes in the Brain

Research has shown that reading begins at the phonemic level (Sousa, 2005), because brains detect and interpret phonemes, independent of viewing letters. Brains detect phonemes all the time when listening to others speaking, and consequently, reading begins, in some fundamental sense, with listening to the language of others, and generating language oneself. Consequently, it should come as no surprise that effective reading interventions impact a brain's actual processing, but only recently have we had various technologies that would allow neuroscientists to measure those changes in brain function (UniSci, 2000). As one example, research has shown only recently actual changes in brain functioning resulting from as few as 15 two-hour reading instruction sessions in a phonologically driven instructional treatment involving systematic instruction in analysis of the structure of spoken and written words (Richards et al., 2000). We are at a point today when measures of actual brain functioning can tell us which reading intervention programs work best, and what this research has shown is that reading programs should be phonemically based. More on these exciting discoveries is presented below in this chapter.

These findings represent only a few of the notable research results from the brain research on reading and are presented only to show the types of insight that can be derived from powerful new research technology. In fact, various authors have identified other reading problems that have been identified using the newly developed fMR1 technologies (Joseph et al., 2001; King & Gurian, 2006; Leonard, 2001; Richards et al., 1999, 2000; Shaywitz et al., 1996; Sousa, 2005; Tallal et al., 1996), and this area of research will continue to lend insight into the reading problems noted among students with reading difficulty.

RESPONSE TO INTERVENTION: THE NATIONAL MODEL

What Is RTI?

Given recent research on the reading brain, coupled with the increasing national emphasis on reading instruction, teachers today must understand the newly emerging response to intervention instructional model. This has become the model for reading interventions across the nation in programs such as Reading First, and RTI is now allowed by the federal government as one option for identification of students with learning disabilities (Bender & Shores, 2007). Although RTI can be used to document a student's learning disability, as described below, the basic emphasis of RTI is remediation of reading problems prior to diagnosis of a disability.

Traditionally, learning disabilities were identified by noting a difference between an IQ score and a reading achievement score for a particular child. Whereas other academic scores were sometimes used, in well over 90% of the cases, learning disabilities were diagnosed on the basis of reading deficits (Bender, 2008). In short, if a child had an IQ score that was considerably higher than his or her reading score, coupled with some indication among the IQ subtest scores of various auditory or visual processing problems, a learning disability was believed to exist. Over the years, many researchers expressed dissatisfaction with this diagnostic procedure, and in 2004, the federal government passed legislation that allowed the use of another procedure, commonly referred to as response to intervention, or RTI. Note that the federal legislation does not mandate RTI, but rather, allows RTI as an indication of a learning disability. Subsequent research (Barkeley, Bender, Peaster & Saunders, in press) has indicated that most states are implementing RTI statewide, or pilot testing RTI as an eligibility tool for documenting a learning disability.

Using an RTI process, schools will be required to document how a child responds to several scientifically based educational interventions. It is hoped that more intensive educational interventions will meet the needs of most children, who will not then be documented as learning disabled. However, should a child not respond to two or more scientifically based reading interventions, that child may be suspected of having a learning disability.

What Does RTI Look Like?

The RTI process is typically described in terms of a pyramid that includes multiple tiers of instructional interventions (Barkeley et al., in press; Bender & Shores, 2007; Fuchs & Fuchs, 2007; Kemp & Eaton, 2007), and most models involve three such intervention tiers, as presented in Figure 1.2. The purpose of the multiple tiers is to document that the child had more than one opportunity to respond to a scientifically based reading curriculum, when instruction was presented in an appropriate fashion, consistent with the instructions in the teacher's manual. To protect the interests of the child, and prevent a diagnosis of learning disability based on only one supplementary instructional intervention, every model used in the various states and described in the instructional literature mandates a minimum of two supplemental instructional interventions prior to a diagnosis of learning disability (Barkeley et al., in press). These multiple intervention tiers are required to ensure that the child had several adequate opportunities to respond to instruction.

In the RTI procedure, a student who is struggling in reading is identified by the general education teacher, who then provides supplementary, more intensive instruction as the tier one intervention. Note that this intervention must be offered as a supplementary intervention in reading—not a replacement for the reading class, and it must be more intensive than the intervention provided for all students in the general education class. As indicated in Figure 6.2, the instruction provided for all students in the general education class is believed to meet the instructional needs of approximately 80% of all students.

Whereas most learning needs for most struggling students can be addressed at the first intervention tier, some students will not progress adequately, even

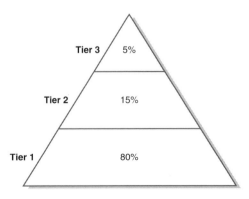

Figure 6.2   RTI Pyramid of Interventions

with the supplemental intervention. These students will require a second, more intensive tier of intervention, which may involve small group instruction for an additional period each day. This tier two intervention, in some school districts, will be a function of the student support team, and while it will be managed by the general education teacher, most districts are providing considerable support for teachers to meet this need for more intensive interventions for a limited number of students in the classroom. While one may expect 20% of students to be exposed to tier two, the tier two intervention adequately will meet the needs of some 15% of the school population (Bender & Shores, 2007).

Finally, for students who do not progress in the first two intervention tiers, another more intensive intervention will be required. In some cases, school districts are viewing this third tier of intervention as an intervention that is provided in the context of special education, and is thus offered only after a child has been identified as learning disabled. Other districts, however, are presenting this third intervention tier as a general education intervention tier that is more intensive than the first two interventions, but still managed by general education teachers, with the support of perhaps a reading specialist or an inclusion teacher who is co-teaching in the same classroom. Approximately 5% of students are expected to need a third intervention tier.

Issues to Consider in RTI

Teachers should be aware of a number of issues when they plan for implementing RTI interventions. First, this is the first time in history in which the interventions managed by the general education teacher will play such a significant role in determining the eligibility of students for learning disability status. Although general education teachers have been sitting on child eligibility teams for decades, only under RTI do general education teachers provide one of the two most critical pieces of data documenting the eligibility—a chart of the child's daily or weekly performance in response to the first targeted intervention.

Next, many different models of RTI currently are being implemented. For example, the three-tier model described above is being used in Texas, whereas both Georgia and North Carolina are implementing a four-tier model. Teachers should check with their own state department of education and school district to obtain a description of the RTI model used in their district.

One issue will be how general education teachers can make the time to undertake these additional interventions. In a typical third grade class, with 24 students, there may be five to six students who are struggling in reading, and those students will need a tier one intervention, which is provided above and beyond their typical reading instruction. Moreover, the general education teacher in that class is expected to provide that intervention, monitor the weekly or daily performance of those students, and be prepared to present those data (which are typically presented in the form of an x-y axis chart with days or weeks at the bottom and achievement on the side) to the student support team in a matter of weeks. Finding or making the time to do that is a critical concern, and fortunately technology can assist. Once teachers identify students who need the tier one or tier two intervention, teachers may be able to find and implement a computer-based reading program, such that the teacher can continue teaching the class, while those five or six students work on computer-assisted instruction on their targeted reading skills.

A final issue to consider involves treatment fidelity, which may also be referred to as treatment validity. This addresses the question, "Did this child receive instruction that was presented as it should have been presented, or in accordance with the instructor's manual for the curriculum used?" Clearly, even the best scientifically validated curriculum is not effective unless it is taught appropriately, and if it is not implemented appropriately, the child will not have an appropriate opportunity to respond to instruction. Thus, educators will have to address the issue of treatment fidelity in the RTI process (Bender & Shores, 2007).

As can be seen from the discussion above, solutions for a number of issues on implementation of RTI have not been determined as yet, and in all likelihood, various districts will develop different approaches to RTI. What is certain is that general education teachers will be playing an increasing role in documentation of the effectiveness of reading instruction for students suspected of having a learning disability, and we must all prepare for that.

One major purpose of this text will be to describe various RTI procedures in reading and relate these to various reading strategies. These case studies will vary according to the content of the chapter. For example, a phonemically based tier of interventions will be presented in the next chapter, while subsequent chapters will present RTI procedures dealing with phonics, reading fluency, or reading comprehension. Also, this text will present a number of instructional procedures that can be the basis for interventions in the RTI process. This should help all general education teachers prepare for the full and complete implementation of RTI.

CONCLUSION

This chapter has presented a series of research-based conclusions on the development of reading skill, as well as several areas within which reading instructional strategies may be discussed: early literacy instruction, brain compatible instruction, and RTI. A series of general research results has been presented in each of those areas, as those results provide a further framework for the strategies discussed throughout this book. Finally, the RTI model presented here will serve as our organizer for the remainder of the book, as we present research-based reading strategies and suggest how those might fit into an RTI procedure. Each subsequent chapter will include at least one RTI case study, and these may be used as models for educators struggling to implement RTI.

WHAT'S NEXT?

In the next chapter, you will find a series of instructional strategies to enhance phoneme awareness and phoneme manipulation skills among students with reading difficulties. These skills are essential for the effective auditory processing of letter sounds, which takes place in the angular gyrus and Wernicke's area of the brain. Further, these skills also serve as a basis for all subsequent reading. The RTI example in that chapter will focus on early literacy skills for kindergarten teachers, involving phonemic recognition activities.

Mathematics Intervention Overview 7

Paul J. Riccomini and Bradley S. Witzel

Mathematics interventions delivered in an RTI framework can have a positive effect on student learning. It is important to choose appropriate interventions and deliver the interventions wisely in order to have the desired effect. If math interventions are developed and the time is used inappropriately, then RTI will be the failure, not the student. It is our belief that if Tier 2 or 3 intervention time is used for homework or extra independent practice only, then RTI is a waste of time. Moreover, if an ineffective curriculum is selected and/or is taught by an ill-informed or unprepared teacher, then RTI is a waste of time. More accurately, instruction and intervention are not possible.

> The NMAP recommends that those responsible for math education have strong math skills.

Mathematics interventions should be taught daily using systematic, explicit, and research-supported instruction and curriculum that includes ongoing assessment and progress monitoring tailored to the specific areas of weakness of each student. By placing students in small groups for Tiers 2 and 3, the instructional delivery options increase. As students are placed into increasing tiers, group size must decrease in order to best meet the individual needs of each student. In small groups, students may be peer grouped and called on individually more often to increase interactions, individualized feedback, and informal assessment. Additionally, decreasing the size of the group allows for easier adaptation of curricular content.

For example, in a class of 25 students, the teacher may spend a great deal of effort and time making certain that everyone is on the same page and accomplishing the same task. When a small group of students are not keeping up or are unable to keep up, it is more difficult to recognize the errors being made and make immediate adjustments for those select few students, all the while keeping the rest of the class at their same pace. In a Tier 2 class of six students, the teacher is more likely to notice the difficulty of a particular student and make immediate adjustments to the instruction so that the student can acquire the skill. In Tier 3, class and group size are even smaller, and thus curriculum, instruction, and assessment are individualized to the specific and immediate need of each student.

Math intervention research has grown in recent years since RTI was first endorsed in government white papers and then with the Individuals with Disabilities Education Act (IDEA) of 2004. As such, some research projects have made claims of being an effective Tier 2 intervention while others have claimed effectiveness for *all* students in Tier 1. Because of the various claims, research reported in this book will use research that supports whole-class curriculum and instruction for struggling students to constitute Tier 1 instruction and research that focuses on small-group curriculum and instruction to constitute intervention research. The focus of this book is to prevent a learning disabilities diagnosis by using highly effective intervention methods. As such, Tier 3 modifications are looked at as more intense renditions of the interventions. Because the focus of RTI is on prevention of disabilities, alternative graduation curriculum, nondiploma track, and work study interventions are not the focus of the interventions explored in this document.

WHO NEEDS INTERVENTION?

We must consider a number of factors when concerning ourselves with who requires intervention in math. Many people focus on struggling groups such as those with a low socioeconomic status (SES), females, those with memory issues, or those who are hyperactive. In reality, it is highly unlikely that any person will never struggle in mathematics. Mathematics, unlike other content areas, is very complex and ever increasing in difficulty and demand. So it is important to look at screening data and make individual recommendations accordingly. Extra attention should be given to the grade level of the struggling student. If a kindergartner or second-grade student is struggling in math early on in their academic career, then the need for intervention is urgent. Weaknesses in early learning concepts can interfere with future math performance. Students who struggle early require immediate and effective interventions to prepare for future success. While the need for early intervention is important, it does not negate the need for intervention of students in upper elementary to secondary levels. In fact, as students progress in grade level, mathematics difficulties become more complex, which requires more complex and intensive interventions.

WHAT DO I TEACH FOR THE INTERVENTION?

Some assessment batteries will help pinpoint specific areas of weakness for students. Knowing exactly in what to intervene is a key to successful intervention. While some assessment batteries provide a detailed picture, other assessment batteries do not. Assessment batteries that provide a percentile or rating only do not provide guidance as to what to intervene in but rather to whom the intervention should occur.

Typical areas of mathematics intervention research, as identified in preassessments, cover the topics of number sense, computation, fractions/decimals/proportions, algebraic equations, and problem solving. Students who exhibit math difficulties early struggle in understanding and task performance with number sense concepts such as counting, quantification or magnitude of number, number-to-numeral identification, base 10 and place value, and fluent arithmetic strategies. Students who continue to struggle in mathematics require intervention in fractions, computation, and problem solving. If problems persist into middle school, interventions with algebraic concepts, such as solving equations; continued work on fractions, decimals, and proportions; along with computation involving negatives are important.

WHO SHOULD INTERVENE?

At any school, the person who is intervening with the students may be a general or special education teacher, a mathematics coach, a mathematic supervisor, or even an instructional assistant (Gersten et al., 2009). No matter who is delivering the intervention, that person requires training in the intervention curriculum, the instructional delivery most effective for the student, and the assessment procedures to best ensure informed instruction for the student. Additionally, the interventionist must possess curricular and content knowledge of the grade level of at least the year before and after the student's current grade and curricular placement so as to make proper goals for the student and work with the material to which the student already has been introduced.

> "Substantial differences in mathematics achievement of students are attributable to differences in teachers. Teachers are crucial to students' opportunities to learn and to their learning of mathematics."
>
> —*NMAP (2008)*

WHERE?

An area free of distractions is required for the intervention. Students with attention or peer pressure concerns require the ability to be allowed to focus on the work and not on others' behavior. For example, a former recess closet accessible only to the outside with one wall conveniently used for ball play by a couple hundred children every afternoon is not appropriate. Special education has come a long way in the past two decades to move special education classes to classes that, at the least, appear like those in the rest of the school. It is conceivable that broom closets would be reopened to provide interventions. Instead of looking for a convenient location, it is better to find the most effective place for students to learn. Although six students and a teacher could fit in a former book room, it is not always conducive to learning. The best place for interventions to take place is an area that is free of distractions, capable of handling and displaying technology appropriate for the selected interventions, and large enough to allow necessary instructional groupings, movement, and interactions. Some example seating arrangements taken from the IRIS Center (n.d.) are displayed in Figure 7.1.

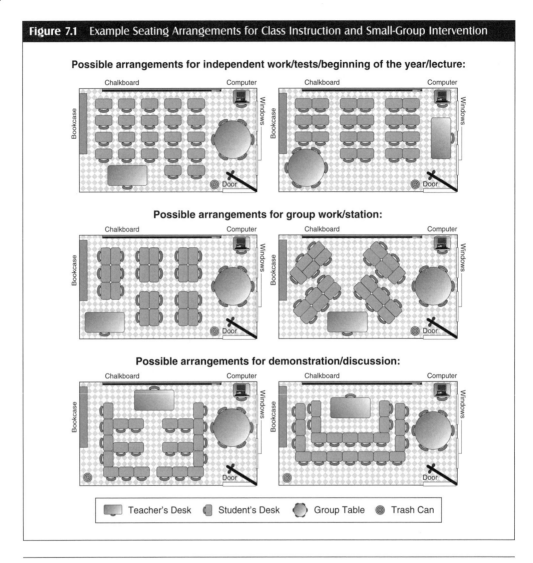

Figure 7.1 Example Seating Arrangements for Class Instruction and Small-Group Intervention

Possible arrangements for independent work/tests/beginning of the year/lecture:

Possible arrangements for group work/station:

Possible arrangements for demonstration/discussion:

Teacher's Desk   Student's Desk   Group Table   Trash Can

Source: Courtesy of the IRIS Center, Peabody College.

HOW LONG?

Interventions should happen 4–5 days per week for a minimum of 20 minutes. Considerable research conducted across many years has consistently demonstrated improved student achievement through the increase of instructional time (Ellis, Worthington, & Larkin, 1994). Although no absolute time recommendations exist, the recommendations that we put forth should be considered starting points and should only increase. Student attention span and instructional delivery will cause fluctuations in the actual time for intervention. Some interventions are preset to last up to 50 minutes for middle school classes. This is fine, but make certain that the delivery varies the activities quickly and maintains frequent interactions to help keep the students focused. The intervention set should occur until the students meet grade-level expectations or the students are assessed to need more intensive instruction.

What kinds of instructional delivery work best with interventions?

> Instructional practice should be informed by high-quality research, when available, and by the best professional judgment and experience of accomplished classroom teachers. High-quality research does not support the contention that instruction should be either entirely "student-centered" or "teacher-directed." Research indicates that some forms of particular instructional practices can have a positive impact under specified conditions. (NMAP, 2008, p. 11)

Students who struggle in mathematics require explicit and systematic instruction (Gersten et al., 2009). Such instruction should be provided in all tiers for struggling students. However, while there are many similarities between tiered instructional deliveries, the extra time allotted in each successive tier provides additional classroom opportunities. Gersten and his colleagues suggest that educators use the time opportunities to provide extra practice and more interactions through the use of clear examples and models, more detailed feedback, and extra and different use of think alouds. The think alouds that are recommended for the teacher to use in Tier 1 can be used more extensively in Tier 2. Not only should teachers use think alouds, but the students should as well. Verbalizations of thought process and understanding have a history of research effectiveness, particularly for students with learning disabilities (Baker, Gersten, & Scanlon, 2002).

Using teacher think alouds can be an awkward means of teaching for someone who is unfamiliar with the process and the research. However, it is highly effective, particularly for students who have not established a means to approach a problem. Thus, it is important for teachers to learn this skill. There are a couple of things to keep in mind when implementing think alouds. The first is that you need to have developed a clear and simple set of sequenced procedures that solves the problem (and hopefully several problems like it). Next, when implementing, it is good to go through at least one whole problem aloud first without student interaction. The students need to see the problem solving in its entirety. Also, depending on the students, you will have to scaffold the steps individually or in groups so that they can be repeated. Finally, provide practice so that the students can name the steps and think aloud accurately and independently.

In Figure 7.2, the teacher is at an intermediate step in showing an integer method for subtraction without regrouping. It is important to verbalize the reasoning rather than simply reading the problem as it would be written on a board. Once a teacher models a problem using a think aloud, he should ask the students to repeat the thought process. This extra step adds instructional time, but the additional interactions are valuable when teaching students who have a history of memorization difficulties.

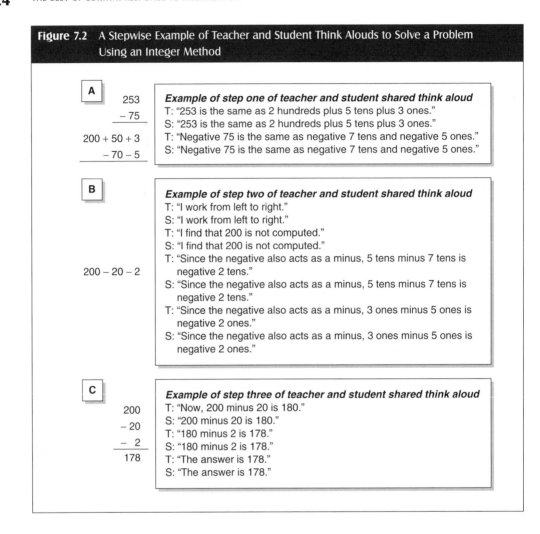

Figure 7.2 A Stepwise Example of Teacher and Student Think Alouds to Solve a Problem Using an Integer Method

A

253
− 75

200 + 50 + 3
− 70 − 5

Example of step one of teacher and student shared think aloud
T: "253 is the same as 2 hundreds plus 5 tens plus 3 ones."
S: "253 is the same as 2 hundreds plus 5 tens plus 3 ones."
T: "Negative 75 is the same as negative 7 tens and negative 5 ones."
S: "Negative 75 is the same as negative 7 tens and negative 5 ones."

B

200 − 20 − 2

Example of step two of teacher and student shared think aloud
T: "I work from left to right."
S: "I work from left to right."
T: "I find that 200 is not computed."
S: "I find that 200 is not computed."
T: "Since the negative also acts as a minus, 5 tens minus 7 tens is negative 2 tens."
S: "Since the negative also acts as a minus, 5 tens minus 7 tens is negative 2 tens."
T: "Since the negative also acts as a minus, 3 ones minus 5 ones is negative 2 ones."
S: "Since the negative also acts as a minus, 3 ones minus 5 ones is negative 2 ones."

C

200
− 20
− 2
178

Example of step three of teacher and student shared think aloud
T: "Now, 200 minus 20 is 180."
S: "200 minus 20 is 180."
T: "180 minus 2 is 178."
S: "180 minus 2 is 178."
T: "The answer is 178."
S: "The answer is 178."

Along the line of increasing frequency of interactions, teachers can use several forms of simple and advanced technology to increase student participation in class. One of the more recent technologies to make it to the classroom is an interactive whiteboard. The SMART Board and other interactive board technologies have options for student input in a couple of formats. Students can answer multiguess questions from a portable keypad, or they can write directly on a portable notepad allowing their original work to be displayed. Contrary to the belief that open discussions can hurt a student's feelings thus causing their work effort to disintegrate, when handled correctly, discussing a student's work can provide the student with clear explanations from other students. In many cases, students are more resistant to teacher feedback than they are to peer feedback. Students need to be taught how to provide constructive and supportive feedback in order to make this work.

Along the lines of increasing peer interactions and appropriate peer feedback, the use of peer-assisted learning strategies (PALS) has had great success in mathematics and reading. Specific to the mathematics, Fuchs, Fuchs, and Karns (2001) found success across achievement levels in kindergartners when PALS was implemented. PALS is enacted by pairing two students of slightly different achievement for 30 minutes three to four times a week. If there are an uneven number of students, then flexible groups of three are a possibility. The intervention is focused on practice of ideas already taught to the students. Each intervention is individually arranged according to the student's needs. Each member of the pair plays the role of coach and student in a reciprocal role play. Additionally, each member of the team is involved in progress monitoring. To learn more about PALS mathematics research, visit the site http://kc.vanderbilt.edu/pals/library/mathres.html.

HOW DO I ORGANIZE MY CURRICULUM?

Information from assessments should provide the teacher/interventionist with a focused outcome on what the student is lacking that may be preventing success in the general education curriculum. With this focused outcome in mind, the teacher can design curricular steps to help the student reach that goal. One such way to break down instruction is through task analysis. Task analysis has long been recognized as a means for taking large and difficult tasks and breaking them down into reasonable, sequential, and learnable chunks (Witzel & Riccomini, 2007). In special education, task analysis has been used for low-incidence special education populations to teach life and work skills. The teacher would start by teaching a small first step of the sequence of things someone must learn. For grade-level mathematics, the approach is similar. With a typical second-grade standard of two-digit addition and subtraction, students must not only know addition and subtraction facts but also know the reasoning behind addition and subtraction and place value in preparation for regrouping and borrowing. To best instruct a standard like two-digit addition and subtraction, teachers need to task analyze the standard to ensure that students are prepared for success and to appropriately teach *all* precursor skills. Some teachers in Tier 1 elect not to task analyze their curriculum to minute steps because of reasons such as concern with instructional time or demands made by preset pacing guides. However, because Tiers 2 and 3 provide more instructional time and many of the intervention curricula available do not incorporate a rigid pacing guide, teachers are more able to task analyze curriculum into "baby steps" to best meet the learning needs of struggling students.

One strategy to help teachers and curricular analysts task analyze a curriculum to more accurately reach a desired outcome and best meet the needs of students is through the use of OPTIMIZE (Riccomini, Witzel, & Riccomini, in press; Witzel & Riccomini, 2007). The eight steps of OPTIMIZE help teachers examine and revise their current curriculum to fill in gaps or reduce unnecessarily spiraled activities. The steps of OPTIMIZE are:

1. O—Organize the math skills of a textbook chapter before teaching.

2. P—Pair your sequence with that of the textbook.

3. T—Take note of the commonalities and differences.

4. I—Inspect earlier chapters and later chapters to see if they cover the differences.

5. M—Match supplemental guides to see if they cover the differences.

6. I—Identify additional instruction to complement the current text/curriculum.

7. Z—Zero in on the optimal sequence with your new knowledge.

8. E—Evaluate and improve the sequence every year.

See the example in Table 7.1 that demonstrates how to enact OPTIMIZE with your curriculum. In this example, a Tier 2 interventionist, Mrs. Hunt, tackles the demand of intervening with a group of students to learn the above-mentioned skill, two-digit addition and subtraction. Reviewing the textbook,

Table 7.1 Example Application of OPTIMIZE to Instructional Sequence for an Algebra Chapter		
Textbook Chapter Sequence	*Alternative Textbook*	*New Instructional Sequence*
1. Comparing real numbers on a number line	1. Ordering real numbers on a number line	1. Pretest for knowledge of integers
2. Adding integers on a number line	2. Adding integers with positive addends	2. Ordering integers
3. Subtracting integers on a number line	3. Adding and subtracting integers with negative and positive addends	3. Adding integers on a number line
4. Adding and subtracting in a matrix	4. Multiplying and dividing integers with one positive product or quotient	4. Adding and subtracting integers on a number line
5. Multiplying integers	5. Multiplying and dividing integers with two negative or positive addends or quotients	5. Rules for positive and negative terms
6. Using the distributive property to simplify expressions		6. Multiplying and dividing integers
7. Dividing real numbers to simplify expressions	6. Application of integers in real-life scenarios	7. Application with distributive property and expressions
8. Solving the probability of an event		*Note:* Include real-life scenarios throughout unit and include maintenance of each successive skill per chapter.

Note: This is just one example sequence and should not be interpreted as the only or correct sequence. The instructional sequence is dependent on state standards, access to curriculum and materials, and, most important, the students' instructional needs. OPTIMIZE was developed by Witzel & Riccomini (2007).

Mrs. Hunt observes several extraneous skills like spatial relations and telling time. Since these are important topics, they can be used as tools to teach this skill rather than as separate lessons. Additionally, this textbook alternated addition and subtraction several times. While examining the alternate textbook, she finds fewer extraneous math skills, but that textbook did not include some ideas, such as fact families. Instead of choosing one textbook or the other, Mrs. Hunt task analyzes a sequence of math skills that leads directly to two-digit addition and subtraction. Her delivery of this task analysis in a Tier 2 setting requires Mrs. Hunt to assess where students are along the task analysis to better know where to start in the sequence.

WHAT TYPES OF CURRICULAR STRATEGIES SHOULD BE USED FOR TIER 2 AND TIER 3 INTERVENTIONS?

There are several instructional approaches that can be used to present curriculum at the Tier 2 or 3 level. Research is in its infancy, but sufficient evidence is emerging to preliminarily endorse certain intervention strategies. Among the research-supported and evidence-supported approaches are explicit instruction for word problems (Wilson & Sindelar, 1991) and computation (Tournaki, 2003), use of visual representations for word problems (Owen & Fuchs, 2002), schema-based problem solving for word problems (Xin, Jitendra, & Deatline-Buchman, 2005), the concrete to representational to abstract (CRA) sequence of instruction for fractions (Butler, Miller, Crehan, Babbitt, & Pierce, 2003), algebra (Witzel, 2005; Witzel, Mercer, & Miller, 2003) and computation (Miller & Mercer, 1993), and meta-cognitive strategy instruction for fraction computation (Hutchinson, 1993). Moreover, in meta-analyses of research findings from studies during the past three decades, Baker, Gersten, and Lee (2002) as well as the National Mathematics Advisory Panel (2008) and RTI Math Practice Guide Panel (Gersten et al., 2009) support these instructional and curriculum interventions.

The repeated conclusion that visual and concrete representations should be incorporated in instruction should not be overlooked. CRA and visual representations are very important strategies for teaching students to learn complex tasks. The NMAP (2008) and RTI Math Practice Guide Panel (Gersten et al., 2009) both supported the use of CRA based on its significant effect size. CRA is a three-stage process of learning whereby students first learn by interacting with concrete objects (see Figure 7.3). Then they use the same steps to solve the problem using pictorial representations. Finally, the students use the same steps again to solve the problem using the abstract or Arabic symbols. It is important to use the same steps for each stage of learning so that students learn the procedures to solving problems.

Some teachers may find it difficult to locate manipulatives that can be used in the manner in which CRA is founded. If so, the National Library of Virtual Manipulatives (NLVM) can be used as a resource to help the teacher peruse the

Figure 7.3 The CRA Sequence of Instruction

Example 8. A set of matched concrete, visual, and abstract representations to teach solving single-variable equations

$$3 + x = 7$$

Solving the Equation With Concrete Manipulatives (Cups and Sticks)	Solving the Equation With Visual Representations of Cups and Sticks	Solving the Equation With Abstract Symbols
		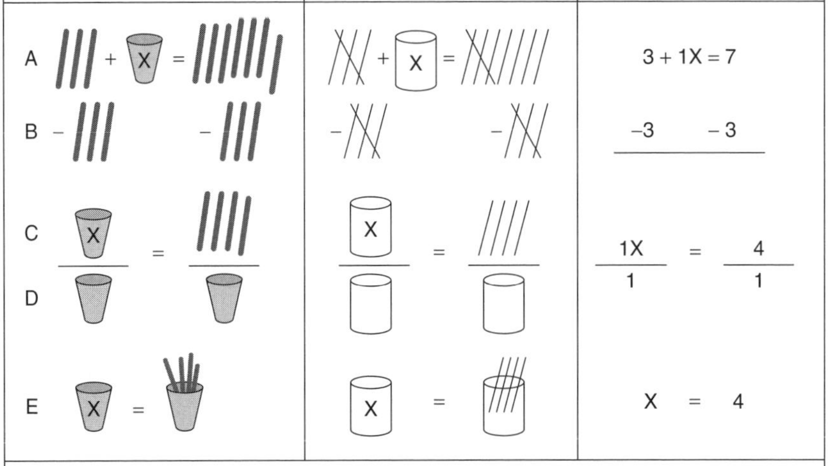 A. $3 + 1X = 7$
		B. $-3 \quad -3$
		C. $\dfrac{1X}{1} = \dfrac{4}{1}$
		D.
		E. $X = 4$

Concrete Steps
A. 3 sticks plus one group of X equals 7 sticks.
B. Subtract 3 sticks from each side of the equation.
C. The equation now reads as one group of X equals 4 sticks.
D. Divide each side of the equation by one group.
E. One group of X is equal to four sticks (i.e., 1X/group = 4 sticks/group; 1X = 4 sticks).

Source: Gersten, R., Beckmann, S., Clarke, B., Foegen, A., Marsh, L., Star, J. R., & Witzel, B. (2009). *Assisting students struggling with mathematics: Response to Intervention (RTI) for elementary and middle schools* (NCEE 2009-4060). Washington, DC: National Center for Education Evaluation and Regional Assistance, Institute of Education Sciences, U.S. Department of Education. Retrieved from http://ies.ed.gov/ncee/wwc/publications/practiceguides.

use of manipulatives (see Figure 7.4). In each math strand and grade-level band, teachers can review several manipulatives designed to help students learn concretely. Once found, the teacher can obtain the manipulatives and use them in a CRA sequence.

The interventions in Chapters 6 through 9 will depict how to enact these curricular strategies with the specific areas of math weakness that are found to be most prevalent with students at risk for learning disabilities in mathematics: number sense, fact computation, fractions and decimals, and problem solving.

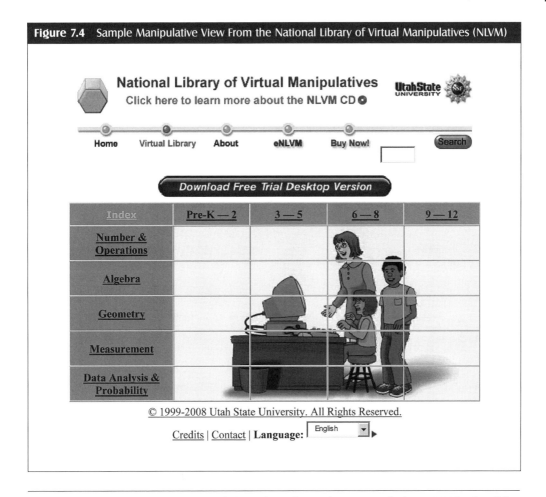

Figure 7.4 Sample Manipulative View From the National Library of Virtual Manipulatives (NLVM)

Source: Reprinted with permission from the National Library of Virtual Manipulatives. Retrieved February 2009 from http://nlvm .usu.edu/en/nav/vlibrary.html.

SUMMARY

Students who exhibit repeated difficulties in math require a different mode of instruction. A knowledgeable interventionist using evidence-supported curricula should explicitly teach deficit skills to mastery in hopes of curbing each student's poor performance. The intervention should cease when assessment data show that the student has begun to succeed in mathematics or when the assessment data show that it is time for more intensive intervention. There are several interventions from which interventionists may choose. It is important to choose interventions for their curriculum support and necessary instructional delivery. The next four chapters will focus on key areas frequently requiring interventions: number sense, computational fluency, fractions and decimals, and problem solving.

List of Mathematics Interventions and Programs

Peer-Assisted Learning Strategies: http://kc.vanderbilt.edu/pals

PALS Reading and PALS Math were developed to help teachers accommodate diverse learners and to promote their academic success. PALS is listed among the best evidence-supported math programs on the Johns Hopkins University website, Best Evidence Encyclopedia (BEE). The What Works Clearinghouse found "The Peer-Assisted Learning Strategies© instructional program to have potentially positive effects on reading achievement" for elementary-age ELL children. For information specifically about Hot Math and other Tier 1 and 2 interventions, contact flora .murray@vanderbilt.edu.

Hot Math: Problem-Solving Program

Hot Math is available in a manual that includes teaching scripts for implementing all five units and provides all necessary materials (e.g., posters, overheads, worked problems, classroom exercises, scoring keys, homework assignments, personal charts, class charts). For information specifically about Hot Math and other Tier 1 and Tier 2 interventions, contact flora.murray@vanderbilt.edu.

Otter Creek Institute: http://www.oci-sems.com

A leading provider in high-quality training and resources, Otter Creek is dedicated to the success of our nation's teachers and students. Specific instructional interventions for Writing Numerals, Mastering Math Facts, and Problem-Solving Strategy Instruction.

Voyageur Learning-VMath: http://www.voyagerlearning.com/vmath/index.jsp

Many students need extra support to succeed in math and pass high-stakes tests. VMath fills critical learning gaps with a balanced, systematic approach, combining print materials, robust assessment, and online technology to create confident, independent learners in math.

Computation of Fractions: Math Intervention for Elementary and Middle Grades Students: http://www.pearsonhighered.com/educator

This intervention is based on the CRA instructional sequence and contains 30 instructional lessons, pretest, and posttest to determine effectiveness. The effectiveness of this instructional sequence is supported by research in which certified teachers provided daily whole-class and/or small-group instruction using concrete manipulative objects, then pictorial representations, and finally abstract representations of fractions.

Computation of Integers: Math Intervention for Elementary and Middle Grades Students: http://www.pearsonhighered.com/educator

This intervention is based on the CRA instructional sequence and contains 30 instructional lessons, pretest, and posttest to determine effectiveness. The effectiveness of this instructional sequence is supported by research in which certified teachers provided daily whole-class and/or small-group instruction using concrete manipulative objects, then pictorial representations, and finally abstract representations of positive and negative integers.

Computation of Simple Equations: Math Intervention for Middle Grade Students: http://www.pearsonhighered.com/educator

This intervention is based on the CRA instructional sequence and contains 30 instructional lessons, pretest, and posttest to determine effectiveness. The effectiveness of this instructional sequence is supported by research in which certified teachers provided daily whole-class and/or small-group instruction using concrete manipulative objects, then pictorial representations, and finally abstract representations of simple algebraic equations.

Core Program: Algebra Readiness: https://www.sraonline.com

SRA Algebra Readiness teaches concepts introduced as early as Grade 2 through Algebra I to ensure that students are brought to mastery of pre-Algebra skills and concepts. SRA Algebra Readiness spirals development needed for success in an Algebra I program.

Core Math Program: Saxon Mathematics Program: www.harcourtachieve.com

Saxon Math, published by Harcourt Achieve, is a scripted curriculum that blends teacher-directed instruction of new material with daily distributed practice of previously learned concepts and procedures. Students hear the correct answers and are explicitly taught procedures and strategies. Other key factors of the program include frequent monitoring of student achievement and extensive daily routines that emphasize practice of number concepts and procedures and use of representations.

Core Math Program: Math Expressions: http://www.hmco.com/indexf.html

Math Expressions, published by Houghton Mifflin Company, blends student-centered and teacher-directed approaches. Students question and discuss mathematics, but are explicitly taught effective procedures. There is an emphasis on using multiple specified objects, drawings, and language to represent concepts, and an emphasis on learning through the use of real-world situations. Students are expected to explain and justify their solutions.

Solving Math Word Problems: Teaching Students With Learning Disabilities Using Schema-Based Instruction: www.proedinc.com

This intervention, developed by Dr. Asha Jitendra, is a teacher-directed program designed to teach critical word problem–solving skills to students with disabilities in the elementary and middle grades. The program is carefully designed to promote conceptual understanding using schema-based instruction (SBI) and provides the necessary scaffolding to support learners who struggle with math word problems.

Solve It! A Practical Approach to Teaching Mathematical Problem-Solving Skills: http://www.exinn.net/solve-it.html

Solve It! is a curriculum designed to improve the mathematical problem-solving skills of students in the upper elementary, middle, and secondary school grades—including students with disabilities who are having difficulties solving mathematical

(Continued)

(Continued)

problems. This program helps teachers help students develop the processes and strategies used by good problem solvers. Explicit instruction in mathematical problem solving is provided in lessons that teach critical cognitive and metacognitive processes. This research-based program is designed for easy inclusion in a standard mathematics curriculum. Solve It! was validated and refined in intervention studies with students with mathematical learning disabilities between 12 and 18 years of age.

Note: This list in not intended to be comprehensive, just a sample selection of programs and interventions to consider for use within your school's RTI math model.

8

Classroom Interventions and Individual Behavior Plans

Bob Algozzine, Ann P. Daunic, and Stephen W. Smith

In this chapter, we

- review relationships between Schoolwide Positive Behavior Support and Response-to-Intervention approaches to prevention,
- define and discuss targeted classroom interventions, and
- define and discuss intensive individual interventions.

Since 1996, there has been an increasing emphasis on the use of Schoolwide Positive Behavior Supports (SPBS) to improve students' social behavior. Chapter 3 of this text provides a thorough overview of the background, essential features, and research findings from the past 10 years of implementing SPBS. A critical feature of this three-tiered model is that school staff must work cohesively in a proactive, strategic manner across the school to enhance social behavior and reduce problem behavior of students.

The purpose of this chapter is to discuss how the techniques of SPBS and the current approach known as Response to Intervention (RTI) can be applied in elementary school classrooms to enhance the social behavior of students. Since schools are now attempting to use RTI as both an academic and behavioral approach, this chapter will discuss the relationship between these RTI and SPBS and show how they can be aligned to meet the needs of students and teachers in classroom situations. Our intention is to provide administrators, educators, and family members with a conceptual model and practical educational techniques. Since Chapter 3 reviewed universal approaches across the first tier of the SPBS model, we focus our discussion on important classroom approaches for teachers to support students with behavior problems.

WHAT EDUCATORS SHOULD KNOW ABOUT THE RTI MODEL

The RTI language in the Individuals with Disabilities Improvement Act of 2004 (IDEIA) requires schools to assess, provide necessary instruction, and evaluate progress of students with learning difficulties prior to identifying the students as having a learning disability. These students would be considered to be receiving Tier II interventions, since their performance at Tier I was found to be lagging behind that of other students in the classroom. When students receive and are responsive to Tier II instructional approaches, according to the RTI model, they are more likely to be receptive to the ongoing academic instruction in their classroom. Tier II interventions are, therefore, able to thwart the development of further, more chronic academic problems that might require special education services.

The behavioral side of the RTI model is analogous to this instructional approach. In short, when a student in a general education classroom is displaying behavior that doesn't meet social expectations and schoolwide behavior program (Tier I), teachers can refer a student for Tier II supports and interventions in an attempt to ameliorate the behavior problem and teach the student more effective behavior for school success. The Tier II intervention should be efficient and accessible and have a standard assessment approach and criteria for entering the intervention. While assessment and intervention approaches vary at present, it is generally agreed that this system should be systematic and accessible within one to two weeks to students in general education (see Hawken, Vincent, & Schumann, 2008).

RTI AS A SCHOOLWIDE AND CLASSROOM MANAGEMENT APPROACH

There is mounting evidence that schools that universally employ an SPBS approach are also high-achieving schools (Horner, 2007). Concurrently, when students demonstrate classroom behavior problems in high-achieving schools, competent teachers are better situated to address the student's behavior problem within their classrooms. These teachers know how to work with school and district colleagues to use behavior plans that link directly to their SPBS system. (We again refer the reader to Chapter 3 for a review of schoolwide procedures that serve as foundational and critical features in improving school environments.) We move beyond Tier I schoolwide approaches to discuss how teachers can improve their classroom management strategies and use Tier II and III approaches with students who have behavior problems.

EFFECTIVE CLASSROOM MANAGEMENT APPROACHES

By *effective classroom management procedures*, we are referring to practices that have been used over the past 30 years that have led to diminished behavior problems in classrooms. The strategies we support are backed by evidence from a number of sources but are nicely summarized and presented in Evertson and Emmer (2009) and Sprick, Garrison, and Howard (1998). Evertson and Emmer have been researching and applying effective classroom management procedures for the past three decades, while Sprick and colleagues integrated these classroom procedures into a classroom system known as CHAMPS. Both approaches have been very useful for improving students' classroom behavior. Table 8.1 shows the essential features that accomplish this outcome.

Table 8.1 Essential Features of Classroom Organization and Management			
Feature	Observed		
	Yes	**No**	**Plan for Improvement**
1. Effective Classroom Arrangement/Layout a. High traffic/low congestion b. Teacher is eye to eye with all students. c. Teaching materials are at hand d. Students see whole class presentations ad displays			
2. Walls and Ceilings Available for the Following: a. Classroom expectations/rules b. Daily schedule/assignments c. Calendar d. Student of the week, other honors e. Emergency procedures			
3. Social Expectations Posted a. Rules/behaviors for the expectations are posted. b. Expectations/rules are frequently discussed.			
4. Transitions Taught and Monitored a. Leaving/entering room b. Beginning/ending day			
5. Classroom Procedures Taught and Monitored a. Small- and large-group instruction b. Independent work c. Materials d. Drinks e. Restroom			
6. Schoolwide Expectations Posted and Taught a. Hallways b. Cafeteria c. PE/specialists d. Playground e. Library			

(Continued)

Table 8.1 (Continued)			
	Observed		
Feature	Yes	No	Plan for Improvement
7. Daily Routines Taught/Practiced a. Attention signal b. Homework in/out c. Classroom assignments d. Assignment standards e. Attendance/tardy procedures			
8. Whole-Group Instruction Emphasizes the Following: a. Prevention of misbehavior b. Managing pace of and on-task behavior through momentum and smoothness c. Maintaining focus through alerting, accountability, and participation			
9. Appropriate Student Behavior Maintained by the Following: a. Monitoring and supervising all student behavior b. Being consistent across behavior c. Identifying and acknowledging students using positive social skills d. Using proximity and eye contact when students are off-task or misbehaving e. Providing reminders and redirection to those off-task f. Verbal statements to stop misbehavior g. Using individual and group reinforcement programs			
10. Clear Communication Skills a. Behaviorally specific b. Calm and direct c. Assertive body posture d. Empathy and concern e. Questioning and problem solving			

In collaborative schools that value peer and administrative guidance and feedback, Table 8.1 can be used as a tool to observe and make a plan of action for a classroom teacher. Some teachers use many of these recommended practices in their classrooms, but when most teachers are observed, they will be found to have some areas in need of improvement. The following example describes how one teacher benefitted from a peer observation.

Example: Classroom Management Observation and Plan

Ms. Tomaz is a third-grade classroom teacher with seven years of teaching experience at Sunset Elementary. She has received positive yearly evaluations from her principal, which typically have included a few comments about improving her classroom management approaches. Until this year, however, Ms. Tomaz has never had specific goals or activities for improving her management skills.

She and another teacher agreed to use some collegial support and supervision around management procedures. With the principal's agreement, they planned observations of each other's classroom for two hours. The principal substituted for the teachers so that they could visit and observe in each other's classroom. The teachers used Table 8.1 during their observations so that they could specify a few items for improvement and develop a plan of action to help each other.

The observing teacher concluded that Ms. Tomaz had discussed and taught social expectations and had a daily schedule, but communicated these only verbally in class. There were no posters or other visual reminders in the room about their Schoolwide Positive Behavior Support program. The observer recommended that the program poster with its social expectations be posted and that a daily schedule be written on the classroom whiteboard. This would give the students and the adults in the room a place to look at and review these items throughout the day when necessary. It would also give Ms. Tomaz referents for students who were misbehaving. She could ask the students to refer to the expectations or schedule to identify what they should be doing at the specific time. The students could respond, make commitments to show expected behavior within the scheduled activity, and then get back to the activity.

This type of reminding about social expectations through posted visual material is helpful in improving classroom management. While this is a brief and straightforward example, one can see that many possible recommendations can come from classroom management observation. Teachers and administrators should use the information to develop goals that are achievable within the classroom, without overwhelming a teacher with too many goals at any one time.

TIER II BEHAVIOR PLANS FOR STUDENTS

Even when teachers have developed a strong, systematic approach to classroom management, some students will need additional behavior supports and interventions. Following an SPBS model, these students are considered to be a targeted group who are at risk of school failure due to their behavior. These students show consistent and somewhat enduring behavior problems. Sometimes this is evident through teacher discussion and nomination. That is, teachers often know in a comparative manner when a student is not meeting classroom and school expectations. They will then refer the student to a school student support team meeting to review progress and brainstorm ideas in the classroom.

Systematic Identification of Tier II Students

Systematic approaches for identifying students for Tier II interventions have been developed over the past 20 years. The two most common approaches are *systematic screening* and *frequency of office discipline referrals*. Walker and Severson (1992) developed the

Systematic Screening for Behavior Disorders (SSBD) to identify students at risk for severe behavior problems. The SSBD requires teachers to nominate students and rate their behaviors to determine if they are at risk for behavioral failure. This screening tool has three assessment steps, or gates, that narrow the pool of students who may need Tier II or III interventions.

1. Teachers rank all of their students for externalizing (e.g., aggression, defiance) or internalizing (e.g., shy, anxious, withdrawn) behavioral characteristics, as defined and explained in the SSBD.

2. Teachers complete rating scales on critical events and maladaptive and adaptive behaviors on the three highest-ranked internalizing and externalizing students.

3. Students who meet criteria based on a normative sample are considered at risk for school failure and, with parent consent, enter the Tier II interventions.

We have used this approach in several intervention studies to identify students. Further elaboration of the SSBD can be found in Walker and Severson (2007); Walker, Cheney, Blum, and Stage (2005); and Cheney, Flower, and Templeton (2008). The SSBD is used early in the school year, in the first 30–45 days, and is an efficient and valid method, taking only about 90 minutes of a teacher's time, for forming a pool of students in need of Tier II intervention.

Irvin and his colleagues (Irvin, Tobin, Sprague, Sugai, & Vincent, 2004; Irvin et al., 2006) have reviewed the use of office discipline referrals (ODR) as a practical and valid approach for identifying students in need of Tier II interventions. This approach can be useful after a school has met all requisites of implementing universal Tier I interventions. Using ODRs requires that teachers and administrators review and align the types of behavior problems that can lead to an office referral and those that can be managed in classrooms. Once this alignment has been made and, for example, only significant behavior problems (e.g., aggression, defiance, peer provocation, repeated noncompliance within a one-day period) are referred to the office, a behavior support team can set criteria for admitting a student into a Tier II intervention. The criterion is typically set at three to five ODR. Use of this procedure has been described and evaluated in several recent studies (e.g., Fairbanks, Sugai, Guardino, & Lathrop, 2007; Filter et al., 2007; Hawken, MacLeod, & Rawlings, 2007).

BEHAVIOR PLANNING FOR TIER II STUDENTS

Once a teacher needs assistance with a student, SPBS requires an approach that is efficient, effective, and accessible. The Tier II strategy and its techniques should also be directly linked to the schoolwide system of social instruction. This integration has led to the development and evaluation of strategies that incorporate several evidence-based practices in the classroom. These include increased supervision and monitoring through the use of daily behavior report cards, regular positive instructional feedback regarding social behavior, increased reinforcement for positive social behavior, improved relationships with adults at school, regular parental involvement, and systematic progress monitoring. This type of behavior planning is based on 15 years of research on established programs (e.g., Check & Connect, Behavior Education Program), which has been described in several articles.

Check & Connect (Sinclair, Christenson, Evelo, & Hurley, 1998) has been identified as an evidence-based intervention by the U.S. Department of Education's What Works Clearinghouse (http://ies.ed.gov/ncee/wwc/). This intervention has been demonstrated to maintain school engagement and reduce problem behavior in general education settings for middle and high school students with learning disabilities and emotional disturbances (ED). C&C relies on an adult mentor to supervise, monitor, provide feedback to, and problem-solve with students regarding their behavior in school.

The *check* component of the program consists of an adult mentor employing daily monitoring procedures for school risk factors: tardiness, absenteeism, behavior referrals, detention, suspension, course grades, and credits. The *connect* refers to the mentors forming positive relationships with students so that they can implement two levels of intervention for monitoring student progress in terms of risk factors. Progress monitoring is shared with students daily and weekly through a report card system. Additional supports are provided to students in the intensive program, including social skills groups, individualized behavior contracts, academic tutoring, problem-solving sessions with parents, and help developing alternatives to out-of-school suspensions with school personnel.

Randomized studies of both elementary- and secondary-level students have found positive improvement for students in C&C in the areas of attendance, school completion, school engagement in academic and social activities, and overall improved social functioning (Lehr, Sinclair, & Christenson, 2004; Sinclair, Christenson, & Thurlow, 2005).

The Behavior Education Program is similar to C&C in that it uses relational, supervisory, and feedback systems, although it was explicitly developed as a Tier II intervention to support students who are at risk of developing more serious behavior problems in meeting schoolwide social expectations while reducing their problematic behavior (Crone, Horner, & Hawken, 2004; Hawken & Horner, 2003). As a Tier II behavioral intervention, BEP has shown promise with elementary and middle school students, reducing ODR and improving teachers' perceptions of student social and academic performance. Hawken (2006), for example, reported that in a small sample of 10 middle school students, 70 percent had a reduction in office discipline referrals after at least eight weeks of BEP intervention. This finding was replicated when Hawken and colleagues (2007) used the BEP to decrease office referrals with a sample of elementary-aged students.

Supervision and Monitoring of Tier II Students

Behavior planning for Tier II students relies on the availability of two adults, a coach/mentor and the classroom teacher, to provide increased supervision and monitoring of students. Students follow prescribed steps like those outlined in the BEP and C&C models. They first get a daily behavior progress report (DPR) card developed by the school's behavior support team. The DPR lists the schoolwide expectations (e.g., respect, responsibility, safety) for at least three grading periods to rate student progress against clearly stated expectations. This card provides a rubric for the teacher to rate the student's behavior during the school day. It is designed to prompt the teachers to provide students with positively stated feedback about their behavior and specific behavior they need to improve to be successful in the classroom. Figure 8.1 provides an example of a DPR.

Figure 8.1   Daily Progress Report for Buzzy Bee Club

Buzzy Bee Club

Checked in	Yes	No
Checked out	Yes	No
Parent Signature	Yes	No

Bee Respectful   Bee Responsible
Bee Safe   Bee a Hard Worker

Student:_____   **Date:**_____   **Goal:**_____

	Reading				Math				Afternoon				
Expectations	Tough Time	OK	Good	Way to Go!	Tough Time	OK	Good	Way to Go!	Tough Time	OK	Good	Way to Go!	Totals
Bee Respectful	1	2	3	4	1	2	3	4	1	2	3	4	
Bee Responsible	1	2	3	4	1	2	3	4	1	2	3	4	
Bee Safe	1	2	3	4	1	2	3	4	1	2	3	4	
Bee a Hard Worker	1	2	3	4	1	2	3	4	1	2	3	4	

DAILY TOTAL _____

Way to Go! (4): Met expectations with positive behavior; worked independently without any reminders or corrections.

Good (3): Met expectations with only 1 reminder or correction.

OK (2): Needed 2–3 reminders or corrections.
Tough Time (1): Needed 4 or more reminders or corrections.

Parent Signature:_____ **Comments:**	**TOTAL:** _____ **Comments:**

In our development and evaluation of the Social Response to Intervention System (SRIS; Cheney & Lynass, 2009), students checked in with their coach daily for an eight-week period, the minimum time allowed for students to benefit from SRIS's instruction, supervision, and reinforcement on social expectations. Check-in, which lasted two to three minutes, occurred before school and accomplished the following:

- Assured that students were ready and had their school materials.
- Reviewed their daily goals.

- Gave students verbal encouragement to meet their goals.
- Checked for parent signatures on the previous day's DPR.

At check-in, students received their daily progress report (DPR) card. The DPR listed the schoolwide expectations (e.g., Bee Respectful, Bee Responsible) for at least three grading periods so that student progress could be rated against the expectations. This card established clear student expectations and provided a rubric for the teacher to rate the student's behavior during the school day. The card was designed to prompt the teachers to provide students with positively stated feedback about their behavior and specific behaviors to improve so they would be successful in the classroom.

Regular Feedback During Instructional Periods

Throughout the school day, teachers are expected to give students regularly scheduled feedback on their social behavior. Teachers rate the student's behavior at set intervals (e.g., morning reading, recess, morning math, lunch, afternoon science/social studies, etc.) on the DPR. Students are rated based on their ability to meet schoolwide expectations without teacher reminders. The teacher meets briefly (two minutes) with students at the end of each period and discusses student behavior, provides positive feedback about what the student did well, and gives corrective feedback if needed. Teacher feedback and a DPR score are given throughout the day at the set times. In our work, we ask teachers to score students based on the number of teacher reminders given to a student on the social expectations. For example, a score of 4 indicates that the student met the expectation without any reminders from the teacher. A 3 represents one teacher reminder, a 2 indicates two to three teacher reminders, and a 1 indicates four or more teacher reminders. (Figure 8.1 presents an example of a DPR developed in the evaluation study of SRIS.)

To learn how to give these reminders and scores, teachers participate in a four-hour training on use of the DPR and giving positive feedback to students. Teachers are first given information on the use of the DPR by watching a DVD produced by the BEP (Hawken, Peterson, Mootz, & Anderson, 2006) and then practice giving feedback in role-plays. After the training session, teachers are observed in classrooms and provided feedback on the use of this system. Our research indicates that most teachers can implement the program with fidelity and report that the system works effectively with students in their classrooms (Cheney, Lynass, Flower, Waugh, & Iwaszuk, in press).

Increased Reinforcement for Positive Social Behavior

Three decades of research has consistently concluded that increasing the rate of positive interactions and tangibles with students results in greater improvements in students' social and academic performance. For Tier II classroom interventions, therefore, it is recommended that teachers increase their rates of acknowledgment and reinforcement to improve students' social behavior in school. This suggests that the teacher and coach need to identify systematic ways to increase the types of verbal and tangible reinforcement. Within the Tier II intervention, the DPR serves as a means to make sure this reinforcement occurs.

The DPR requires teachers to give students points after identified time periods. The points are used to set daily goals for the student. Daily goals are typically set between 75 and 85 percent of the total points. In Figure 8.1, for example, there are 48 total points on the DPR, so a student would have to earn 36 points if the daily criteria/goal was 75 percent. The number of points expected is written on the point card for students to see. After each period, students can calculate the points they have earned. When a student meets his or her daily goal, the student receives a daily reinforcer, which is either verbal praise, a sticker, or a visible acknowledgment on a string of beads or a bar graph. As students meet their goals over a week or month, the coach and student celebrate these larger stretches of success in more socially valid and valuable ways. For example, a one-week celebration may be additional free time with peers, while a one-month reinforcer might be a special lunch with the teacher or coach.

Progress Monitoring

The hallmark of determining a student's progress in Tier II interventions is the collection and close monitoring of performance data. In reading programs, we often use fluency data of words read per minute. Results are then charted, and teachers can review the progress of students by how students increase their words per minute in relation to a target or goal. The same is true for social behavior in a Tier II intervention. When students have a DPR, the data from it can be charted, performance criteria set, and goals for program success set at a four- to eight-week intervals.

This process starts when the coach enters students' DPR data into a database, such as an Excel file or an online database system that can chart student progress. The number of points earned daily on the DPR is converted to a percentage of total points and then charted. Weekly goals can be set that are equal to or slightly higher than the points earned in a student's baseline period. Figure 8.2 shows a chart for one student in the Social Response to Intervention System (Cheney & Lynass, 2009). The example shows that the student initially had difficulty earning daily points and after the first seven days had earned 64 percent of points. Days when the student did not meet criteria were below the vertical goal line, which was set at 75 percent. The team determined the daily criteria should be lowered for the student, and it was set at 70 percent. After that, the student started having success with the daily point card and gradually improved his performance to averaging over 80 percent of points earned by the 10th week of the program. While the chart does not show all of the student's data, this student's criteria were shifted from 75 to 80 and finally to 85 percent of daily points. The student was successful with the program and finally graduated after 15 weeks of the intervention.

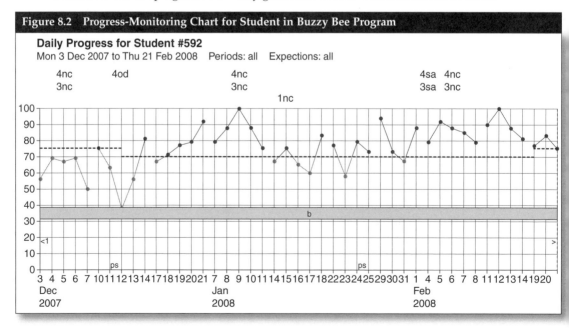

Figure 8.2 Progress-Monitoring Chart for Student in Buzzy Bee Program

This use of charted data for progress monitoring demonstrates how Tier II interventions can be based on wise use of daily performance data. Data are used for the decision-making process, and students, teachers, and parents are kept informed about how the student progressing in the program and toward ultimate goals. The data can be collected efficiently, and once a mentor checks the student out daily, student data can be entered in 15-minutes using a Web-based application.

Improved Relationships With Adults at School

Researchers have concluded that the *quality* of students' relationships with staff and faculty is connected to their school outcomes (Finn, 1989; McPartland, 1994). Sinclair and her colleagues (1998) emphasized this in their discussion of why building connections with students is important in school (see Chapter 5). The type of interpersonal relationships that teachers and students develop and the types of school activities a student becomes involved in are major factors in a child's positive social development (Connell & Welborn, 1991; McPartland, 1994). Additionally, when children do not develop positive relationships with their parents or guardians, they are likely to develop behavior problems at home and in school. Finally, behavior problems are related to poor academic performance and school failure (Anderson, Christenson, & Sinclair, 2004; Sinclair et al., 1998).

Developing relationships with children in a Tier II intervention may be perplexing sometimes, rewarding at other times, and very challenging with a few students. This is due to the backgrounds and experiences of children, some of which may make the child hesitant in or resistant to forming relationships with adults. Trust with these children has to be developed over time and comes from repeated interactions that are consistent and positive.

Interviews with at-risk children indicate that they value coaches or mentors who are trustworthy, attentive, empathetic, available, positive, respectful, and virtuous. Behaviors that illustrate these characteristics include doing what you say you will, putting the child at the center of concern, looking at how the child feels, willingly making time for the child, genuinely saying positive things about the child, involving children in decisions that affect them, and being a role model. When you couple the notion of being strength based with the values and actions above, you will be developing what psychologists refer to as "unconditional positive regard."

This is not always an easy stance to take with a child who is displaying a behavior problem. When a student has shoved another student, knocked over a desk in classroom, or argued with the teacher, a typical adult reaction might be to blame the child for misbehavior and then punish him or her for the behavior. We are encouraging coaches to take another approach, considered "authoritative," which is neither overly "authoritarian" nor overly "permissive." When students misbehave, we expect the coach to be available and attentive to the children's needs. We expect that the coach would spend time listening to the children explain their perceptions of any problems they encountered and attempt to have the children discuss how they behaved and what they "got" from the misbehavior. This is often called identifying the "function" or "purpose" of a child's behavior. The following suggestions are provided for coaches to improve their relationships with students:

- Use appropriate volume, tone of voice, and language.
- Do not take the student's frustration personally.
- Tell the student, "I am listening to you so we can solve the problem together."
- Let the student explain his or her feelings, without interrupting, while maintaining safety.

- Calmly explain why some things cannot happen or are not allowed in school.
- Offer alternatives to students when necessary.
- Use empathetic words like "I can see that you're frustrated."

Regular Parental Involvement

Whenever students are exhibiting classroom behavior problems that merit behavioral interventions, it is important to involve parents, family members, or guardians in the intervention work. In Tier II BEP and SRIS, it is recommended that a daily home note goes to parents/guardians so that they can review student progress and participate in reinforcing and encouraging school success. Communication among the coach, teachers, and parents is not always easy to accomplish, but it should be maintained as an important goal in behavior plans and planning process.

Many parents of students with behavior problems have received countless telephone calls relating problems that occurred at school. Communication with parents attempts to build greater trust, collaboration, and cooperation. Therefore, it makes sense that phone calls and home notes should emphasize the positive aspects of students' social progress. Even if the child has had difficult day, the teacher or coach involved with the parent should stay positive and suggest ways to help the student learn and use positive social skills. When there are significant behavioral issues at school, we suggest that the teacher or coach make a personal call to the parent and review the issues and make any further program adjustments with the parents involvement. Overall, it is good practice to coordinate communication efforts to families with other staff members, such as office staff, the teacher, and/or the counselor, to ensure that families are not overwhelmed or confused by multiple contacts.

SUMMARY OF TIER II BEHAVIOR PLANNING

This section has presented the steps and examples for implementing a Tier II Behavior Plan. To summarize, Tier II interventions are embedded in and consistent with a SPBS system. In this case, we described the Buzzy Bee program from the SPBS and then showed how it can be applied systematically with one to three students in a classroom. The students are identified through teacher nomination, systematic screening, or from review of ODR data. Once a student is identified, he or she is assigned to a coach, who explains the DPR, the system of checking in and out, and how points can be exchanged for reinforcement. The coach supervises and monitors student progress by charting data daily or weekly and by having frequent discussions with the teacher. The coach and teacher work hard to improve the student's social relationships with them as adults and with other peers in the classroom. Finally, the coach, teacher, and parents/guardians work collaboratively to have a unified system for improving student social skills. This approach has been shown to be highly effective with about 75 percent of students who use the intervention within a school practicing SPBS (see Cheney et al., in press; Hawken et al., 2008; Todd, Campbell, Meyer, & Horner, 2008).

INDIVIDUALIZED BEHAVIOR INTERVENTION PLAN (BIP)

The Tier II intervention approach described above, with a coach, daily report card, daily goals, reinforcement, and progress monitoring, was developed for students with emerging behavior problems that put them at risk of school failure. SRIS and BEP approaches are for groups of students and, thus, are typically not individualized to any great extent so they can be quickly and efficiently implemented with any student. When a student is not responsive to a Tier II intervention, however, teachers should work with their school behavior support teams to modify and develop an individualized behavior plan for the student.

Individualized behavior plans have been emphasized in both the Individuals with Disabilities Education Act (IDEA) of 1997 and IDEIA of 2004 within the language of Positive Behavioral Supports (PBS) "in the case of a child whose behavior impedes the child's learning or that of others" (20 U.S.C. § 1414[d][3][B][I]). Behavior intervention plans (BIP) should be strength based (Horner, Sugai, Todd, & Lewis-Palmer, 2000) and based on results from a functional assessment (FA). The goal of the BIP is to develop interventions that will significantly decrease problem behaviors while concurrently teaching and sustaining positive social skills. Development of the BIP requires the involvement of behavior support team members, who will assist the teacher so that the student be more successful over the course of his or her academic career (Bambara & Kern, 2005).

Roles and Input for Behavior Plans

Classroom teachers should rely on the expertise of other professionals and family members of the student. A typical behavior support team consists of parents/guardians, the student when appropriate, general education teacher(s), special education teacher, an administrator, school psychologist, and school counselor (Horner, Sugai, Todd, & Lewis-Palmer, 2000). Other members from the community and school may be involved when they can provide additional insight into the student's behaviors and ideas for effective strategies. Each team member is important, offering valuable information for the development and implementation of an effective behavior intervention plan.

Formal and Informal Assessment by Team Members

At the initial team meeting, each member should be assigned the task of collecting some baseline information on the student's functioning. This information will be used to help develop an effective BIP. Information collected falls into two categories: formal assessments and informal assessments. Formal assessments are any materials that document the student's behaviors, abilities, or personal history. Examples are a list of medications, legal proceedings with family and/or child, expulsions/suspensions, disciplinary actions, absences, staff/parent/student interviews, office discipline referrals, and any direct observations of the student. Just as important is informal information, which is any undocumented life changes, naturalistic observations of the child, interactions with community members, student self-reports, and discussions between teachers and school staff (Sugai, Lewis-Palmer, & Hagan-Burke, 2000). To be effective and efficient for the classroom and, possibly, home settings, assessments should occur within a two-week period and reported back to the team so that initial intervention work can begin.

The assessments enable the team to answer multiple questions in relation to each problem behavior. Team members should be able to describe the behaviors of concern; identify when, where, and to what extent each behavior occurs or does not occur in multiple environments; classify different consequences that maintain or deter the behaviors; and write a summary statement for each behavior. Such assessments will allow the team to develop clear descriptions for each problem behavior.

Example: Addressing Student Behavior Problems

Returning to the work done by Ms. Tomaz at Sunset, recall that she had followed the schoolwide Buzzy Bee program, had made some environmental improvements after a peer observation, and had used the Tier II Bee program with three of her students. After reviewing the progress-monitoring notes for the students, she concluded that two of her three students were successful and meeting classroom social expectations on a daily basis. However, one student, Laurence, was not successful, and after eight weeks of using the DPR and charting daily performance data, he was still only meeting his daily goals about 50 percent of the time. Laurence was, therefore, a candidate for a Tier III behavior plan. The teacher met with the behavior support team, and all agreed to start the Tier III planning and intervention process for Laurence.

The first step was to agree on clear descriptions of each problem behavior that would be addressed in the Behavior Intervention Plan. Clear, objective definitions enabled team members to understand what the behavior clearly looked like. The team used clear behavioral definitions for discussing when, where, and to what extent they had or had not seen the specific behaviors. It is important to acknowledge when and where behaviors occur because this information dictates the types of interventions that will ultimately developed by the team. Next, the team discussed current consequences that maintain the identified behaviors. With this information, the team helped the teacher write a summary statement (also known as a hypothesis statement), which concisely identified the antecedent events that triggered the behavior, described the problem behavior, and identified the consequence (Bambara & Kern, 2005; O'Neill et al., 1997). Summary statements provide a clear picture of the behavior to facilitate the team's development of interventions focused on decreasing problem behaviors while providing school-appropriate replacement/alternative behaviors.

Developing and Evaluating Interventions

Once all summary statements are completed, the team can begin developing interventions for each problem behavior. It is important that all members of the team are encouraged to contribute ideas or recommendations. Allowing parents, community members, and school staff to participate will support the incorporation of culturally appropriate strategies (Kea, Cartledge, & Bowman, 2002). Using culturally appropriate strategies will support the plan, along with maintaining the student's and family's beliefs and values.

Prior to the meeting, support parents in becoming involved by brainstorming techniques they have used in the past to reduce their child's problem behaviors. These solutions will be discussed during the brainstorming part of the meeting. During brainstorming, which should be around 15 minutes, write down everyone's ideas on a board, computer screen, or someplace else where the entire group can see everyone's ideas. Once brainstorming is complete, the group starts analyzing each idea for appropriateness and effectiveness. Both appropriateness and effectiveness can be analyzed by making sure strategies are supported in peer-reviewed literature (i.e., journal articles or books). The ideas must also be culturally significant and beneficial to the individual student, family, and community (Kea et al., 2002). Multicultural research offers many interventions, which are peer reviewed, to support a child. Thus, school team members should review culturally appropriate, peer-reviewed literature prior to the meeting.

Using Evidence-Based Practices

The Individuals with Disabilities Education Improvement Act of 2004 (IDEIA) requires interventions "based on peer-reviewed research to the extent practicable" (20 U.S.C. § 1414[d][1][A][i][IV]). *Peer-reviewed research*, as defined in IDEIA, is research that has been published in a scholarly journal article that is reviewed and edited by experts in the field (peers). The interventions or strategy suggested by an article will not be published if peers do not find the research valid and reliable. Many Positive Behavior Supports for students needing a behavioral intervention plan are published in peer-reviewed literature.

Some ideas for the BIP may come from the student or family or community members with little or no basis in peer-reviewed research. These interventions should not be dismissed, as it is important to incorporate culturally appropriate interventions that work in terms of the student's diverse and individual needs. The team can compromise by making small modifications of the peer-reviewed intervention to incorporate the student's culture.

While collaborating on culturally appropriate and peer-reviewed interventions, the group should also remember there is more than one solution to a problem behavior. Multiple solutions may be needed due to different environments, times of day, and other student factors. If multiple interventions exist for a problem behavior, there is nothing wrong with picking one to start off with, then changing to a different intervention if data show the first intervention is unsuccessful (Walker, Ramsey, & Gresham, 2004).

To help keep everyone focused providing appropriate interventions for the student's problem behaviors, the case manager or special education teacher should create a summary of the plan. This plan should define specific behaviors, strategies to use for each problem behavior, replacement/alternative skills the student will learn, person/people responsible for implementing/using particular intervention, and a re-evaluation schedule.

Table 8.2 is the BIP that was developed by Ms. Tomaz and her team for Laurence. The team worked with Ms. Tomaz to narrow areas of concern down to two primary behaviors. The first was a class or group of behaviors that was defined as "refusing to do work"; these included arguing, talking back, being out of his seat, and disrupting peers with talking during math time. The second was fighting on the playground during recess. The team proposed two beginning interventions for Laurence: one in class, which included self-monitoring and reinforcement of cooperative classroom skills, and the other on the playground, which included instruction and reinforcement of game skills. The team planned to meet and evaluate Laurence's progress during a scheduled weekly evaluation time.

Table 8.2 Behavior Intervention Plan	
BEHAVIOR INTERVENTION PLAN	Date Created: 07/06/2009
Student's Name: Laurence Shiro	Grade: 3
Section A	
Description of Problem Behaviors	1. Refuses to work (argues with teacher, talks back, is out of seat, and disrupts peers by talking) on individual math assignments, such as worksheets. 2. Fights (yells, physically pushes, or places his body in close proximity to others' faces) with peers on the playground during recess.

(Continued)

Table 8.2 (Continued)

Section A	
Antecedents	1. Laurence struggles with math. It is his hardest subject. He also struggles with staying focused during individual time.
	2. Laurence does not understand how to share, ask to enter into a game, or play by someone else's rules.
Consequences of Behaviors	1. When Laurence does not complete his individual math assignments, he is removed from the classroom and put in the hallway. He gains the teacher's attention, and she works through assignment with him.
	2. Laurence loses recess privilege and stands on "wall." Students give Laurence the item and walk away. Students fight back with Laurence.
Behavioral Objectives	1. Laurence will work on grade-level individual math assignments during designated time and finish assignments.
	2. Laurence will interact positively with his peers by sharing school equipment, asking to play with others, and participating in a game with someone else's rules during recess.

Data to Be Collected: Discipline referrals from recess fights, amount of individual math work completed, frequency of disruptions during individual math time

Section B		
Antecedent/Environment: (Individual Math Time)	Replacement/ Alternative Skill:	Contact:
1. Self-Management: Monitor his behavior (Smith & Sugai, 2000).	1. Laurence will self-monitor behaviors during math class and check in with teacher at the end of math period. He will receive positive reinforcements for using cooperative class skills when he meets his predetermined criteria.	1. Ms. Block, School Counselor 2. Ms. Tomaz, General Education Teacher 3. Mr. & Mrs. Shiro, Parents

Evaluation Schedule: General education teacher and school counselor will review progress weekly and report to parents via e-mail or phone call.

Antecedent/Environment (Recess):	Replacement/ Alternative Skill:	Contact:
1. Teach cooperative play skills. 2. Assign peer buddy. 3. Use point card and reinforcement for cooperative play.	1. Laurence will use cooperative play skills to join and play games at recess. 2. Laurence will listen to and talk with his peer buddy about game rules. 3. Laurence will follow game rules and participate appropriately in game for 10–20 minutes.	1. Ms. Block, School Counselor 2. Ms. Tomaz, General Education Teacher 3. Mr. & Mrs. Shiro, Parents 4. Laurence, Student Carter, Peer Buddy

Evaluation Schedule: The school team (school counselor, behavior support team, recess staff, and general education teacher) will review Laurence's progress weekly, and the school counselor will check in with both Laurence and his peer buddy. Laurence's parents will be notified through e-mail or a phone call on Laurence's progress each week.

Addressing the Function of Behavior

Interventions to address the problem behaviors should focus on answering the question "Why?" Why was Laurence, for example, refusing to work on individual math homework and fighting with peers during recess? Students may use these behaviors because they do not have positive social skills to obtain a teacher's or peers attention or to escape situations, such as a difficult or uncomfortable task. Students can have many reasons for obtaining and escaping; interventions must gradually work toward desirable social skills while considering the preferred function for the behavior.

Table 8.3 displays how the two interventions chosen for Laurence can meet the perceived function of his behavior. If Laurence is seeking attention, then both the self-monitoring and the peer assistance approaches should increase the amount of attention by the teacher and peers. The teacher can attend to this issue by positioning the student closer to her and checking in with him more often. Peers can be used in the process by serving as buddies and tutors. If Laurence is finding math too difficult or frustrating, he may be refusing to work because he thinks he will ultimately fail anyway and feel embarrassed. His arguing, defiance, and peer interruptions may be a result of his motivation to escape the math work. Ms. Tomaz can use this knowledge to design the intervention by decreasing his frustration and giving him work that is closer to his level.

Table 8.3	Evidence-Based Strategies Matching Interventions by Function (Obtain Attention/Objects or Escape From Difficult/Unwanted Tasks)		
Function	**Intervention Strategy**	**Example**	**Research**
Attention	Student support	• Answer questions as a team with a peer or peers. • Engage in peer tutoring/learning.	Armendariz & Umbreit, 1999; Bacon & Bloom, 2000; Morrison, Kamps, Garcia, & Parker, 2001; Shukla, Kennedy, & Cushing, 1999
	Increased proximity to student	• Move seating arrangement. • Use explicit routines and expectations within the classroom.	Scott & Nelson, 1999; Shukla et al., 1999
	Self-management of activities	• Student tallies behaviors and receives reward when levels achieved. • Completes work and demonstrates appropriate behaviors.	Barry & Messer, 2003; Brooks, Todd, Tofflemoyer, & Horner, 2003; Callahan & Rademacher, 1999; Lee, Simpson, & Shogren, 2007; Smith & Sugai, 2000; Todd, Horner, & Sugai, 1999
Function	**Intervention**	**Example**	**Research**
Escape	Modifing difficulty of the task	• Shorten sentences required for paragraph. • Provide breaks during lesson. • Reduce number of pages required. • Provide more challenging work.	Moore, Anderson, & Kumar, 2005; Umbreit, Lane, & Dejud, 2004

(Continued)

Table 8.3 (Continued)			
Function	Intervention	Example	Research

	Providing choices	• Allow student to choose
		  ○ sequence of completing tasks.
		  ○ where to work on task.
		  ○ whom to work with on task (peer).
			Dunlap et al., 1994; Vaughn & Horner, 1997

	Self-monitoring of activities/behaviors	• Student monitors work and checks off when completed. • Reinforced after completion of predetermined number.	Smith & Sugai, 2000; Stahr, Cushing, Lane, & Fox, 2006; Todd et al., 1999

Addressing Skill Deficits

The interventions listed above along with others developed by the team can only be successful if the student has learned the appropriate behaviors necessary to replace the problem behaviors. Many students do not have the necessary skills to demonstrate appropriate school behaviors. Alternative skills provide students with replacement behaviors to use during situations they they may want to obtain attention or escape situations. Replacement skills (behaviors) teach students effective, socially acceptable behaviors that allow the student to obtain the desired outcomes without using an inappropriate problem behavior. These skills may provide students with coping, tolerance, or general adaptive skills (Bambara & Knoster, 1998). Students with problem behaviors can acquire these skills by receiving social skills lessons. Social skills training is an effective intervention to help students learn alternative and/or replacement skills, resulting in a decrease in problem behaviors (Cook, Gresham, Kern, Barreras, & Crews, 2008). Providing a student with a set of school-appropriate social skills can increase his or her chances of success in future academic work.

Developing and implementing behavior intervention plans with Positive Behavior Supports sets up the team to support the student in being successful in school. The multidisciplinary team works together to provide the student with culturally relevant, peer-reviewed interventions that decrease problem behaviors. Decreasing the problem behaviors will increase the student's prosocial behaviors, which has been correlated to increase in academic engagement in the classroom (Kilian, Fish, & Miniago, 2007). The student increases his or her chances of decreasing problem behaviors when the team works together to provide an effective behavior intervention plan.

CONCLUSION

This chapter has provided a process for developing behavior plans for teaching positive, prosocial skills while reducing problem behaviors. We recommended and provided examples of using the SPBS model and have attempted to show how it is similar to an RTI model. Figure 8.3 summarizes the building blocks of the process we have discussed. The foundation is a block of schoolwide features that are formulated, monitored, and evaluated by a leadership team and implemented by all staff. Within classrooms, teachers need to focus on the next block, effective classroom management. When schoolwide features and classroom management approaches don't reach a few students, Tier II and III interventions need to be implemented. These four blocks form the primary structures and strategies for impacting positive school social behavior. Teachers who follow these recommendations should see an improved classroom environment and enhanced student social and academic performance.

Figure 8.3   Building Blocks of Effective Behavior Plans

Tier 3—Individualized Behavior Plans: Clear behavior, concise summary statement, evidence-based practices, function based

Tier 2—Behavior Intervention: Adult mentor, increased supervision and daily report card, positive relationships, progress monitoring and reinforcement, parent involvement

Classroom Management: Class layout; wall/ceiling displays; social expectations posted; transitions, procedures, and routines taught; effective instruction; social behavior maintained; clear communication

Schoolwide Features: Leadership team, clear social expectations, social expectations posted throughout school, social expectations taught and reinforced, strategies for reducing problem behaviors, disciplinary system aligned with classroom and school procedures, data collected and analyzed for social behavior, data-based decision making

9

Fidelity of Implementation

Daryl F. Mellard and Evelyn S. Johnson

M any failures of education reforms and practices can be attributed to poor implementation (Gresham, 1989). When schools
adopt new initiatives without fidelity to essential program design
features, the results are often discouraging (Kovaleski, Gickling, &
Marrow, 1999). Other chapters of this text provide information about
design features and how to implement RTI. This chapter focuses
on helping schools recognize how consistent and detailed measures
of fidelity of implementation support the efficacy of an RTI model.
Fidelity of implementation refers to how closely the prescribed procedures of a process are followed. Without fidelity to the process, it is
impossible to determine the cause of poor performance, which jeop-
ardizes the effectiveness of the RTI process.

The three-dimensional model of fidelity of implementation presented here can help schools ensure that RTI is implemented well.
A listing of resources to support these efforts is also provided.

Definitions and Features

What Is Fidelity of Implementation?

Fidelity of implementation refers to the delivery of instruction in the way in which it was designed to be delivered (Gresham, MacMillan, Beebe-Frankenberger, & Bocian, 2000). For example, a published reading curriculum may require teachers to teach decoding skills in a prescribed sequence and fashion. If teachers do not follow the sequence or the method, a student may not learn to decode accurately. However, it would be unclear whether the failure to learn was due to a problem with instruction (e.g., the teacher didn't follow the curriculum procedures) or a problem the student faces with learning. In an RTI model, fidelity is important at both the school level (e.g., implementation of the process) and the teacher level (e.g., implementation of instruction and progress monitoring).

Several studies on various interventions confirm the importance of fidelity of implementation to maximize program effectiveness (see, for example, Foorman & Moats, 2004; Foorman & Schatschneider, 2003; Gresham et al., 2000; Kovaleski et al., 1999; Telzrow, McNamara, & Hollinger, 2000; Vaughn, Hughes, Schumm, & Klingner, 1998). Specifically, the results suggest that positive student outcomes may be attributed to one of three related factors:

1. *Fidelity of Implementation of the Process (at the School Level).* In an RTI model, this refers to the consistency with which the various components are implemented across classrooms and grade levels.

2. *Degree to Which the Selected Interventions Are Empirically Supported.* If an intervention or instructional practice has a strong

evidence base, it is more likely to help improve student learning than is an intervention with an unknown outcome.

3. *Fidelity of Implementation of the Intervention at the Teacher Level.* If teachers do not implement the intervention in the way in which it was designed, students may not benefit, and a child assistance team may conclude that the problem lies with the student (as opposed to poor quality of instruction).

A Three-Dimensional Model of Fidelity of Implementation

When school staffs administer a standardized assessment, the assumption is that the test is administered according to the directions in the accompanying manual and that the examiner is appropriately qualified. Implementation of RTI must meet the same standard. As described in the research literature, direct and frequent assessment of an intervention for fidelity is considered to be best practice.

Descriptions of fidelity checks in the existing literature tend to focus on research perspectives rather than on practice. When researching the effectiveness of an intervention, it is critical to be able to report the fidelity with which it was implemented: (a) so that any resulting gains in student achievement can be accurately attributed to the intervention under scrutiny and (b) so that the intervention can be replicated. Similarly, when implementing an intervention, it is critical to know whether it is being implemented as designed, so that if the intervention is initially unsuccessful, schools can take appropriate measures to remedy the deficiency rather than abandoning the entire reform.

The ultimate aim of a fidelity system is to ensure that both the school process of RTI and the classroom instruction at various tiers are implemented and delivered as intended. This aim must be balanced with the school's existing resources. In recognition of this reality, we have conceptualized an approach to ensuring fidelity that is based on three dimensions. Figure 9.1 illustrates the model; each of the dimensions is described below.

- *Dimension 1: Method.* This dimension includes the tools and approaches a school uses to provide various kinds of feedback on how RTI is being implemented.
- *Dimension 2: Frequency.* How often checks are conducted will vary depending on the situation. A combination of approaches that includes annual, monthly, and, in some cases, weekly observations and review will provide the most thorough evaluation of how RTI is being implemented.

Figure 9.1   Three Dimensions of Ensuring Fidelity

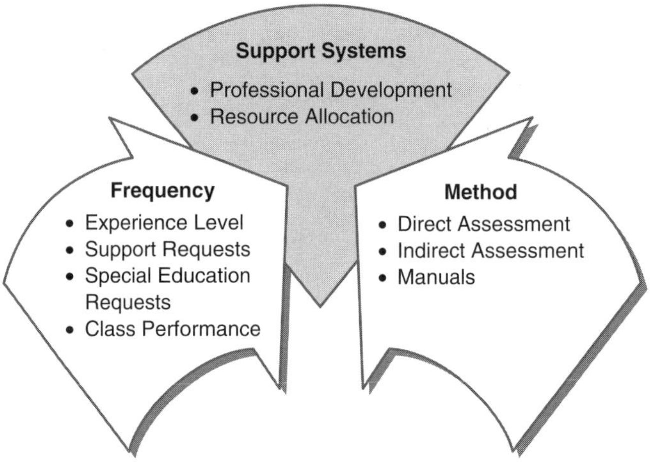

Support Systems
- Professional Development
- Resource Allocation

Frequency
- Experience Level
- Support Requests
- Special Education Requests
- Class Performance

Method
- Direct Assessment
- Indirect Assessment
- Manuals

SOURCE: Johnson, Mellard, Fuchs, & McKnight (2006).

- *Dimension 3: Support Systems.* This dimension includes the feedback and professional development opportunities needed to implement a process with fidelity. Support systems should be selected and developed in response to school needs. For example, a school will need to develop professional development on their system of RTI for new staff, as well as a system of continued development in the instructional methods, interventions, and related assessments. An ongoing, flexible, and multifaceted support system will provide the best professional development response.

Implementation

Implementation of RTI places demands on a school's resources. Ensuring fidelity of implementation represents yet another demand. However, without fidelity checks, if RTI is not successful either in part or whole, it is difficult to take the appropriate steps to improve implementation, and the school may abandon the process altogether.

To keep fidelity manageable for schools, it is conceptualized here as a three-dimensional model that takes a proactive approach to implementing RTI the way in which it was intended. First, each of the three fidelity dimensions is explained. Next, we provide some indicators that schools can use to select the methods, the frequency with which they use the methods, and the support systems chosen to remedy areas of deficiency. Finally, we provide a detailed planning tool for schools to use as they implement the process to check fidelity of implementation.

Dimension 1: Method

Checking the implementation of a process for fidelity can be a complex and resource-intensive undertaking. In the research literature, checks for fidelity typically involve frequent observations and recording of behavior, teacher questionnaires, and self-reports or videotaping of lessons. The tools available to achieve fidelity may be divided into three main categories—direct assessment, indirect assessment, and manualized treatment (Gresham et al., 2000).

Direct Assessment

Using this approach, the components of an intervention are clearly specified in operational terms within a checklist, and a qualified staff member observes the intervention, counting the occurrence of each component to determine the percentage correctly implemented and identifying teachers who need retraining.

Indirect Assessment

Indirect assessment methods include self-reports, rating scales, interviews, and permanent products. Of these, permanent product assessment is thought to be the most reliable and accurate. Permanent products might include samples of student work or student performance on assessments. Each product would be related to a particular component of the intervention.

Manualized Treatments

Essentially, this represents a step-by-step guide or checklist to implementation. Although such guides are helpful in detailing the steps required for implementation, unless they are accompanied by completed checklists, accompanying student work, and assessment data, or one of the other methods included above, they are by themselves not sufficient for ensuring fidelity.

Direct assessments of an intervention are considered to be best practice because they provide immediate feedback on how instruction is being delivered. However, direct assessments are the most time consuming, so schools likely will have to prioritize the ways in which they plan to ensure fidelity of implementation of the various components of RTI. Many of the tools to begin a process of fidelity checks might already exist within a school or might be built into the RTI process. For example, classroom level reports of progress monitoring provide an indication of the number of students achieving at desired benchmarks. If a teacher has an unusually high number of students who do not meet benchmarks, this could be an indication that she requires support in delivering instruction, administering assessments, or other related classroom or instructional management process.

Dimension 2: Frequency

As mentioned above, the frequency with which fidelity checks are conducted will vary depending on several factors, including the following:

1. The experience level of the teacher

2. A teacher request for support in implementing a particular component of RTI

3. Overall class performance on progress monitoring, screening, and other assessments

4. The degree to which special education referrals do or do not decrease

As noted under Dimension 1 (Method), schedules for checking, reviewing, and analyzing data may already exist within a school or district and can be used in the process of checking for fidelity of RTI. For example, principals are required to evaluate new staff, state and district assessment results generally arrive at a given time in the school year, schoolwide screenings are routinely scheduled, child study teams meet on a regularly scheduled basis, and information on student performance and teacher instruction can be included as part of these meetings.

Table 9.1 lists different kinds of fidelity checks along a frequency continuum (from ongoing to annual) to demonstrate how this frequency dimension might operate within the larger context of fidelity of implementation. If used as a planning tool, it offers schools a comprehensive view of the amount, type, and regularity of feedback and data they are collecting on fidelity of implementation.

Dimension 3: Support Systems

As applied by schools, fidelity of implementation checks serve the purpose of identifying areas of strength on which schools can build and areas of deficiency that need to be remedied. For example, a

Table 9.1　　Frequency and Fidelity Checking Methods Continuum

Task	Ongoing	Weekly	Monthly	3 Times a Year	Annually
Review state/district assessment results					X
Conduct screening				X	
Review progress monitoring		X			
Conduct teacher evaluations	X				
Solicit teacher comments/input	X				
Evaluate new staff				X	

newly hired teacher may not be familiar with the school's reading curriculum. This teacher might require professional development opportunities to become acquainted with the principles and procedures of the curriculum. Through previous fidelity checks, a teacher who is especially skilled with the particular curriculum may have been identified and can be paired with the new staff member to serve as a mentor or coach. At the class level, fidelity checks may reveal that a particular classroom may not have sufficient resources to implement and sustain a system of progress monitoring. This deficiency would require the subsequent attainment or redistribution of resources within the school. The kinds of support systems that are required to correct areas of deficiency likely will fall into one of two categories:

1. *Professional Development and Training.* This may include formal opportunities for workshops and inservice training, as well as for partnership with teacher mentors or coaches.

2. *Resource Allocation.* If teachers do not have the proper resources to implement the intervention, it is incumbent on the school leadership to obtain or redistribute resources.

Putting the Model Together

RTI represents a significant instructional shift for many schools that requires a coordination of processes at the school and teacher levels. Fidelity of implementation is critical for RTI or any education intervention to be successful. We recognize that schools have limited resources with which to implement the many initiatives and policy requirements they face. In this section, we have attempted to streamline the process of fidelity of implementation by noting indicators and applying the three-dimensional model (Table 9.2).

Table 9.2   Fidelity of Implementation Sample Application of the Three-Dimensional Model

Indicator	Method	Frequency	Support System
New staff has been hired.	Evaluations or observations.	Ideally three times a year, once early on.	Pair with mentor or coach; provide training in curriculum program.
Screening results show class averages are lower than school average, or a high percentage of kids are identified as at risk.	Review of data, direct observations, teacher logs, review any supporting evidence from parents, student work samples.	Same schedule as screening, with more frequent checks to resolve problems.	Have teacher work with mentor coach to problem solve, identify areas of strength and weakness; offer training opportunities.
Teacher evaluations highlight deficiency in instructional methods.	Follow-up observations, dialogues with other teachers, teacher logs/ self-reports.	As needed.	Identify problem to be able to either require professional development and/or allocation of resources.

Essential Task List for Implementation

Table 9.3 provides an essential task list for fidelity of implementation. While certainly not exhaustive, the list represents important steps in initial implementation. The first column describes the specific task required. The second column asks you to identify, by name, who has overall responsibility for overseeing this task. In some cases, more than one individual may be responsible. The final column allows you either to set target dates for completion or to indicate the status of progress related to the task.

Table 9.3   Essential Task List for Fidelity of Implementation

Directions

In the second column, *Responsible Person(s)*, write the name(s) of the individual or team who will assume responsibility for the task identified in the first column. In the third column, *Timeline/Status*, write the deadline for the task and/or its status.

Task	Responsible Person(s)	Timeline/Status
Develop a system of professional development and training as the school begins RTI implementation, and as the school hires new staff.		
Collect or create methods to ensure fidelity.		
Coordinate master schedules to conduct fidelity checks (e.g., teacher evaluations, walk-through checks, trainings).		
Develop a plan to systematically review results of information collected.		
Develop criteria to indicate when a teacher may require additional supports.		
Develop a plan to provide additional supports or professional development.		

Standards for Judging High-Quality
Fidelity of Implementation

Methods of ensuring fidelity must be aligned with the requirements of the district, school, and curriculum. Therefore, we do not make any recommendations here on specific approaches. Regardless of the tools selected to implement and operate a system of fidelity, however, several criteria may be used to judge the quality of the system. Table 9.4 presents standards for judging high-quality fidelity of implementation that are based on the research in this area and that were used as part of a national effort to identify model RTI sites (Mellard, Byrd, Johnson, Tollefson, & Boesche, 2004). The checklist is formatted so that you can indicate current and planned implementation. If the practice has been implemented, indicate that with a checkmark. If the practice is being developed, rank its priority of focus; 1 = highest priority, 3 = lowest priority.

Fidelity of implementation is arguably the most important component of an RTI process because it serves as the means by which a school can evaluate and respond to professional development needs, resource acquisition and distribution, and infrastructure development.

Changing Structures and Roles

In an era of increasing demands for teacher accountability, a system of fidelity of implementation may be viewed as a negative development by school staff. However, ensuring fidelity of implementation can integrate the following three components of a school:

1. Instructional tools and strategies

2. Student achievement

3. Professional development

Such integration cannot occur if teachers are threatened by the system of observation and evaluation that accompanies this process. In many cases, accountability measures related to state assessments and NCLB (2001) have placed an emphasis on punitive measures for teachers. This need not be the case. Through the use of positive approaches to accountability, schools have the opportunity to implement a system of fidelity checks within a collaborative environment that promotes teacher improvement. As a part of that approach, accountability for implementation involves active participation and shared participation among teachers, administrators, students and

Table 9.4   Standards for Judging High-Quality Fidelity of Implementation

Directions

Read each of the standards that have been identified as mechanisms for judging high-quality fidelity of implementation. The checklist is formatted so that you can indicate current and planned implementation.

- If the practice has been implemented, indicate that with a checkmark (✓).
- If the practice is being developed, rank by priority. Indicate 1 = of highest priority through 3 = of lowest priority. (Thus, practices ranked as "1" would be implemented before those ranked as "2" and those ranked as "2" would be implemented before those ranked as "3.")

	Status	
Standard	*In Place* (✓)	*Priority* (1–2–3)
Specific, qualified staff member or members are designated to observe instructional methods.		
Staff members are trained in fidelity procedures and have authoritative status (i.e., can take action if necessary).		
To document fidelity of instruction, a teacher who is using a newly learned instructional method is observed immediately and then weekly or bi-weekly, as needed. A "master teacher" may be observed less frequently (three times a year or less).		
Classroom observation data are collected at least three times a year for Tier 1 and two times a year for Tier 2 to document implementation of strategies addressed in professional development activities.		
Observers complete a written checklist comprising the specific critical features of the instructional methods to document the degree of fidelity.		
Specific criteria (e.g., percentage of critical features observed) are used to judge methods as having or lacking fidelity.		
Feedback to instructional staff members includes one or more of the following: a scheduled conference, written information about problematic key features of the checklist, a plan for improvement, and a videotape of exemplary implementation with fidelity.		

SOURCE: Mellard & McKnight (2006).

parents (Neill, 2004). Honest and open communication with mentors or coaches, or both, can help a school tailor its professional development resources to support staff and ultimately improve student achievement. Evaluations and observations of teachers are approached in a positive manner that emphasizes problem solving rather than blaming. No important decisions about teachers, individual students, or the instructional program should be made solely on one type of evidence (Neill). Schools must be accountable for implementing procedures using information to guide decision making by teachers, students, parents, and administrators to improve the quality of schools and learning (Neill).

Teacher mentors also can play a larger role in the school environment to ensure fidelity. In order to make this process work, mentors or coaches must have authority to act. Mentors who have proven ability in the relevant area should be selected to serve as coaches to new staff. Mentors may require some training for their new role, especially if they now find themselves evaluating their peers.

Table 9.5 outlines some possible roles and structures for ensuring fidelity of implementation. Schools may choose to organize their process differently. For example, they may organize their process in ways that are consistent with their shared vision and implementation of RTI.

Challenges to Implementation

Although both common sense and research support the concept of fidelity of implementation to ensure an intervention's successful outcome, the practical challenges associated with achieving high levels of fidelity are also well documented. Gresham et al. (2000) noted several factors that may reduce the fidelity of implementation of an intervention, including complexity, materials and resources required, and perceived versus actual effectiveness.

Complexity

The more complex the intervention, the lower the fidelity of implementation. While many of the individual components of RTI are not complex, the coordination of numerous components into a seamless, integrated model presents challenges for schools. For example, the development, selection, implementation, and evaluation of Tier 2 interventions is a complex process that may require closer attention and scrutiny than implementation of screening measures.

Table 9.5   Changing Roles and Structures for Fidelity of Implementation

---

Teachers

- Collect the indirect assessments that can help corroborate manualized and direct observation results.
- Review existing checklists and manuals for implementation.
- Implement necessary changes to instructional practices (as result of faculty check).
- If requested, complete teacher reflections or teacher logs.
- If requested, videotape and review delivery of instruction.
- Review fidelity of implementation observation result with supervisor.

Mentor Teachers and School Coaches

- Monitor progress of teachers in delivering instruction in the content area.
- Provide professional development, coaching, and training.
- Evaluate results of observations and collected work samples to provide meaningful and specific feedback to teachers.
- Respond to teacher requests for assistance or information.

Administration

- Lead effort to create infrastructure for a cooperative fidelity of implementation process.
- Provide required resources to include access to the curriculum, opportunities to interact with mentors and coaches, and other material and equipment.
- Conduct teacher observations according to schedule and include the evaluation of evidence-based instructional practice.
- Monitor the special education referral rates and average class performance of teachers.
- Ensure fidelity of implementation through routine, periodic walk-throughs, observations, and discussions with staff.
- Coordinate for needed professional development.
- Determine if classroom performance warrants intervention (i.e., entire class performance is considerably lower than other classes in the same grade level).

NOTE: *Teachers* includes general and special education teachers. *Administration* includes building principals and assistants, as well as curriculum and/or assessment specialists at building or district levels.

Materials and Resources Required

If new or substantial resources are required, they must be readily accessible. Access includes both having the resources available (physical access), and providing the initial and ongoing support to teachers for their use (conceptual or cognitive access). Periodic reviews of material and resource requirements help improve and sustain implementation efforts.

Perceived and Actual Effectiveness

Even with a solid research base, if teachers believe an approach will not be effective, or if it is inconsistent with their teaching style, they will not implement it well. RTI represents a paradigm shift for many teachers. The focus on ongoing progress monitoring, the increased reliance on the general education teacher to provide support to students at risk, and the routine collection and analysis of data to support instructional decision making are all very different from what many teachers may have been trained to do. As a result, staffs will need to continue to discuss their perceptions of RTI and to be encouraged to openly communicate if specific components present significant challenges to their teaching approaches or philosophy. These discussions can help find workable solutions to implementation.

Schools are encumbered by numerous policy initiatives, increasingly diverse student needs, and limited resources. RTI has the potential to help a school make better use of its resources for increasing overall student achievement and for serving students with learning disabilities by the following:

- Allowing for early identification of students at risk through screening and progress monitoring, along with appropriate Tier 2 interventions.
- Aligning assessment procedures with instruction to develop a more comprehensive system of assessment to include both standardized measures and formative assessment of student progress.
- Providing multiple data points on which decisions are based to include screening results, regular progress monitoring data, and supporting student work.
- Ensuring access to appropriate instruction through the use of progress monitoring and evidenced-based instruction. Decision making is based on individual student needs as well as empirically supported practices.

However, these potentials cannot be realized if interventions are not properly implemented. Initially, ensuring fidelity will be a fairly resource-intensive process and will continue to require resources as schools receive new staff and students. We have attempted to consider the existing tools and procedures available to schools in developing a system of ensuring fidelity that supports but does not overwhelm schools as they implement RTI. As you read through the accompanying sample tools, you should consider additional resources that may have been overlooked in this chapter.

Summary

RTI is a schoolwide framework that integrates curriculum, instruction, intervention, and assessment. To be implemented well, it requires a strong collaborative relationship among school staff. Without assurances that instruction has been delivered as intended, that screening and progress monitoring tools have been administered with fidelity, and that related interventions have been provided consistent with the research base, the ability to support student learning will be compromised. Fidelity of implementation as described in this chapter is a way for schools to align a process of accountability with a supportive environment of professional development and growth.

Resources

The following resources may support your implementation of fidelity of implementation.

- **Washington State K–12 Reading Model Implementation Guide (Geiger, Banks, Hasbrouck, & Ebbers, 2005) (http://www.k12.wa.us/CurriculumInstruct/Reading/default.aspx)**

  This document was developed by the Washington State Office of Public Instruction to inform the implementation of RTI to reading instruction. It provides details on assessment, intervention, and instruction, as well as checklists that may be used as part of a fidelity check of implementation.

(Continued)

(Continued)

- **Principal's Reading Walkthrough
  (http://www.fcrr.org/staffpresentations/SNettles/
  PrincipalWalkthroughContent.pdf)**

  This presentation and related documents (Nettles, 2006)
  were developed at the Florida Center for Reading Research, with
  individual checklists for kindergarten and first, second, and
  third grades. A thorough checklist of implementation at both
  classroom and school levels is included.

- **Intervention Validity Checklist (Vaughn, Linan-Thompson,
  Kouzekanani, Bryant, Dickson, & Blozis (2003)**

  The Intervention Validity Checklist was developed by
  researchers at the Texas Center for Reading and Language Arts
  in the College of Education at The University of Texas at Austin
  (Vaughn et al., 2003) to ensure (a) implementation consistency
  across teachers and (b) treatment fidelity.

- **Foorman and Moats (2004)**

  Foorman and Schatschneider (2003) and Foorman and Moats
  (2004) have developed observation protocols for measuring
  instructional effects on primary-grade literacy outcomes.

- **The Consortium on Reading Excellence
  (http://www.corelearn.com)**

  The Consortium on Reading Excellence has developed a
  number of reading-focused coaching and instructional implementation materials.

- **Fuchs and Fuchs (2006)**

  Fuchs and Fuchs (2006) identify dimensions and recommendations for RTI implementation in this publication.

References

Chapter 1

Batsche, G., Elliott, J., Graden, J. L., Grimes, J., Kovaleski, J. F., Prasse, D., et al. (2006). *Response to intervention: Policy considerations and implementation* (4th ed.). Alexandria, VA: National Association of State Directors of Special Education, Inc.

Bergan, J. R. (1977). *Behavioral consultation*. Columbus, OH: Charles E. Merrill.

Bradley, R., Danielson, L., & Doolittle, J. (2005). Response to intervention. *Journal of Learning Disabilities, 38*(6), 485–486.

Butler, F. M., Miller, S. P., Crehan, K., Babbitt, B., & Pierce, T. (2003). Fraction instruction for students with mathematics disabilities: Comparing two teaching sequences. *Learning Disabilities Research and Practice, 18,* 99–111.

Cass, M., Cates, D., Smith, M., & Jackson, C. (2003). Effects of manipulative instruction on solving area and perimeter problems by students with learning disabilities. *Learning Disabilities Research and Practice, 18,* 112–120.

Deno, S., & Mirkin, P. (1977). *Data-based program modification*. Minneapolis, MN: Leadership Training Institute for Special Education.

Fletcher, J. M., Denton, C., & Francis, D. J. (2005). Validity of alternative approaches for the identification of learning disabilities: Operationalizing unexpected underachievement. *Journal of Learning Disabilities, 38,* 545–552.

Fuchs, L. S. (2003). Assessing intervention responsiveness: Conceptual and technical issues. *Learning Disabilities Research and Practice, 18*(3), 172–186.

Fuchs, L. S., Compton, D. L., Fuchs, D., Paulsen, K., Bryant, J., & Hamlett, C. L. (2005). Responsiveness to intervention: Preventing and identifying mathematics disability. *TEACHING Exceptional Children, 37*(4), 60–63.

Fuchs, D., & Fuchs, L. S. (2005). Responsiveness-to-intervention: A blueprint for practitioners, policymakers, and parents. *Teaching Exceptional Children, 38*(1), 57–61.

Fuchs, D., & Fuchs, L. S. (2006). Introduction to Response to Intervention: What, why, and how valid is it? *Reading Research Quarterly, 41*(1), 93–98.

Fuchs, L. S., Fuchs, D., Hamlett, C. L., Hope, S. K., Hollenbeck, K. N., Capizzi, A., et al. (2006). Extending responsiveness-to-intervention to math problem-solving at third grade. *TEACHING Exceptional Children, 38*(4), 59–63.

Fuchs, L. S., Fuchs, D., Prentice, K., Burch, M., & Paulsen, K. (2002). Hot Math: Promoting mathematical problem solving among third-grade students with disabilities. *TEACHING Exceptional Children, 31*(1), 70–73.

Fuchs, D., Fuchs, L. S., Thompson, A., Svenson, E., Yen, L., Al Otaiba, S., et al. (2001). Peer-assisted learning strategies in reading: Extension for kindergarten, first grade, and high school. *Remedial and Special Education, 22*, 15–21.

Gersten, R., & Dimino, J. A. (2006). RTI (Response to Intervention): Rethinking special education for students with reading difficulties (yet again). *Reading Research Quarterly, 41*(1), 99–108.

Good, R. H., & Kaminski, R. A. (Eds.), (2001). *Dynamic indicators of basic early literacy skills* (5th ed.). Eugene, OR: Institute for the Development of Educational Achievement.

Grimes, J., & Kurns, S. (2003, December). *An intervention-based system for addressing NCLB and IDEA expectations: A multiple tiered model to ensure every child learns.* Paper presented at the National Research Center on Learning Disabilities Responsiveness-to-Intervention Symposium, Kansas City, MO

Heller, K. A., Holtzman, W. H., & Messick, S. (1982). *Placing children in special education: A strategy for equity.* Washington, DC: National Academy Press.

Individuals With Disabilities Education Act of 2004. (2004). Federal Register 71, pp. 46539–46845. Retrieved August 30, 2006, from www.ed.gov/policy/speced/guid/idea2004.html

Jankowski, E. A. (2003, Fall). Heartland Area Education Agency's problem solving model: An outcomes-driven special education paradigm. *Rural Special Education Quarterly.* Retrieved July 25, 2006, from www.findarticles.com/p/articles

Kukic, S., Tilly, D., & Michelson, L. (Presenters). (2006). *Addressing the needs of students with learning difficulties through the Response to Intervention (RtI) strategies.* Retrieved January 26, 2007, from the National Association of State Directors of Special Education, Inc., website: http://www.nasdse.org/publications.cfm

Marston, D. (2005). Tiers of intervention in responsiveness to intervention: Prevention outcomes and learning disabilities identification patterns. *Journal of Learning Disabilities, 38*(6), 539–544.

Marston, D., Muyskens, P., Lau, M., & Canter, A. (2003). Problem-solving model for decision making with high-incidence disabilities: The Minneapolis experience. *Learning Disabilities Research & Practice, 18*(3), 187–200.

Mastropieri, M. A., & Scruggs, T. W. (2005). Feasibility and consequences of Response to Intervention: Examination of the issues and scientific evidence as a model for the identification of individuals with learning disabilities. *Journal of Learning Disabilities, 38*(6), 525–531.

McCook, J. E. (2006). *The RTI guide: Developing and implementing a model in your schools.* Horsham, PA: LRP Publications.

McMaster, K. L., Fuchs, D., Fuchs, L. S., & Compton, D. L. (2003, December). *Responding to nonresponders: An experimental field trial of identification and intervention methods.* Paper presented at the National Research Center on Learning Disabilities Responsiveness-to-Intervention Symposium, Kansas City, MO.

Mercer, C. D., Jordan, L., & Miller, S. P. (1996). Constructivistic math instruction for diverse learners. *Learning Disabilities Research and Practice, 11*, 147–156.

National Research Center on Learning Disabilities (2002). *Common ground report.* Reston, VA: Author.

National Research Center on Learning Disabilities (2005). *Core concepts of RTI.* Retrieved July 25, 2006, from www.nrcld.org

President's Commission on Excellence in Special Education (2002). *A new era: Revitalizing special education for children and their families.* Retrieved July 26, 2006, from www.ed.gov/inits/commissionsboards/index.html

Reschly, D. J., Hosp, J. L., & Schmied, C. M. (2003, August 20). *And miles to go: State SLD requirements and authoritative recommendations.* Retrieved July 20, 2006, from www.nrcld.org, pp. 3–10.

Scruggs, T. W., & Mastropieri, M. A. (2002). On babies and bathwater: Addressing the problems of identification of learning disabilities. *Learning Disability Quarterly, 25*(2), 155–168.

Siegel, L. S. (1989). IQ is irrelevant to the definition of learning disabilities. *Journal of Learning Disabilities, 22,* 469–486.

Tilley, W. D. (2003, December). *How many tiers are needed for successful prevention and early intervention? Heartland Area Education Agency's evolution from four to three tiers.* Paper presented at the National Research Center on Learning Disabilities Responsiveness-to-Intervention Symposium, Kansas City, MO.

U.S. Office of Education. (1977). *Assistance to states for education of handicapped children: Procedures for evaluating specific learning disabilities.* Federal Register 42, pp. 65082–65085.

Vaughn, S., & Fuchs, L. S. (2003). Redefining learning disabilities as inadequate response to instruction: The promise and potential problems. *Learning Disabilities Research & Practice, 18*(3), 137–146.

Vaughn, S., Linan-Thompson, S., & Hickman, P. (2003). Response to treatment as a means of identifying students with reading/learning disabilities. *Exceptional Children, 69*(4), 391–409.

Vellutino, F. R., Scanlon, D. M., Sipay, E. R., Small, S., Chen, R., et al. (1996). Cognitive profiles of difficult to remediate and readily remediated poor readers: Early intervention as a vehicle for distinguishing between cognition and experiential deficits as basic cause of specific reading disability. *Journal of Educational Psychology, 88,* 601–638.

Vellutino, F. R., Scanlon, D. M., Small, S., & Fanuele, D. P. (2006). Response to intervention as a vehicle for distinguishing between children with and without reading disabilities: Evidence for the role of kindergarten and first-grade interventions. *Journal of Learning Disabilities, 39*(2), 157–169.

Ysseldyke, J. (2005). Assessment and decision making for students with learning disabilities: What if this is as good as it gets? *Learning Disability Quarterly, 28,* 125–128.

Chapter 2

The Access Center (2004, October). *Concrete-representational-abstract instructional approach.* Retrieved August 2007 from http://www.k8accesscenter.org/training_resources/CRA_instructional_approach.asp

Alberto, P. A., & Troutman, A. C. (2006). *Applied behavior analysis for teachers* (7th ed.). Upper Saddle River, NJ: Prentice Hall.

Armbruster, B. B., & Anderson, T. H. (1987). Improving content-area reading using instructional graphics. *Reading Research Quarterly, 26*(4), 393–416.

Bandura, A. (1977). *Social learning theory.* New York: General Learning Press.

Beecher, J. (1988). *Note-taking: What do we know about the benefits: ERIC DIGEST #37.* Bloomington, IN: ERIC Clearinghouse on Reading, English, and Communications. (ERIC Document Reproduction Service No. EDO CS 88 12).

Bretzing, B. H., & Kulhary, R. W. (1979, April). Notetaking and depth of processing. *Contemporary Educational Psychology, 4*(2), 145–153.

Brown, A. L., Campione, J. C., & Day, J. (1981). Learning to learn: On training students to learn from texts. *Educational Researcher, 10,* 14–24.

The Center for the Improvement of Early Reading Achievement (2001, September). *Put reading first: The research building blocks for teaching children to read.* Retrieved July 2007 from http://www.nifl.gov/partnershipforreading/publications/reading_first1.html

Comprehensive School Reform Program Office. (2002, August). *Scientifically based research and the comprehensive school reform program.* Retrieved September 2007 from http://www.ed.gov/programs/compreform/guidance/appendc.pdf

Cotton, K. (1991, May). *Computer assisted instruction.* Retrieved September 2007 from http://www.nwrel.org/scpd/sirs/5/cu10.html

Davey, B. (1983). Think alouds: Modeling the cognitive processes of reading comprehension. *Journal of Reading, 27*(1), 44–47.

Eaker, R., DuFour, R., & DuFour, R. (2002). *Getting started: reculturing schools to become professional learning communities.* Bloomington, IN: National Educational Service.

Fleer, M. (1992). Identifying teacher-child interaction which scaffolds scientific thinking in young children. *Science Education, 76,* 373–397.

Fuchs, D., & Fuchs, L. S. (2005). Responsiveness to intervention: A blueprint for practitioners, policymakers, and parents. *Exceptional Children, 38*(1), 57–61.

Fuchs, L. S., & Fuchs, D. (2007). A model for implementing responsiveness to intervention. *TEACHING Exceptional Children, 39*(5), 14–20.

Fuchs, L. S., Fuchs, D., Prentice, K., Burch, M., Hamlett, C. L., Owen, R., et al. (2003). Enhancing third-grade students' mathematical problem solving with self-regulated learning strategies. *Journal of Educational Psychology, 95*(2), 306–315.

Fuchs, L. S., Fuchs, D., Prentice, K., Hamlett, C. L., Finelli, R., & Courey, S. J. (2004). Enhancing mathematical problem solving among third-grade students with schema-based instruction. *Journal of Educational Psychology, 96*(4), 635–647.

Gentner, D., & Markman, A. B. (1994). Structural alignment in comparison: No difference without similarity. *Psychological Science, 5*(3), 152–158.

Harrison, M., & Harrison, B. (1986). Developing numeration concepts and skills. *Arithmetic Teacher, 33,* 1–21.

Heacox, D. (2002). *Differentiating instruction in the regular classroom: How to reach and teach all learners, grades 3–12.* Minneapolis, MN: Free Spirit Publishing.

Hidi, S., & Anderson, V. (1987). Providing written summaries: Task demands, cognitive operations, and implications for instruction. *Reviewing Educational Research, 56,* 473–493.

Jacobs, G. (2001). Providing the scaffold: A model for early childhood/primary teacher preparation. *Early Childhood Education Journal, 29*(2), 125–130.

Jitendra, A. (2002). Teaching students math problem-solving through graphic representation. *Teaching Exceptional Children, 34*(4), 34–38.

Jitendra, A. K., Griffin, C., Haria, P., Leh, J., Adams, A., & Kaduvetoor, A. (2007). A comparison of single and multiple strategy instruction on third grade students' mathematical problem solving. *Journal of Educational Psychology, 99,* 115–127.

Johnson, M. (1987). *The body in the mind: The bodily basis of meaning, imagination, and reason.* Chicago: University of Chicago Press.

Jones, B., Pierce, J., & Hunter, B. (1989). Teaching children to construct graphic representations. *Educational Leadership, 46,* 20–25.

Kounin, J. S. (1970). *Discipline and group management in classrooms.* New York: Holt, Rinehart & Windston.

Lakoff, G., & Johnson, M. (1980). *Metaphors we live by.* Chicago: University of Chicago Press.

Marzano, R., Pickering, D., & Pollock, J. (2001). *Classroom instruction that works: Research-based strategies for increasing student achievement.* Alexandria, VA: McREL.

Marzano, R. J. (2003). *What works in schools: Translating research into action.* Alexandria, VA: Association for Supervision and Curriculum Development.

Marzano, R. J., Marzano, J. S., & Pickering, D. J. (2003). *Classroom management that works: Research based strategies for every teacher.* Alexandria, VA: Association for Supervision and Curriculum Development.

Miller, S. P. (1998, September). Validated practices for teaching mathematics to students with learning disabilities: A review of literature. *Focus on Exceptional Children, 31*(1), 1–24.

Montague, M. & Jitendra, A. K. (2006). *Teaching Mathematics to Middle School Students with Learning Difficulties.* New York, NY: The Guilford Press.

National Council of Teachers of Mathematics. (2000). Principles and standards for school mathematics. Reston, VA: Author.

No Child Left Behind Act. (2001). Section 9101[37]. Retrieved March 12, 2008, from http://www.ed.gov/policy/elsec/leg/esea02/index.html

Nye, P., Crooks, T. J., Powlie, M., & Tripp, G. (1984). Student note-taking related to university examination performances. *Higher Education, 13*(1), 85–97.

Oczkus, L. D. (2005). *Reciprocal teaching strategies at work: Improving reading comprehension, grades 2–6: Videotape viewing guide and lesson materials.* Retrieved September 2007 from http://www.reading.org/publications/bbv/videos/v500/

OSEP Technical Assistance Center on Positive Behavioral Interventions. (2007). *School wide positive behavioral supports.* Retrieved July 2007, from http://www.pbis.org/schoolwide.htm

Palincsar, A. S., & Brown, A. L. (1984). Reciprocal teaching of comprehension fostering and comprehension monitoring activities. *Cognition and Instruction, 1*(2), 117–175.

Promising Practices Network. (2005). *Programs that work: Reciprocal teaching.* Retrieved September 10, 2007 from http://www.promisingpractices.net/program.asp?programid=144

Rosenshine, B., & Meister, C. (1994). Reciprocal teaching: A review of the research. *Review of Educational Research, 64*(4), 479–530.

Saenz, L. M., Fuchs, L. S., & Fuchs, D. (2005). Peer-assisted learning strategies for English language learners with learning disabilities. *Exceptional Children, 71*(3), 231–247.

Smith, P. L., & Wedman, J. F. (1988). Read-think-aloud protocols: A new data source for formative evaluation. *Performance Improvement Quarterly, 1*(2), 13–22.

Sprick, R. S., Garrison, M., & Howard, L. (1998). *CHAMPs: A proactive and positive approach to classroom management.* Longmont, CO: Sopris West.

Stennett, R. G. (1985). *Computer assisted instruction: A review of the reviews*. London: The Board of Education for the City of London. (ERIC Document Reproduction Service No. ED 260 687.)

Tomlinson, C. A. (1999). *The differentiated classroom: Responding to the needs of all learners*. Alexandria, VA: ASCD.

Tomlinson, C. A. (2001). *How to differentiate instruction in mixed-ability classrooms* (2nd ed.). Alexandria, VA: ASCD.

University of Kansas Center for Research on Learning. (2008). *Strategic Instruction Model*. Retrieved April 7, 2008, from http://www.kucrl.org/sim/index.shtml

U.S. Department of Education. (2006, August 14). Assistance to states for the education of children with disabilities and preschool grants for children with disabilities; Final rule. *Federal Register, 71*(156), 46786–46787.

U.S. Surgeon General. (2000). *Executive summary youth violence: A report of the surgeon general*. Washington, DC: Public Health Service. Retrieved March 1, 2008 from http://www.surgeongeneral.gov/library/youthviolence/summary.htm

Vaughn, S., & Roberts, G. (2007). Secondary interventions in reading: Providing additional instruction for students at risk. *TEACHING Exceptional Children, 39*(5), 40–46.

Vygotsky, L. S. (1978). *Mind in society*. Cambridge, MA: Harvard University Press.

Weaver, R. (1967). *A rhetoric and handbook*. New York: Halt, Rinehart, and Winston.

Wolfgang, C. H. (2004). *Solving discipline and classroom management problems: Methods and models for today's teachers* (6th ed.). Hoboken, NJ: John S. Wiley and Sons, Inc.

Wright, S. P., Horn, S. P., & Sanders, W. L. (1997). Teacher & classroom context effects on student achievement: Implications for teacher evaluation. *Journal of Personnel Evaluation in Education, 11*, 57–67.

Chapter 3

Baca, L. M., & Cervantes, H. (Eds.). (2003). *The bilingual special education interface* (4th ed.). New York: Prentice Hall.

Bender, W. N., & Shores, C. (2007). *Response to intervention: A practical guide for every teacher*. Thousand Oaks, CA: Corwin.

Berkeley, S., Bender, W. N., Peaster, L. G., & Saunders, L. (2009). Implementation of response to intervention: A snapshot of progress. *Journal of Learning Disabilities, 42*, 85–95.

Bradley, R., Danielson, L., & Doolittle, J. (2005). Response to intervention: 1997. *Journal of Learning Disabilities, 38*, 485–486.

Collier, C. (2009). *Separating difference from disability* (4th ed.). Ferndale, WA: CrossCultural Developmental Education Services.

Collier, C., Brice, A. E., & Oades-Sese, G. V. (2007). Assessment of acculturation. In G. B. Esquivel, E. C. Lopez, & S. Nahari, (Eds.), *Handbook of multicultural school psychology: An interdisciplinary perspective* (pp. 353–380). Mahwah NJ: Lawrence Erlbaum.

Collier, V. P., & Thomas, W. P. (2007). Predicting second-language academic success in English using the prism model. In C. Davison & J. Cummins (Eds.), *International handbook of English language teaching* (pp. 333–348). New York: Springer.

Freeman, D. E., & Freeman Y. S. (2007). *English language learners: The essential guide.* New York: Scholastic.

Fuchs, D., Mock, D., Morgan, P. L., & Young, C. L. (2003). Responsiveness-to-intervention: Definition, evidence, and implications for the learning disabilities construct. *Learning Disabilities Research & Practice, 18,* 157–171.

Hoover, J. J., Baca, L. M., & Klingner, J. J. (2007). *Methods for teaching culturally and linguistically diverse exceptional learners.* Upper Saddle River, NJ: Prentice Hall.

Johnson, E., Mellard, D. F., Fuchs, D., & McKnight, M. A. (2006). *Responsiveness to intervention (RTI): How to do it.* Lawrence, KS: National Research Center on Learning Disabilities.

Kavale, K. (2005). Identifying specific learning disability: Is responsiveness to intervention the answer? *Journal of Learning Disabilities, 38,* 553–562.

Padilla, E. R., Padilla, A. M., Morales, A., Olmedo, E. L., & Ramirez, R. (1979). Inhalant, marijuana, and alcohol abuse among barrio children and adolescents. *International Journal of the Addictions, 14,* 945–964.

Reschly, D. J. (2005). Learning disabilities identification: Primary intervention, secondary intervention, then what? *Journal of Learning Disabilities, 38,* 510–515.

Semrud-Clikeman, M. (2005). Neuropsychological aspects for evaluating learning disabilities. *Journal of Learning Disabilities, 38,* 563–568.

Siegel, J., & Shaughnessy, F. M. (1994). Educating for understanding: An interview with Howard Garder. *Phi Delta Kappan, 76,* 563–566.

Tomsho, R. (2007, August 16). Is an early-help program shortchanging kids? *The Wall Street Journal,* p. B1 [Electronic version]. Retrieved from http://online.wsj.com/article/SB118721849477198989.html

U.S. Department of Education. (2007, July). *Special education and rehabilitation services: IDEA's impact.* Retrieved November 4, 2009, from http://www.ed.gov/policy/speced/leg/idea/history30.html

Vaughn, S., Linan-Thompson, S., & Hickman, P. (2003). Response to treatment as a means of identifying students with reading/learning disabilities. *Exceptional Children, 69,* 391–409.

Chapter 5

Covey, S. R. (2004). *The 7 habits of highly effective people.* Roseburg, OR: Free Press.

DuFour, R., DuFour, R., Eaker, R., & Many, T. (2006). *Learning by doing: A handbook for Professional Learning Communities at work.* Bloomington, IN: Solution Tree.

Elmore, R. (2007). *Educational improvement in Victoria.* Victoria, Canada: Office of Government, School, Education, Department of Education. Retrieved July 5, 2009, from http://www.eduweb.vic.gov.au/edulibrary/public/staffdev/schlead/Richard_Elmore-wps-v1–20070817.pdf

Fuchs, D., & Deshler, D. D. (2007). What we need to know about responsiveness-to-intervention (and shouldn't be afraid to ask). *Learning Disabilities Research and Practice, 22*(2), 129–136.

Lachat, M. A. (2001). *Data-driven high school reform: Breaking ranks model.* Providence, RI: Northeast and Islands Regional Educational Laboratory.

Lashway, L. (2003). Distributed leadership. *Research Roundup, 19,* 4. Eugene, OR: ERIC Clearinghouse on Educational Management.

Mellard, D. F., & Johnson, E. S. (2008). *RTI: A practitioner's guide to implementing Response to Intervention.* Thousand Oaks, CA: Corwin.

National Association of Secondary School Principals. (1996). Breaking ranks: Changing an American institution. *NASSP Bulletin, 80*(578), 55–66.

Portin, B. S., DeArmond, M., Gundlach, L., & Schneider, P. (2003). *Making sense of leading schools: A national study of the principalship.* Seattle: University of Washington, Center on Reinventing Public Education.

Reid, W. A. (1987). Institutions and practices: Professional education reports and the language of reform. *Educational Researcher, 16*(8), 10–15.

Chapter 6

Armstrong, T. (2007). *The multiple intelligences of reading and writing: Making words come alive.* Alexandria, VA: Association for Supervision and Curriculum Development.

AutoSkill. (2004). *Focus on research: A paper on the scientific validation of effective reading programs and the development of the AutoSkill Academy of Reading.* Ottawa, Canada: Author.

Barkeley, S., Bender, W. N., Peaster, L., & Saunders, L. (in press). Implementation of responsiveness to intervention: A snapshot of progress. *Journal of Learning Disabilities.*

Bender, W. N. (2001). *Learning disabilities: Characteristics, identification and teaching strategies* (4th ed.). Boston: Allyn & Bacon.

Bender, W. N. (2008). *Differentiating instruction for students with learning disabilities* (2nd ed.). Thousand Oaks, CA: Corwin.

Bender, W. N., & Shores, C. (2007). *Response to intervention: A practical guide for every teacher.* Thousand Oaks, CA: Corwin.

Bhat, P., Griffin, C. C., & Sindelar, P. T. (2003). Phonological awareness instruction for middle school students with learning disabilities. *Learning Disability Quarterly, 26*(2), 73–88.

Bos, C. S., Mather, N., Silver-Pacuilla, H., & Narr, R. F. (2000). Learning to teach early literacy skills collaboratively. *Teaching Exceptional Children, 32*(5), 38–45.

Bradley, R., Danielson, L., & Doolittle, J. (2007). Responsiveness to intervention: 1997 to 2007. *Teaching Exceptional Children, 39*(5), 8–13.

Chard, D. J., & Dickson, S. V. (1999). Phonological awareness: Instructional and assessment guidelines. *Intervention in School and Clinic, 34*(5), 261–270.

Dayton-Sakari, M. (1997). Struggling readers don't work at reading: They just get their teachers to! *Intervention in School and Clinic, 32*(5), 295–301.

Fuchs, L. S., & Fuchs, D. (2007). A model for implementing responsiveness to intervention. *Teaching Exceptional Children, 39*(5), 14–23.

Goldstein, B. H., & Obrzut, J. E. (2001). Neuropsychological treatment of dyslexia in the classroom setting. *Journal of Learning Disabilities, 34*, 276–285.

Good, R. H., & Kaminski, R. (2002). *DIBELS: Dynamic Indicators of Basic Early Literacy Skills* (6th ed.). Longmont, CO: Sopris West.

Gregory, G. H., & Chapman, C. (2002). *Differentiated instructional strategies: One size doesn't fit all.* Thousand Oaks, CA: Corwin.

Haager, D. (2002, October 11). *The road to successful reading outcomes for English language learners in urban schools.* A paper presented at the annual meeting of the Council for Exceptional Children, Denver, CO.

Joseph, J., Noble, K., & Eden, G. (2001). The neurobiological basis of reading. *Journal of Learning Disabilities, 34*(6), 566–579.

Kame'enui, E. J., Carnine, D. W., Dixon, R. C., Simmons, D. C., & Coyne, M. D. (2002). *Effective teaching strategies that accommodate diverse learners* (2nd ed.). Upper Saddle River, NJ: Merrill-Prentice Hall.

Kemp, K. A., & Eaton, M. A. (2007). *RTI: The classroom connection for literacy: Reading intervention and measurement.* Port Chester, NY: Dude Publishing.

King, K., & Gurian, M. (2006). Teaching to the minds of boys. *Educational Leadership, 64*(1), 56–61.

Langdon, T. (2004). DIBELS: A teacher friendly basic literacy accountability tool for the primary classroom. *Teaching Exceptional Children, 37*(2), 54–58.

Larkin, M. J. (2001). Providing support for student independence through scaffolded instruction. *Teaching Exceptional Children, 31*(1), 30–35.

Leonard, C. M. (2001). Imaging brain structure in children: Differentiating language disability and reading disability. *Learning Disability Quarterly, 24,* 158–176.

McCutchen, D., Abbott, R. D., Green, L. B., Beretvas, N., Cox, S., Potter, N. S., et al. (2002). Beginning literacy: Links among teacher knowledge, teacher practice, and student learning. *Journal of Learning Disabilities, 35*(1), 69–86.

National Institute of Child Health and Development. (2000). *Teaching children to read: An evidence-based assessment of the scientific research literature on reading and its implications for reading instruction* (Report of the National Reading Panel). Retrieved May 23, 2002, from http://www.nichd.nih.gov/publications/nrp/findings.cfm

Patzer, C. E., & Pettegrew, B. S. (1996). Finding a "voice": Primary students with developmental disabilities express personal meanings through writing. *Teaching Exceptional Children, 29*(2), 22–27.

Posse, S., Dager, S. R., & Richards, T. L. (1997). In vivo measurement of regional brain metabolic response to hyperventilation using magnetic resonance proton echo planar spectroscopic imaging (PEPSI). *Research in Medicine, 37,* 858–865.

Prigge, D. J. (2002). Promote brain-based teaching and learning. *Intervention in School and Clinic, 37,* 237–241.

Raskind, W. H. (2001). Current understanding of the genetic basis of reading and spelling disability. *Learning Disability Quarterly, 24,* 141–157.

Richards, T. L. (2001). Functional magnetic resonance imaging and spectroscopic imaging of the brain: Application of the fMRI and fMRS to reading disabilities and education. *Learning Disability Quarterly, 24*(3), 189–204.

Richards, T. L., Corina, D., Serafini, S., Steury, K., Echeland, D. R., Dager, S. R., et al. (2000). The effects of a phonological-driven treatment for dyslexia on lactate levels as measured by proton MRSI. *American Journal of Neuroradiology, 21,* 916–922.

Richards, T. L., Dager, S. R., Corina, D., Serafini, S., Heide, A. C., Steury, K., et al. (1999). Dyslexic children have abnormal brain lactate response to reading-related language tasks. *American Journal of Neuroradiology, 20,* 1393–1398.

Rourke, B. P. (2005). Neuropsychology of learning disabilities: Past and future. *Learning Disability Quarterly, 28*(2), 111–114.

Shaker, P. (2001). Literacies for life. *Educational Leadership, 59*(2), 26–31.

Shaywitz, B. A., Shaywitz, S. E., Pugh, K. R., Sukdlarski, P., Fulbright, R. K., Constable, R. T., et al. (1996). The functional organization of brain for reading and reading disability (dyslexia). *The Neuroscientist, 2*, 245–255.

Smith, S. B., Baker, S., & Oudeans, M. K. (2001). Making a difference in the classroom with early literacy instruction. *Teaching Exceptional Children, 33*(6), 8–14.

Sousa, D. A. (2001). *How the special needs brain learns.* Thousand Oaks, CA: Corwin.

Sousa, D. A. (2005). *How the brain learns to read.* Thousand Oaks, CA: Corwin.

Sylwester, R. (2001). *A biological brain in a cultural classroom: Applying biological research to classroom management.* Thousand Oaks, CA: Corwin.

Tallal, P., Miller, S. L., Bedi, G., Bvma, G., Want, X., Nagarajan, S., et al. (1996). Fast-element enhanced speech improves language comprehension in language-learning impaired children. *Science, 271*, 81–84.

UniSci. (2000, May). Brain shown to change as dyslexics learn. *Daily University Science News,* p. 26.

Winn, J. A., & Otis-Wilborn, A. (1999). Monitoring literacy learning. *Teaching Exceptional Children, 32*(1), 40–45.

Wood, F. B., & Grigorenko, E. L. (2001). Emerging issues in the genetics of dyslexia: A methodological review. *Journal of Learning Disabilities, 34*, 503–511.

Wright, B. A., Bowen, R. W., & Zecker, S. G. (2000). Nonlinguistic perceptual deficits associated with reading and language disorders. *Current Opinion in Neurobiology, 10*, 482–486.

Chapter 7

Baker, S., Gersten, R., & Lee, D. (2002). A synthesis of empirical research on teaching mathematics to low-achieving students. *The Elementary School Journal, 103*, 51–73.

Baker, S., Gersten, R., & Scanlon, D. (2002). Procedural facilitators and cognitive strategies: Tools for unraveling the mysteries of comprehension and the writing process, and for providing meaningful access to the general curriculum. *Learning Disabilities Research and Practice, 17*, 65–77.

Butler, F. M., Miller, S. P., Crehan, K., Babbitt, B., & Pierce, T. (2003). Fraction instruction for students with mathematics disabilities: Comparing two teaching sequences. *Learning Disabilities Research and Practice, 18*, 99–111.

Ellis, E. S., Worthington, L., & Larkin, M. J. (1994). *Executive summary of research synthesis on effective teaching principles and the design of quality tools for educators.* (Tech. Rep. No. 6). Retrieved July 17, 2004, from University of Oregon, National Center to Improve the Tools of Educators website: http://idea.uore gon.edu/~ncite/ documents/ techrep/other.html.

Fuchs, L. S., Fuchs, D., & Karns, K. (2001). Enhancing kindergarteners' mathematical development: Effects of peer-assisted learning strategies. *Elementary School Journal, 101*, 495–510.

Gersten, R., Beckmann, S., Clarke, B., Foegen, A., Marsh, L., Star, J. R., & Witzel, B. (2009). *Assisting students struggling with mathematics: Response to Intervention (RTI) for elementary and middle schools* (NCEE 2009-4060). Washington, DC: National Center for Education Evaluation and Regional Assistance, Institute of Education Sciences, U.S. Department of Education. Retrieved from http://ies.ed.gov/ncee/wwc/publications/practiceguides.

Hutchinson, N. L. (1993). Second invited response: Students with disabilities and mathematics education reform—let the dialog begin. *Remedial and Special Education, 14*(6), 20–23.

IRIS Center for Training Enhancements. (n.d.). *Algebra (part 1): Applying learning strategies to beginning algebra.* Retrieved on March 5, 2007, from http://iris .peabody.vanderbilt.edu.

IRIS Center for Training Enhancements. (n.d.). *Algebra (part 2): Applying learning strategies to intermediate algebra.* Retrieved on March 5, 2007, from http://iris .peabody.vanderbilt.edu.

IRIS Center for Training Enhancements. (n.d.). *Comprehension & vocabulary: Grades 3–5.* Retrieved on March 5, 2007, from http://iris.peabody.vanderbilt.edu.

IRIS Center for Training Enhancements. (n.d.). *Effective room arrangement.* Retrieved on March 5, 2007, from http://iris.peabody.vanderbilt.edu/gpm/chalcycle.htm.

Miller, S. P., & Mercer, C. D. (1993). Using data to learn about concrete-semiconcrete-abstract instruction for students with math disabilities. *Learning Disabilities Research & Practice, 8,* 89–96.

National Mathematics Advisory Panel (NMAP). (2008). *Foundations for success: The final report of the National Mathematics Advisory Panel.* U.S. Department of Education Washington, DC. Retrieved March 2008 from www.ed.gov/MathPanel.

Owen, R. L., & Fuchs, L. S. (2002). Mathematical problem-solving strategy instruction for third-grade students with learning disabilities. *Remedial and Special Education, 23,* 268–278.

Riccomini, P. J., Witzel, B. S., & Riccomini, A. E. (in press). Maximize development in early childhood math programs by optimizing the instructional sequence. In N. L. Gallenstein & J. Hodges (Eds.), *Mathematics for all.* Olney, MD: ACEI.

Tournaki, N. (2003). The differential effects of teaching addition through strategy instruction versus drill and practice to students with and without disabilities. *Journal of Learning Disabilities, 36,* 449–458.

Wilson, C. L., & Sindelar, P. T. (1991). Direct instruction in math word problems: Students with learning disabilities. *Exceptional Children, 57,* 512–518.

Witzel, B. S. (2005). Using CRA to teach algebra to students with math difficulties in inclusive settings. *Learning Disabilities: A Contemporary Journal, 3*(2), 49–60.

Witzel, B. S., Mercer, C. D., & Miller, M. D. (2003). Teaching algebra to students with learning difficulties: An investigation of an explicit instruction model. *Learning Disabilities Research and Practice, 18,* 121–131.

Witzel, B. S., & Riccomini, P. J. (2007). OPTIMIZE your curriculum for students with disabilities. *Preventing School Failure, 52*(1), 13–18.

Xin, Y. P., Jitendra, A. K., & Deatline-Buchman, A. (2005). Effects of mathematical word problem-solving instruction on middle school students with learning problems. *Journal of Special Education, 39,* 181–192.

Chapter 8

Anderson, A. R., Christenson, S. L, & Sinclair, M. F. (2004). Check & connect: The importance of relationships for promoting engagement with school. *Journal of School Psychology, 42*(2), 95–113.

Armendariz, F., & Umbreit, J. (1999). Using active responding to reduce disruptive behavior in a general education classroom. *Journal of Positive Behavior Interventions, 1,* 152–158.

Bacon, E., & Bloom, L. (2000). Listening to student voices. *Teaching Exceptional Children, 32,* 38–43.

Bambara, L. M., & Kern, L. (2005). *Individualized supports for students with problem behaviors: Designing positive behavior plans.* New York: Guilford Press.

Bambara, L. M., & Knoster, T. (1998). Designing Positive Behavior Support plans. In *Innovations* (No. 13). Washington, DC: American Association on Mental Retardation.

Barry, L. M., & Messer, J. J. (2003). A practical application of self-management for students diagnosed with attention-deficit/hyperactivity disorder. *Journal of Positive Behavior Interventions, 5,* 238–248.

Brooks, A., Todd, A. W., Tofflemoyer, S., & Horner, R. H. (2003). Use of functional assessment and a self-management system to increase academic engagement and work completion. *Journal of Positive Behavior Interventions, 5,* 144–152.

Callahan, K., & Rademacher, J. A. (1999). Using self-management strategies to increase the on-task behavior of a student with autism. *Journal of Positive Behavior Interventions, 1,* 117–122.

Cheney, D., Flower, A., & Templeton, T. (2008). Applying response to intervention metrics in the social domain for students at risk of developing emotional or behavioral disorders. *Journal of Special Education, 42,* 108–126.

Cheney, D., & Lynass, L. (2009). *Social Response to Intervention System.* Seattle: University of Washington.

Cheney, D., Lynass, L., Flower, A., Waugh, M., & Iwaszuk, W. (in press). The Check, Connect, and Expect program: A targeted, tier two intervention in the School-wide Positive Behavior Support model. *Preventing School Failure.*

Cook, C. R., Gresham, F. M., Kern, L., Barreras, R. B., & Crews, S. D. (2008). Social skills training for secondary students with emotional and/or behavioral disorders. *Journal of Emotional and Behavioral Disorders, 16,* 131–144.

Crone, D. A., Horner, R. H., & Hawken, L. S. (2004). *Responding to problem behavior in schools: The behavior education program.* New York: Guilford Press.

Evertson, C., & Emmer, E. (2009). *Classroom management for elementary teachers* (8th ed.). Upper Saddle River, NJ: Pearson.

Finn, J. D. (1989). Withdrawing from school. *Review of Educational Research, 59,* 117–142.

Dunlap, G., DePerczel, M., Clarke, S., Wilson, D., Wright, S., White, R., et al. (1994). Choice making to promote adaptive behavior for students with emotional and behavioral challenges. *Journal of applied behavior analysis, 27,* 505–518.

Fairbanks, S., Sugai, G., Guardino, D., & Lathrop, M. (2007) Response to Intervention: Examining classroom behavior support in second grade. *Exceptional Children, 73,* 288–310.

Filter, K. J., McKenna, M. K., Benedict, E. A., Horner, R. H., Todd, A. W., & Watson, J. (2007). Check in/check out: A post-hoc evaluation of an efficient, secondary-level targeted intervention for reducing problem behaviors in schools. *Education and Treatment of Children, 30*(1), 69–84.

Hawken, L. S. (2006). School psychologists as leaders in the implementation of a targeted intervention: The behavior education program. *School Psychology Quarterly, 21*, 91–111.

Hawken, L. S., & Horner, R. (2003). Implementing a targeted intervention within a school-wide system of behavior support. *Journal of Behavioral Education, 12*, 225–240.

Hawken, L. S., MacLeod, K. S., & Rawlings, L. (2007). Effects of the Behavior Education Program (BEP) on office discipline referrals of elementary school students. *Journal of Positive Behavior Interventions, 9*, 94–101.

Hawken, L. S., Peterson, H., Mootz, J., & Anderson, C. (2006). *The Behavior Education Program video: A check-in, check-out intervention for students at risk.* New York: Guilford Press.

Hawken, L., Vincent, C., & Schumann, J. (2008). Response to Intervention for social behavior. *Journal of Emotional and Behavioral Disorders, 16*, 213–225.

Horner, R. (2007). *Is School-wide Positive Behavior Support an evidence-based practice: A research summary.* Eugene: Technical Assistance Center on PBIS, University of Oregon.

Horner, R., Sugai, G., Todd, A., & Lewis-Palmer, T. (2000). Elements of behavior support plans: A technical brief. *Exceptionality, 8*, 205–215.

Individuals with Disabilities Education Act (IDEA) of 1997, 20 U.S.C. § 1400 *et seq.*

Individuals with Disabilities Education Improvement Act (IDEIA) of 2004, 20 U.S.C. § 1400 *et seq.*

Irvin, L. K., Horner, R. H., Ingram, K., Todd, A. W., Sugai, G., Sampson, N., et al. (2006). Using office discipline referral data for decision-making about student behavior in elementary and middle schools: An empirical investigation of validity. *Journal of Positive Behavior Interventions, 8*, 10–23.

Irvin, L. K., Tobin, T., Sprague, J., Sugai, G., & Vincent, C. (2004). Validity of office discipline referral measures as indices of school-wide behavioral status and effects of school-wide behavioral interventions. *Journal of Positive Behavioral Interventions 6*, 131–147.

Kea, C. D., Cartledge, G., & Bowman, L. J. (2002). Interventions for African American learners with behavioral problems. In B. A. Ford & F. Obiakor (Eds.), *Creating successful learning environments for African American learners with exceptionalities* (pp. 79–94). Austin, TX: Pro-ED.

Kilian, J. M., Fish, M. C., & Maniago, E. B. (2007). Making schools safe: A system-wide school intervention to increase student prosocial behaviors and enhance school climate. *Journal of Applied School Psychology, 23*, 1–30.

Lee, S., Simpson, R. L., & Shogren, K. A. (2007). Effects and implications of self-management for students with autism: A meta-analysis. *Focus on Autism and Other Developmental Disabilities, 22*, 2–13.

Lehr, C. A., Sinclair, M. F., & Christenson, S. L. (2004). Addressing student engagement and truancy prevention during the elementary years: A replication study of the Check & Connect model. *Journal of Education for Students Placed at Risk, 9*(3), 279–301.

McPartland, J. M. (1994). Dropout prevention in theory and practice. In R. J. Rossi (Ed.), *Schools and students at risk: Context and framework for positive change* (pp. 255–276). New York: Teachers College. (ERIC Document Reproduction Service No. ED366695)

O'Neill, R. E., Horner, R. H., Albin, R. W., Sprague, J. R., Storey, K., & Newton, J. S. (1997). *Functional assessment and program development for problem behavior: A practical handbook.* Pacific Grove, CA: Brooks/Cole.

Scott, T. M., & Nelson, C. M. (1999). Using functional behavioral assessment to develop effective intervention plans: Practical classroom applications. *Journal of Positive Behavior Interventions, 1,* 242–251.

Sinclair, M. F., Christenson, S. L., Evelo, D. L., & Hurley, C. M. (1998). Dropout prevention for high-risk youth with disabilities: Efficacy of a sustained school engagement procedure. *Exceptional Children, 65*(1), 7–21.

Sinclair, M. F., Christenson, S. L., & Thurlow, M .L. (2005). Promoting school completion of urban secondary youth with emotional or behavioral disabilities. *Exceptional Children, 71*(4), 465–482.

Smith, B. W., & Sugai, G. (2000). A self-management functional assessment-based behavior support plan for a middle school student with EBD. *Journal of Positive Behavior Interventions, 2,* 208–217.

Sprick, R., Garrison, M., & Howard, L. (1998). *CHAMPs: A proactive and positive approach to classroom management,* Longmont, CO: Sopris West.

Stahr, B., Cushing, D., Lane, K., & Fox, J. (2006). Efficacy of a function-based intervention in decreasing off-task behavior exhibited by a student with ADHD. *Journal of Positive Behavior Interventions, 8,* 201–211.

Sugai, G., Lewis-Palmer, T., & Hagan-Burke, S. (2000). Overview of the functional behavioral assessment process. *Exceptionality, 8,* 149–160.

Todd, A. W., Campbell, A. L., Meyer, G. G., & Horner, R. H. (2008). The effects of a targeted intervention to reduce problem behaviors. *Journal of Positive Behavior Interventions, 10,* 46–55.

Todd, A. W., Horner, R. H., & Sugai, G. (1999). Self-monitoring and self-recruited praise: Effects on problem behavior, academic engagement, and work completion in a typical classroom. *Journal of Positive Behavior Interventions, 1*(2), 66–122.

Umbreit, J., Lane, K. L., & Dejud, C. (2004). Improving classroom behavior by modifying task difficulty: Effects of increasing the difficulty of too-easy tasks. *Journal of Positive Behavior Interventions, 6*(1), 13–20.

Vaughn, B. J., & Horner, R. H. (1997). Identifying instructional tasks that occasion problem behaviors and assessing the effects of student versus teacher choice among these tasks. *Journal of Applied Behavior Analysis, 30,* 299–312.

Walker, B., Cheney, D., Stage, S., & Blum, C. (2005). Schoolwide screening and Positive Behavior Support: Identifying and supporting students at risk of school failure. *Journal of Positive Behavior Interventions, 7,* 194–204.

Walker, H. M., Ramsey, E., & Gresham, F. M. (2004). *Antisocial behavior in school: Evidence-based practices.* Belmont, CA: Thomson/Wadsworth.

Walker, H. M., & Severson, H. H. (1992). *Systematic screening for behavior disorders* (2nd ed.). Austin, TX: Pro-Ed.

Walker, H. M., & Severson, H. H. (2007). Proactive, early screening to detect behaviorally at-risk students: Issues, approaches, emerging innovations, and professional practices. *Journal of School Psychology, 45,* 193–223.

Chapter 9

Consortium on Reading Excellence (CORE). (2006). Retrieved March 9, 2006, from http://www.coreread.com/Downloads.htm.

Foorman, B. R., & Moats, L. C. (2004). Conditions for sustaining research-based practices in early reading instruction. *Remedial and Special Education, 25*(1), 51–60.

Foorman, B. R., & Schatschneider, C. (2003). Measuring teaching practices in reading/language arts instruction and their relation to student achievement. In S. Vaughn & K. Briggs (Eds.), *Reading in the classroom: Systems for observing teaching and learning*. Baltimore: Brookes Publishing Co.

Fuchs, L. S., & Fuchs, D. (2006). Implementing responsiveness-to-intervention to identify learning disabilities. *Perspectives on Dyslexia, 32*(1), 39–43.

Geiger, S., Banks, A., Hasbrouck, J., & Ebbers, S. (2005, January). *Washington state K–12 reading model: Implementation guide*, Office of the Superintendent of Public Instruction, Publication No. 05–0001, Olympia, WA. Retrieved on March 9, 2006, from http://www.k12.wa.us/curriculumInstruct/ reading/default.aspx.

Gresham, F. M. (1989). Assessment of treatment integrity in school consultation and prereferral intervention. *School Psychology Review, 18*(1), 37–50.

Gresham, F. M., MacMillan, D. L., Beebe-Frankenberger, M. E., & Bocian, K. M. (2000). Treatment integrity in learning disabilities intervention research: Do we really know how treatments are implemented? *Learning Disabilities Research & Practice, 15*, 198–205.

Individuals with Disabilities Education Act (IDEA). (2004). Public Law 108-446.

Johnson, E. S., Mellard, D. F., Fuchs, D., & McKnight, M. (2006) Response to intervention: How to do it. National Research Center on Learning Disabilities, Lawrence, KS.

Kovaleski, J. F., Gickling, E. E., & Marrow, H. (1999). High versus low implementation of instructional support teams: A case for maintaining program fidelity. *Remedial and Special Education, 20*, 170–183.

Mellard, D. F., Byrd, S. E., Johnson, E., Tollefson, J. M., & Boesche, L. (2004). Foundations and research on identifying model responsiveness-to-intervention sites. *Learning Disability Quarterly, 27*, 243–256.

Mellard, D. F., & McKnight, M. A. (2006). RTI implementation tool for reading: Best practices [Brochure]. Lawrence, KS: National Resource Centeron Learning Disabilities.

Neill, M. (2004). Leaving no child behind: Overhauling NCLB. In Meier, D., & Wood, G. (Eds.), *Many Children Left Behind*, 101–120. Boston: Beacon Press.

Nettles, S. (2006). *Principal's reading walkthrough presentation and documents*. Florida Center for Reading Research. Retrieved March 9, 2006, from http://www .fcrr.org/staffpresentations/SNettles/PrincipalWalkthroughContent.pdf.

No Child Left Behind Act (NCLB). (2001). Public Law 107-110.

Rowan, B., Camburn, E., & Correnti, R. (2004). Using teacher logs to measure the enacted curriculum in large-scale surveys: A study of literacy teaching in 3rd grade classrooms. *Elementary School Journal, 105*, 75–102. Retrieved March 9, 2006, from http://www.sii.soe.umich.edu/documents/Enacted Curr04.pdf.

Telzrow, C. F., McNamara, K., & Hollinger, C. L. (2000). Fidelity of problem-solving implementation and relationship to student performance. *School Psychology Review, 29*, 443–61.

Vaughn, S., Hughes, M. T., Schumm, J. S., & Klingner, J. (1998). A collaborative effort to enhance reading and writing instruction in inclusion classrooms. *Learning Disability Quarterly, 21*(1), 57–74

Vaughn, S., Linan-Thompson, S., Kouzekanani, K., Bryant, D. P., Dickson, S., & Blozis, S. A. (2003). Reading instruction grouping for students with reading difficulties. *Remedial and Special Education, 24*(5), 301–315.

CORWIN
A SAGE Company

The Corwin logo—a raven striding across an open book—represents the union of courage and learning. Corwin is committed to improving education for all learners by publishing books and other professional development resources for those serving the field of PreK–12 education. By providing practical, hands-on materials, Corwin continues to carry out the promise of its motto: **"Helping Educators Do Their Work Better."**